HV
8978
.G38
B33
2000

Bacon, Margaret
Hope.

Abby Hopper Gibbons.

son charging th   ok is
ble for its retu
g Resources   LP
' Communi
e P rk

W9-BMN-214

Abby
Hopper
Gibbons

SUNY series in
Women, Crime, and Criminology

Meda Chesney-Lind and Russ Immarigeon, editors

Abby Hopper Gibbons

Prison Reformer and Social Activist

Margaret Hope Bacon

STATE UNIVERSITY OF NEW YORK PRESS

Published by
State University of New York Press, Albany

© 2000 State University of New York

All rights reserved

Printed in the United States of America

No part of this book may be used or reproduced in any manner
whatsoever without written permission. No part of this
book may be stored in a retrieval system or transmitted
in any form or by any means including electronic,
electrostatic, magnetic tape, mechanical, photocopying,
recording, or otherwise without the prior permission in
writing of the publisher.

For information, address the State University of New York Press,
State University Plaza, Albany, NY 12246

Production by Kristin Milavec
Marketing by Dana E. Yanulavich

Library of Congress Cataloging-in-Publication Data

Bacon, Margaret Hope.
    Abby Hopper Gibbons : prison reformer and social activist /
Margaret Hope Bacon.
        p.   cm. — (SUNY series in women, crime, and criminology)
    Includes bibliographical references (p.   ) and index.
    ISBN 0-7914-4497-X (hc. : alk. paper). — ISBN 0-7914-4498-8 (pb.
: alk. paper)
    1. Gibbons, Abby Hopper, 1801–1893.   2. Prison reformers—United
States Biography.   3. Women social reformers—United States
Biography.   4. Quaker women—United States Biography.   I. Title.
II. Series.
HV8978.G38B33   2000
365'.7'092—dc21
    [B]   99-39701
                                                                                                 CIP

10 9 8 7 6 5 4 3 2 1

Contents

———

Acknowledgments

I first thought of writing about Abby Gibbons after I had completed a junior biography of her father, Isaac T. Hopper, in 1970. Abby Gibbons's story seemed so intertwined with her father's that it appeared a logical next step. But other projects intervened, and it was almost twenty years until I returned to the Hopper family.

Meanwhile, I had kept in touch with Hopper descendants, especially Sarah Dunning Schear, a great-great-granddaughter of Isaac, and her brother, William Dunning. It was the latter who kept urging me to consider a book on Abby. Finally, in 1989, he offered to loan me her voluminous correspondence and other private papers, which had remained in the family. I suggested instead that these be given to the Friends Historical Library at Swarthmore College, where other Hopper papers had been gathered. In consequence, William Dunning, Sarah Dunning Schear, and Frances Dunning Beebe, great-grandchildren of Abby Hopper Gibbons, made the library a gift of this valuable correspondence. Without these papers, and the continuing support and generous aid of Sarah Dunning Schear, I would never have been able to complete this biography.

I am grateful also to Mary Ellen Chijioke, curator of the Friends Historical Library, for permitting me to borrow segments of this correspondence before it was catalogued, and her aid in every step of the preparation of this manuscript.

Other research libraries were also generous in making manuscripts available to me. I would like to express appreciation to Emma Lapsansky and Elizabeth Potts Brown, of the Quaker Collection at Haverford College, to Elizabeth Moger, former archivist for New York Yearly Meeting Records, to the archivist of the Sophia Smith Collection of Smith College, to the Department of Rare Books and Manuscripts of the Boston Public

Library, to the archivists of the Historical Library of Pennsylvania and the Library Company of Philadelphia. The staff of the Manuscripts and Archives Division of the New York Public Library, where the papers of the Women's Prison Association are deposited, were generous in allowing me research privileges. And I wish to thank the New-York Historical Society for answering many questions, and lending me, through Swarthmore College Library, the journal of James Herbert Morse.

My gratitude in the final preparation of the manuscript to Holley Webster for proofreading. And as always, my thanks to my husband, S. Allen Bacon, for his continuing support.

Introduction

In the 1870s the New York legislature began apportioning money from an Excise Fund to the support of charities. Legislators soon came to know a determined lobbyist for women prisoners. She was a small, elderly woman, dressed in Quaker costume, who commuted to Albany from her home in New York City and called upon each of them, letters of introduction in hand. She was simple, forthright, and direct in what she wanted, and she was generally successful. A friend accompanying her on the train home heard a stranger remark, "When those people want anything they would do better to send the little Quaker lady. The rest of them could stay home."[1]

Abby Hopper Gibbons was one of a small band of nineteenth-century middle-class women who turned their energies into the twin fields of reform and benevolence, using the nineteenth-century concept of woman's separate sphere to empower their efforts to aid their less fortunate sisters. By building networks of women who shared their ideals and their goals, they enhanced both their own effectiveness and their self-image. Their efforts enlarged the role of women in the larger society and laid the groundwork for progress in the twentieth century.[2]

Lori Ginzberg, in her excellent book, *Women and the Work of Benevolence*, outlines stages in the development of the politics and rhetoric of the nineteenth-century women reformers. At the beginning of the century, many of the women came from relatively humble backgrounds and were abolitionists; some adopting the radical social views of William Lloyd Garrison and his colleagues. By the middle of the century, as a younger and more affluent group of women emerged, some of the early radicalism was discarded, and women turned their efforts to the building of institutions to express their benevolent aims. Following the Civil War, a third

ix

Abby Hopper Gibbons. Courtesy of Friends Historical Library, Swarthmore College.

generation, many of whose members came from well-to-do families, emphasized efficiency rather than good motives alone, worked in alliance with government, and began to urge a professional approach. While some of the former abolitionist/feminists or their daughters turned their attention to an ever-narrowing focus on suffrage for women, others concentrated on using their position to raise money to influence legislation in support of women's causes.[3]

Abby Hopper Gibbons(1801–1893), whose life all but spanned the nineteenth century, illustrates these three stages. Born in a relatively poor family, Gibbons played a role in the Garrisonian movement and subscribed to many radical views until 1845. She then became involved in the creation and nurture of two institutions, a halfway house for women prisoners and an industrial school for German immigrant girls. Like many of the other nineteenth century women reformers, she served as a nurse during the Civil War and used her growing prominence and political influence from the battlefield. After the war she helped to develop several additional charities, and turned her attention to fund raising and lobbying for the institutions she supported and for the development of a women's reformatory.[4]

As the years passed, Gibbons abandoned some of the radicalism of her youth. In 1842 she resigned from the Religious Society of Friends in protest against its disowning her father and husband for their radical antislavery views. Thereafter, she began to move away from the Quaker testimonies. Her father, whom she emulated, had been a strong advocate of nonresistance and a foe of capital punishment. Abby Gibbons, however, abandoned her pacifism in the 1850s and supported the Civil War. After Lincoln's assassination in 1865 she wrote her daughter, "I never would give my voice in favor of capital punishment, but in this case, would not dare raise my voice against it."[5]

Her relationship to the women's rights movement is more complicated. Her daughter, Sarah Emerson, who published her biography in 1897, was very conservative and painted Abby Gibbons as conservative on the women's rights issue, and subsequently historians have accepted this as gospel. However, a careful reading of her own papers suggests more ambivalence. She attended the antislavery conventions of American women, where the issue of women's rights was first raised publicly, and served in 1860 as vice president of the Woman's Rights Convention held in New York City. In 1868 she protested when Susan B. Anthony and Elizabeth Cady Stanton used her name without permission for an appeal to the Democratic National Convention. But it was her more conservative daughters who insisted that she do so. Gibbons's only concern was that as a strong Republican she did not want to be "hitched on to the Democratic Party." And though she did not work actively on the suffrage issue, she said she would certainly vote if suffrage were obtained for women. Through the years she remained loyal to the Grimké sisters, Lucretia Mott, and others from the abolitionist/feminist network.[6]

In the post–Civil War era, Gibbons was certainly influenced by the growing wealth and conservatism of the women she worked with, and of her own husband, James Gibbons. Yet she maintained her contacts with former black colleagues, with ex-slaves, and with women convicts, all of whom kept her in touch with ordinary women and men and gave her greater faith in "the people" than her conservative daughters.[7]

Like many of her contemporaries, Gibbons tended to see the women she worked with through eyes shaded by Victorian morality and believed that a return to true womanliness would save the alcoholics, prostitutes, and petty thieves on whose behalf she campaigned. The women's reformatory movement of the nineteenth century, in which she played a significant role, as well as the related Social Purity movement she headed in New York City, were based on the premise that women needed different treatment than men because of their different natures, and that women in trouble with the law should be treated as wayward girls. As an unintended result of these attitudes, as Nicole Rafter has pointed out, in *Partial Justice*, the reformatories institutionalized a double standard, holding women who previously would have served brief jail sentences for drunkenness or prostitution for longer periods of time than comparable male misdemeanants.[8]

But Gibbons cannot be understood exclusively as a product and exponent of nineteenth-century middle-class values. Her birth and upbringing place her also in a long tradition of Quaker belief in gender equality and Quaker concern for prisoners. Estelle Freedman, in *Their Sisters Keepers*, counted some thirty women who worked to improve prison conditions in the nineteenth century. Of these nine, or just under 33 percent, were Quaker. In addition, three other Quaker women pioneered in this field: Mary Waln Wistar, who organized the first society of women prison visitors in Philadelphia, Elizabeth King, who did the same in Baltimore, and Susan Lloyd, who developed and served as first director of the Howard Institution, a halfway house for women prisoners in Philadelphia in 1853. Other Quaker women visited prisons as part of their role as public ministers. Elizabeth Comstock of Michigan was an active prison visitor. Lucretia Mott had preached at Auburn Prison just before attending the Seneca Falls Woman's Rights Convention of 1848.[9]

The tradition of Quaker women's concern for prisoners goes back to the beginning of the movement in England in the middle of the seventeenth century. Elizabeth Hooton, the first disciple of founder George Fox, was imprisoned in Lincoln Castle in 1655, and wrote a scathing letter to Oliver Cromwell:

> O thou that artt sett in Authoryty to doe Justice and Judgmente, and to lett the opporessed goe free, thease things are required att thy hands, looke vpon the pore prissoners, heare is that hath not an[y] [al]lowance all though thear be a greatte sume of mony comes osut of the country suffic[ient]tt to hellpe them all that is in want, both theare dew allowance and to sett them aworke which would labor. . . . And it is a place of g]reate dissorder and of wickedness, so that for oppression and prophaines J neuer came in such a place, because a milignant woman keeps the gole.[10]

While individual voices like Hooton's raised concerns for humanitarian issues in the first hundred years of the history of the Religious Society of Friends, the Quakers as a body did not devote themselves to social concerns until the second half of the eighteenth century. Following a midcentury crisis, Friends in Pennsylvania and elsewhere withdrew from government and turned their attention to the abolition of slavery, fair treatment for Native Americans, humane care of the mentally ill, and prison reform. The Society for the Alleviation of the Miseries of the Public Prisons, organized in 1793 by a group of prominent Quakers and Episcopalians in Philadelphia, gave initial leadership to public concern for improving the conditions of prisoners.[11]

One aspect of the Quaker reformation involved the strengthening of the position of women in the Religious Society of Friends. Though Quaker women had been encouraged by George Fox to travel as ministers and to develop their own business meetings parallel to those of the men, some resistance to women asserting authority within the Society had developed, especially in England, and remnants of that resistance had persisted. One of the goals of the mid-eighteenth-century Quaker reformers was to reestablish the principle of women's role in church business and to provide an equal education to Quaker women in the newly developed academies for higher education.[12]

Thus, at the beginning of the nineteenth century, at the time of Gibbons's birth, Quaker women were receiving an education parallel in most respects to that of their brothers,[13] were playing a stronger role in the Society's affairs, and were sharing the humanitarian concerns that were being developed by their fathers and husbands. They were not expected to participate in the all-male societies the Quaker men were developing to express these concerns, but were given encouragement in developing their own female societies, such as the Female Society of Philadelphia for the Relief and Employment of Poor Women, organized in 1795, and the New York Female Association for the Relief of the Sick Poor in 1798, which developed the first public school in New York City.[14]

The Quaker reformation, begun in the American colonies, spread to England. The first Quaker woman to organize prison reform was Elizabeth Gurney Fry (1780–1845), who first visited Newgate Prison in 1813 and was appalled by the conditions she found among the women prisoners. In 1816 she returned with a group of women determined to make a difference. They established themselves as the Ladies Association for the Improvement of Female Prisoners at Newgate and organized workshops, Bible classes, and a system of discipline based on rules that the inmates themselves agreed to. They also hired a matron, and developed an establishment, Westminister Asylum, where young female prisoners could go on their release. These changes produced a noticeable difference in the prison conditions, and Fry became an advocate for prison reform through parliamentary action, addressing herself particularly to the conditions on prison ships. Her pamphlet, *Observations in Visiting, Superintendence and Government of Female Prisoners,* published in 1827, urged women to enter the field of prison reform.[15]

A member of a wealthy and privileged family and married into another, Fry was no radical. She had no interest in the women's rights movement that was burgeoning in the United States, and pointedly avoided Lucretia Mott when the latter came to London for the 1840 World Anti-Slavery Convention.[16] Nevertheless, her belief that women prisoners should be under the control of matrons was eagerly adopted by the nineteenth-century women reformers, especially in the United States.

Inspired by Fry, a group of Quaker women in Philadelphia, under the leadership of Mary Waln Wistar (1765–1843),[17] established themselves as the Society of Women Friends and began visiting women prisoners in the Arch Street prison in 1823, reading the Bible to them, and supplying them with clothing. Their first ventures met with resistance. Roberts Vaux, a member of the Pennsylvania Prison Society and Mary Wistar's son-in-law, wrote a letter intended to discourage their efforts:

> The unhappy females whom you visited yester-day form a cir-culating medium of poverty and vice, alternately to be found in the wards of the Alms House & within the walls of the Prison—They are known to almost every watch-man in the City & their names are to be found on the docket of almost every magistrate. Their habits have become chronic, & I fear in most instances past restoration. If many of them were *"arrayed in purple & fine linnen"* by an unbounded charity, & set at lib-erty through the agency of a generous sympathy, such is the de-pravity of their minds, that in a few hours their garments would be surrendered as the price of some sensual appetite, the indulgence of which in a few more hours would insure their re-turn to Prison.—of consequence it follows, from a knowledge of these circumstances, that *great caution* be observed in ad-ministering assistance to habitual offenders, lest such be ren-dered more comfortable than those who subsist by honest industry, and thus unintentionally, tho in effect, offer a bounty for crime, and present a reward for vice.[18]

Undeterred by this warning and bolstered by support from Thomas Wistar, Mary's husband, the women continued their visiting and began to offer the women prisoners classes in reading and sewing. Later they pressed for a home for juvenile offenders. As a result, in 1828 the House of Refuge was established. Their next campaign, for a matron, met with success several years later. In 1835, when the Moyamensing Prison was opened in South Philadelphia, the women divided into two groups, one continuing to visit the women in Arch Street and the other making the long trip to Moyamensing. In 1853, under the leadership of Susan H. Lloyd (1801–1857), they established the Howard Institution for Discharged Prisoners, which operated until 1917.[19]

In 1846, the year Gibbons organized the Female Department of the Prison Association of New York, a third group of Quaker women prison visitors was developed in Baltimore by a twenty-six-year-old woman, Elizabeth T. King (1820–1856).The Women Friends Asso-ciation for Visiting the Penitentiary set about teaching women prison-ers to read and write and organized a prison school and library. They later began a campaign for the proper placement of discharged women prisoners, for the classification and separation of women prisoners, and for a matron.[20]

In addition to these groups of Quaker women, there were many individuals involved in prison reform. An early example is Eliza Wood Farnham, who became matron of the Mt. Pleasant prison for women, a division of Sing Sing, at Ossining, New York, in 1844 and introduced a series of reforms until forced to resign in 1848. Following the Civil War, Quaker women interested in prison reform turned their attention to the development of reformatories for women. In Indiana an evangelical Quaker woman, Rhoda Coffin (1826–1909), with her husband, Charles, began visiting prisons, jails, and workhouses in 1865 and helped to establish the first reformatory for women, which opened its doors in 1873. As first director, Rhoda Coffin chose a Quaker Civil War nurse, Sarah Smith, who served as head of the facility until 1882.[21]

When the second reformatory for women opened in Sherborn, Massachusetts, in 1877, Eliza Mosher (1846–1928), a Quaker woman doctor, was invited to serve as physician to the 350 inmates. She organized the prison dispensary and hospital, as well as serving as surgeon, obstetrician, and even dentist to the women. In 1880 she was asked to become superintendent of the new facility and remained in the position for three years, making many reforms in medical care. A severe injury to her knee caused her to retire from the reformatory after the three years but she maintained a lifelong interest in good penal care for women.[22]

A contemporary and friend of Gibbons, Quaker Elizabeth Buffum Chace (1806–1899), began her career in reform as an abolitionist and, after the Civil War, campaigned for prison matrons and for women to be appointed to the state prison boards. In 1870 she was named by the governor of Rhode Island to a Board of Lady Visitors. She shortly discovered that this board lacked influence and resigned in protest but was reappointed when more power was given to the Visitors.[23]

Carrying on the tradition into the early twentieth century, Martha Falconer (1862–1941) became a probation officer for the Cook County Juvenile Court in 1899, where she worked with Jane Addams and Florence Kelley, the latter a Friend, the former, closely affiliated. After working for several years in Chicago for the Children's Home and Aid Society as a probation social worker, she moved to Philadelphia to take over the old House of Refuge established in 1828 by the Society of Women Friends, moved it to a location near Lima, Pennsylvania, and developed it into a model school for delinquent girls, Sleighton Farm.[24]

Of these twelve Quaker women, ten were married, although two of the ten were separated. Many had large families; Wistar, for example, bore thirteen children. In the Quaker tradition, married women with children were expected to play a public role. Many travelled as ministers, though usually after the age of childbearing. Many also participated in the Quaker women's business meetings, learning to raise money, keep accounts, write petitions, and reach a sense of the meeting. Of the twelve women, eight appear to have had supportive husbands.

Because of the strong ties within the Quaker community, most of these women knew of each other; some were related by friendship, kinship, or marriage. Despite separations within the Society of Friends in the nineteenth century, these relationships held. Thus, Susan Lloyd, representing the conservative and wealthy Orthodox branch of Quakerism in Philadelphia, was well aware of the work of radical Hicksite Abby Gibbons and her colleagues in New York. Sharing a commitment to women's equality and to human betterment as aspects of their religious heritage, they encouraged one another and found support for their prison work in their Quaker traditions, meetings, publications and family networks. Gibbons can be seen as a Victorian woman reformer; she can also be seen as representative of Quaker women's philanthropy in the nineteenth century.

The Quaker women reformers were not exempt from the class attitudes of the larger society. Abby Gibbons was sometimes condescending, and often controlling, in her work with her poorer clients. But she was also a trail blazer, following her conscience where it led her, to new developments in work with women prisoners. Her story illuminates the work of nineteenth-century women prisoner reformers and their political strategies.

1

Her Father's Daughter

The black cook had refused an order and answered back and, although this was the Union Army in the midst of the Civil War, a black man was still called "a nigger" in tidewater Maryland and must be kept in his place. The man was accordingly sent to the guard house and tied to a tree in the front yard for three hours. Here he was seen by the chief nurse of the army hospital, a woman from the North, who asked what his offense was, expressed her sympathy, and upbraided the officer in charge in the presence of his subordinates. She said that there ought to be some changes made in the administration of the post and threatened to publish an account of the affair in the press.[1]

As a volunteer nurse, Abby Hopper Gibbons had no authority to interfere in matters of army discipline. But she regarded it her prerogative to intervene anyway, especially to defend the black escaped slaves or contrabands as they were called, who worked at the army base. She may not have thought of it at the time, but the scene duplicated many in which her father had been involved more than sixty years earlier. Isaac Tatem Hopper was credited with helping more than one thousand slaves obtain their freedom, arguing with their pursuing masters, serving as their spirited advocate before magistrates, or concealing them if need be. Gibbons identified with him, devoted her life to his causes, and was widely known as Isaac Hopper's daughter. Their lives are so intertwined that I have found it impossible to tell Gibbons's story without telling Hopper's.[2]

Abigail Hopper, universally known as Abby, was born in Philadelphia on December 7, 1801, the third daughter of Isaac and Sarah Tatum Hopper. While Sarah, the oldest daughter, was rather like her mother and Rachel, the second, was quiet and retiring, Abby was in every sense her father's daughter, a fighter for what she perceived to be justice. One

1

Isaac T. Hopper. Courtesy of Friends Historical Library, Swarthmore College.

might speculate that Isaac Hopper had hoped his third child would be a son and treated her as such, involving her in his crusades. Many of the nineteenth-century reforming women had strong fathers as role models. Gibbons identified with her father's crusades for the rights of blacks, prisoners, and prostitutes. According to a tribute paid to her at the time of her death, Gibbons "combined a man's confidence with a woman's tenderness."[3]

Isaac Hopper's interest in slavery began early. At ten he made the acquaintance of an African slave named Mingo, who worked on a neighboring farm and described to Isaac what it had been like to be snatched from his home village by the slave catchers. As a child Hopper was indignant, and later in life credited this episode as creating the sympathy he came to feel for the escaping slave or imperiled freedman. While some of his fellow Quakers were opposed to slavery on principle but had little feeling for the individual African American, Isaac Hopper was apparently motivated by his identification with the oppressed, person by person. When Lydia Maria Child, the nineteenth-century feminist and author, wrote his biography, she found herself writing primarily about the men and women he helped.[4]

Isaac Hopper disliked authority and welcomed a good fight with those in command, traits that his daughter Abby Hopper incorporated into her being. He was short of stature, as was she, and something of a dandy, according to Lydia Maria Child. He was mischievous, entertained a lively sense of humor, was quick to anger. His contemporaries perceived him as either a saint or a scatterbrain. After his death and the publication of his biography he became legendary as a nineteenth-century philanthropist.[5]

The Hoppers came from Woodbury, New Jersey, and were of Quaker ancestry. Isaac's father had been disowned for marrying a Presbyterian woman, Rebecca Tatem, so Isaac grew up as a Presbyterian, but had many Quaker cousins and friends. Eventually his mother joined and his father rejoined the Religious Society of Friends. In 1787, at the age of sixteen, Isaac went to Philadelphia to serve as an apprentice in the tailoring shop of his mother's brother, Joseph Tatem.[6]

Philadelphia was the site of the Constitutional Convention that year, and Isaac Hopper often saw General George Washington on the streets. He also saw many African Americans. At that time Philadelphia had the largest population of free blacks in the United States. Remembering Mingo, Hopper became interested in making their acquaintance, and from them learned of the problems of slaves who tried to escape from their southern masters when brought to Philadelphia.[7]

Isaac Hopper's uncle, Joseph Tatem, was a member of the Society for Alleviating the Miseries of the Public Prisons, a prison reform group formed in 1787 by Quakers and Episcopalians. He often took his apprentices to watch public executions, believing it a good way to warn them against a life of crime. Isaac Hopper, however, noted the way the crowd seemed to relish the savage spectacle and concluded that watching an execution might have an opposite effect, hardening the audience to violence. He became in later life a strong opponent of capital punishment.[8]

Joseph Tatem also took him to the public prison when Dr. William White and Dr. William Rogers, both members of the Society, were to preach to the prisoners. This event was also turned into a public spectacle, the prison keeper having placed a loaded cannon on the platform, aimed at the prisoners, to emphasize how dangerous they were. Again, Isaac drew the opposite conclusion, believing that fear in the keepers was itself a destructive ingredient.[9]

After seven years of apprenticeship, Isaac Hopper was ready to launch his own business as a tailor and to marry his childhood sweetheart. Sarah Tatum (no relation to Isaac's mother, Rebecca Tatem, despite the similarity of name) was also of pre-Revolutionary Quaker descent, the daughter of a well-to-do farmer from Woodbury, New Jersey. In order to be allowed to marry Sarah Tatum it would be necessary for Isaac to become a Quaker. He joined the Philadelphia Monthly Meeting of the Religious Society of Friends in September 1792; three years later he and Sarah were wed under the care of the Woodbury, New Jersey, Monthly Meeting, to which the Tatums belonged and which Isaac's parents had recently joined. The young couple settled at 39 Pine Street in Philadelphia and became members of the Philadelphia Monthly Meeting for the Southern District, at Pine Street.[10]

A few months after his marriage, Isaac Hopper became a member of the Acting Committee of the Pennsylvania Abolition Society, a largely Quaker group formed in 1775, which lobbied the Constitutional Convention to abolish slavery in the new nation. Failing in this, it advocated the abolition of slavery state by state, as well as other legislation protecting the rights of blacks. Under the Fugitive Slave Act of 1793, a slave became free after living for six months on free soil. Many slaves did not know about this right and failed to claim liberty. Also, many slave owners hired slave catchers who came North looking for slaves and sometimes kidnapped free blacks who bore some resemblance to the slaves they were searching for. The Acting Committee was assigned the duty of rescuing blacks from entrapments. As his partner in this work, Isacc Hopper had a man called Thomas Harrison, another well-known abolitionist. Harrison was also an overseer of the African School, run by the Society of Friends for black children, at which Isaac Hopper taught.[11]

Together, Hopper and Harrison also arranged manumissions for slaves brought to Pennsylvania and often indentured them to local farmers so that they could pay for their own purchase. Such was the case with a slave called William Anderson, whom Thomas Harrison bought and then indentured to Jacob Downing of Downingtown, a son-in-law of Elizabeth Drinker. Sometimes the slave himself had already saved the purchase price. Isaac Hopper arranged for the self-purchase of a slave named Manuel from Joseph Spears of Halifax County in the state of North Carolina for the price of $100.[12]

As agents of the Pennsylvania Abolition Society, Harrison and Hopper sued the owners of Pennsylvania vessels illegally involved in the foreign slave trade. In 1804 they brought to court the Pennsylvania owners of the vessels *Eliza* and *Sally.* The former had picked up six young slaves in Antigua and sold them in Havana, while the latter had acquired a hundred slaves in Gambia and sold them in St. Thomas. In 1805 they brought legal action against the owner of a third vessel, the brig *Tyrphrena,* which had transported twelve slaves to Havana and there sold them.[13]

In 1840 Isaac Hopper began publishing a series of "Tales of Oppression" in the *National Anti-Slavery Standard*, describing some of the escaped slaves he aided. Verification for some of these *Tales* can be found in the Minutes of the Acting Society of the Pennsylvania Abolition Society, in court records, and in contemporary newspapers. In other instances, Hopper seems to have acted on his own, as a freelance advocate for the escaping slave. Elizabeth Drinker, a prominent Quaker who kept a diary from 1758 to 1807, records an occasion when constables came after her daughter's black servant, Harry, and she immediately sent for Isaac Hopper.[14]

In addition to his work for the Abolition Society, Hopper was involved in other philanthropies. In 1799 he was made a Guardian of the Poor, in charge of taking care of all cases of need in a geographical district adjacent to his home. The Guardians operated on a budget of approximately $40,000 a year, raised by a "poor tax" levied on property. With this sum they maintained, on city relief, all those who were destitute, operated a city almshouse, and distributed wood and bread during the winter months. Isaac was assigned to one district and dealt with such problems as seeing to it that fathers supported their illegitimate children and that young boys were apprenticed to good masters. In the course of his work, he again involved himself personally in several of his cases.[15]

The following year he joined the Society for Alleviating the Miseries of the Public Prisons, to which his uncle belonged, and was made an inspector of the prisons. In this role he began working on such problems as piping water from a clean source into the jail, ordering new linens for the infirmary, and changing the regulations of the debtors prison.[16]

The Pennsylvania Prison Society, as it later came to be called, was involved in an effort to convert the old Walnut Street jail into a penitentiary, where prisoners might be classified and separated as much as possible, and thus be given an opportunity to meditate upon their sins, with the help of regular and constant visits from persons designated as prison visitors. The concept of the penitentiary had been developed by a British reformer, John Howard, but was first given expression by this Pennsylvania group.[17]

Separate confinement was never more than an idea at the Walnut Street jail, because overcrowding made it virtually impossible. (Later, the Society built the Eastern State Penitentiary, the first such structure in the world.) There were, however, many other reforms which the Society worked for: the separation of male and female prisoners, the employment of prisoners in useful work, the beginnings of educational and religious training, the first attempts at classification.[18]

Isaac Hopper's interest, however, was always more the individual than the philosophy. In his *Tales of Oppression* and in Child's biography are listed several cases of prisoners he helped. At the Walnut Street jail he befriended two adolescent boys who had been confined for giving false evidence against a neighbor, at the insistence of their irrational father. Isaac Hopper objected to their being housed with adult prisoners and finally persuaded the board of inspectors to allow him to apprentice them to masters, a sort of early work release. Isaac himself oversaw the boys and entertained them once a week in his home until they had finished their apprenticeships and were established in their own businesses. He frequently brought them home for dinner at the crowded Hopper table.[19]

That table was becoming even more crowded as more young Hoppers were born. Elizabeth joined the family in 1803. Hannah and John, born in 1805 and 1807, both died at the age of one year; next came Isaac in 1809, Edward in 1810, Josiah in 1813, John in 1815. Abby Hopper and her sisters helped with this stream of infants, but so also did Isaac, who sometimes took care of the babies while their mother was away, and often took the older children off her hands for a day at a time.[20]

While Gibbons identified with her father, she idealized her mother, Sarah Tatum Hopper, as the epitome of womanly traits. Gibbons described Sarah Hopper to her children and grandchildren as a handsome woman, with a pink complexion, blue eyes, and hair inclined to curl. She remembered her as an excellent housewife, a person who had a place for everything and everything in its place, but also as a very thoughtful, "care-taking" woman, possessing her own quiet sense of humor. She was a talented cook and seamstress, who managed to stretch Isaac Hopper's meager earnings to feed and clothe an enormous household.[21]

The family into which Abby Hopper was born, already a large one, was often augmented by the presence of her father's proteges: escaping slaves, released prisoners, sometimes young "fallen women" for whom Isaac Hopper had a soft spot in his heart. There were, in addition, the apprentices from the Hopper tailor shop and sometimes visitors from the Philadelphia African American community. Richard Allen, the founder of Mother Bethel African-Episcopal Church, was a guest, as well as David Mapps, a black Quaker sea captain. Isaac Hopper's entertaining of blacks was unusual for his day; most philanthropists kept the objects of their concern at arm's length. Abby Hopper's mother welcomed this abundance of guests, but many in the Quaker community frowned on the little tailor's propensity to involve himself in everyone's business but his own.[22]

While Gibbons's father was an activist, her mother was devout and inward, often speaking in the silence of Quaker meeting. At first, Sarah Hopper was too busy with her large family of children to have much time to devote to the ministry, but in 1816 she was recognized as a minister by her meeting, as close as Friends came to ordination, and thereafter sometimes travelled to other meetings in the surrounding states to preach the gospel, while Isaac Hopper took care of the children. She also helped finance the family by keeping a tea shop in her parlor. Thus, while she taught her daughters household arts, she also passed down to them the legacy of the independence of Quaker women, which had been a part of the movement since the birth of Quakerism in Puritan England in the middle of the seventeenth century. In the nineteenth century this legacy flowered in large numbers of Quaker women taking the lead in reforms, in professions such as medicine, and in the movement for women's rights. Gibbons's career as an abolitionist and prison reformer can be seen as part of this flowering.[23]

According to Gibbons's later and idealized recollections, discipline in the large Hopper family was maintained by high expectations. Each child was expected to perform some task and to obey household rules, such as not speaking until spoken to at the table. If a child was disobedient, he was usually reasoned with rather than punished and made to feel he had disappointed his parents. The Quaker community reinforced the expectations of the parents, so that children were urged both at home and meeting to be good and obedient. It worked especially well when a child chose a parent as a role model, as Abby Hopper did Isaac.[24]

One of Abby Hopper's favorite possessions throughout her lifetime was an Indian china bird given to her when she was about ten by a freed slave in gratitude for her helpfulness and sympathy. Abby Hopper's identification with her father led her to interest herself at an early age in his proteges. She was rather like him: short of stature, fun loving, courageous, a fighter. William Lloyd Garrison, a friend of the family, thought that she resembled Isaac in certain features. Her daughter describes her as a handsome child, with blue eyes, pink cheeks, and curling hair. The only extant pictures are of her at middle age, looking serious, with slanting brows over large eyes, a prominent nose, a strong chin, and a straight mouth, at the corners of which lurk a touch of humor. [25]

Like her father, Abby Hopper did not like pomposity. One of the family stories about her concerns her dressing herself and a younger brother in the plain clothes of the Quakers of that period and going to "deal with" young friends who indulged in frivolous amusements, thus making fun of the elders at Quaker meeting, whose duty it was to reprove the frivolous. Despite the Quaker simplicity of the household, Abby Hopper liked clothes and once went away on a week's visit taking eight dresses, an unheard-of number in those days. On the other hand, according to family legend, she was generous with attire. On another occasion, when a young woman, Elizabeth Hicks, was travelling with her and complained that she had forgotten to bring a "best dress," Abby Hopper lent her her only extra outfit. Elizabeth did not realize that she was depriving Abby Hopper of her own favorite dress. When she learned of this, she sent Abby Hopper a beautiful dress of turk silk. It was so pretty that Abby Hopper put it carefully away for an appropriate time to use it.[26]

Also in keeping with her father, Abby Hopper often had a sharp and witty retort to criticism. Once her mother was telling her she must be more careful and added, "Thee will not always have me to tell thee these things." Abby Hopper replied, "Well, Mother, thee can write it down." Both mother and daughter laughed over the incident.[27]

Abby Gibbons's childhood memories were collected by Sarah Emerson from a series of letters Gibbons wrote to her granddaughter Bonnie

Morse in 1878. They were highly idealized. Among the happiest memories she related was spending time with her father on Saturdays. In July 1811, Isaac Hopper took his older children and their schoolmates, eleven in all, for a ferry ride across the Delaware River to Kaign's Point, through the woods to Newtown Meeting house, and on to Joseph Kaign's farm. Here they visited an elderly African American woman, old Nancy, who sold gingerbread and homemade root beer. After they ate, the children scattered to gather flowers and berries, which they took home to Philadelphia and supper for the entire crew at the Hopper home. As Abby Hopper remembered the day, her mother made shortcakes to go with the berries, and after they had eaten in the usual silence, Sarah Hopper sat at the table listening to her children's account of the outing.[28]

Another source of joy to Abby Hopper as a child were visits to her grandparents. Both the Tatums and the Hoppers lived on farms in New Jersey, not far from each other. Visiting the Tatums, Abby Hopper and her sisters were often taken by horse and buggy to visit the Hoppers. At the Tatum farm, Abby Hopper delighted in walking across the velvety front lawn, feeding the chickens, picking cherries, watching the cows being milked, playing house in a hole in the ground, making rush baskets, or driving with her grandfather to the mill. One younger uncle, Josiah Tatum, had a scholarly nature, took a book along when he plowed, and liked to read poetry.[29]

Brothers of Isaac Hopper also had farms in New Jersey, which the Hopper children visited. Abby Hopper particularly remembered that of her Uncle George and his wife, Aunt Beulah, who lived at Mullica Hill. This aunt and uncle often came to Philadelphia with produce from the farm in the summer and, in the winter, sometimes a little roast pig. Aunt Beulah had a little dark-eyed baby who delighted Abby Hopper, and on really cold days the mother would rub the child with applejack before setting out on the long trip to the city.[30]

Philadelphia was itself an interesting place for a growing girl. Along the banks of the Delaware River were the docks of oceangoing sailing ships and the warehouses of the merchants who used the ships for commerce. Front Street was lined with the houses of the merchants as well as small shops and taverns. The city stretched westward, when Gibbons was born, as far as Eighth street, slowly filling out the neat squares that William Penn had planned for his Greene Countrie Towne. At Sixth and Chestnut, Independence Hall, the seat of the federal government until 1801 and of the state government thereafter, drew politicians from all over. Lenni Lenape Indians came there to plead their case. Free blacks were beginning to settle as far south as Lombard Street. At Center Square there was an occasional circus or hot air balloon to be seen.[31]

The education of daughters was important to the Hoppers. The Monthly Meeting for the Southern District, at Pine Street, to which they belonged, operated a "select" school for girls. Sarah Tatum Hopper was often appointed to the committee to supervise this school, which Sarah, Rachel, and Abby Hopper attended. Sarah Hopper also served on a committee to oversee the schools for black children operated by the meeting. In 1799 the Philadelphia Yearly Meeting had established a boarding school at Westtown, Pennsylvania, about twenty-five miles from Philadelphia, to provide higher education for Quaker young people. The Hoppers were interested in this school and enrolled their oldest daughter, Sarah, there for the year 1810–1811. Here she studied grammar, penmanship, arithmetic, and science. She wrote her parents that she was learning to make maps, and that she wished they would send her some sweet cakes. She also asked for a historical romance, but her mother, who was on a committee to supervise the reading material of Quaker children, did not approve. [32]

Abby Hopper, at age nine, wrote to her big sister at Westtown:

> I want to write to thee very much but I hardly know what to tell thee we are all prity well little brother Isaac runs a bout and is very hearty. I should like to come and see thee very much give my love to Esther Morton I do not go to school we have got no mistress Grandfather is unwell he was not in town today but cousin Joseph Whitall come to see us—accept my love, Abigail Hopper.[33]

A year later, when she wrote to Sarah again she had learned to punctuate:

> I take up my pen to write a few lines to tell thee I am well and hope thee is the same. Edward has been very sick and Mother thinks he is better. I think thee might make me a bag or something before thee comes home. Rachel wrote to Ellen last first day. Isaac has been bravely and can say anything at all.[34]

The Hoppers may have expected to send Rachel and then Abby to Westtown. (Elizabeth was evidently handicapped and was always kept at home.) But in 1811 disaster struck the household. Isaac's wide-ranging interests often outran his meager income as a tailor. He sometimes advanced money for the manumission of a slave or to stake an ex-prisoner, optimistically believing that he would be repaid. Some times he wasn't and to make ends meet, was forced to borrow money. He moved his shop and residence in 1805 from 39 Pine Street to the corner of Dock Street and Walnut, possibly as an effort to save. As early as 1804 there is a note in the minutes of the Pennsylvania Prison Society that Isaac Hopper was in its debt. While he kept his good health he was always able to survive by working harder. But in 1811 he fell ill and his business declined. His creditors became alarmed and demanded payment instantly. He was bankrupt.[35]

The elders of the Society of Friends had watched and worried over Isaac Hopper's precarious financial position for some time. Quakers had a strong aversion to borrowing, feeling it discredited the entire community in the eyes of outsiders and thus damaged "the reputation of truth," as they called it. It was a greater sin in Quaker eyes of the period to become bankrupt than to ignore social issues. Other members of the community were involved in the Abolition Society and the Prison Society, but these were generally prosperous men who had the leisure to devote to such enterprises. Now Isaac Hopper was visited with the harsh punishment of expulsion or disownment, "for departing at times from the truth in his assertions, and failing in the discharge of his just debts." His community standing was also injured. The Pennsylvania Abolition Society, for which he had worked long and faithfully, frostily accepted his resignation. He was a ruined man.[36]

Sarah Hopper had meanwhile been selected as an overseer at the Pine Street Meeting. Feeling her position untenable in light of her husband's disownment, she offered to resign. But the meeting made it clear that they had no argument with her, and she continued to be active on several committees. The family had to move in order to retrench. To help her husband she appealed to her father, John Tatum, who allowed the Hopper family to occupy a building he owned on Spruce Street. It was here she opened a tea shop in the parlor to help her husband pay off his many debts.[37]

There was, consequently, no money for Westtown when Abby Hopper might have gone in 1815. Instead, she continued to attend the select school supervised by her mother. The head teacher that year was Rebecca Bunker, a Quaker from Nantucket, assisted by her younger cousin Lucretia Coffin Mott, who taught at the school in 1815 and 1816. Born on the island of Nantucket, educated at Nine Partners boarding school near Poughkeepsie, Mott was a brilliant woman, a grammarian, able to speak French, and a talented teacher, who probably offered her pupils, including Abby Hopper, as much as Westtown could provide. We know at least that Abby left this school able herself to be a teacher, and with such skills that she later helped prepare young women for college. Whether she resented the fact that Sarah went to Westtown and she did not we do not know. There is an occasional edge in her letters about Sarah, suggesting that she was jealous of her father's regard for this older sister, though she hid these feelings behind a facade of admiration.[38]

In addition to being Abby Hopper's teacher, Lucretia Mott was a close friend of the family. She and Isaac Hopper shared a concern about the abolition of slavery as well as prison reform. Some years later Abby's brother Edward married Lucretia Mott's daughter Anna, making Lucretia a sort of honorary aunt to the Hopper children. Scarcely five feet tall, with a sweet voice, a heart-shaped face, and an indomitable will, Lucretia Mott was a role model for many nineteenth-century women. The Hopper daughters followed her into the antislavery struggle.[39]

When she had completed all the courses the Pine Street select school had to offer, Abby Hopper began to assist her mother in the tea shop on Spruce Street, which was by now a modest success. After a year of this, she decided she might do better teaching school and opened a small school for the children of Friends at No. 1 School Avenue, Comptroller Street, charging a tuition of $3.00 a quarter or $12.00 a year. The pupils were mostly from families she knew, and she taught reading, writing, arithmetic, spelling, geography, and, for the girls, sewing. She was soon so successful that she was able to support herself and make small contributions to her father's purse.[40]

Abby Hopper's school was independent, not under the control of a Quaker meeting, and therefore not the responsibility of a Quaker committee. Friends nevertheless took a lively interest in what subjects were being taught, too lively an interest for Abby Hopper's taste, as she wrote a sister.

> Prissy Doves got up in Meeting this morning, and said she could not "approve of those schools where they painted *picters* and *larned* beadwork, and all that kind of thing." I thought to myself, she would raise her hands at the sight of the samplers in my school just now. They are splendid, and when you come, you shall have a sight of them, for they are nearly finished.[41]

Gradually, Isaac Hopper paid off his debts. In 1816 he made an apology to the meeting for having "engaged in pursuits which occasioned embarrassment in his circumstances and in that situation was induced to make promises he was unable to comply with," stated he was sorry for his conduct, and asked to be readmitted. The meeting, however, must have found that he was still in debt, for not until February 23, 1820, was his apology accepted.[42]

Fresh troubles, however, awaited the Hopper family. While some Quaker families of the period appeared able to control the number of their offspring, the Hoppers did not. Sarah had a baby girl, Susannah, in 1817, and a baby boy, Willie, in 1820, when she was forty-five. Sarah did not recover as quickly from his birth as she had the others and grew ill with what was described at the time as a severe dyspepsia, but may have been an ulcer, or even stomach cancer. When baby Willie died in January 1822, having lived just a year, Sarah Hopper grieved and became increasingly sick. On the 18th of June, she died.[43]

Abby Hopper had been aware of the loss of a baby sister, Hannah, when she was five, and of a baby brother, John, two years later. She was, however, twenty-one when her mother died, able to experience the full range of adult grief. Because she so identified with her father, she also participated in his deep sense of loss. For a time Isaac Hopper could do nothing but go over his keepsakes of Sarah and mourn. It was a hard time for the young woman. Her older sister, Sarah, had married a local merchant, Jonathan Palmer, in 1822, and given birth to her first child, also named Sarah. Sarah Palmer remained supportive to her father and did what she could, but she was no longer a member of the household. Rachel, the second daughter, seems to have been overshadowed by her older sister, Sarah, and vigorous Abby. Rachel was devoted to her father but the responsibility for the household seems to have devolved on Abby.[44]

More pain was to come. Isaac, the oldest living son, was fifteen. A quiet, sedate boy, he had been devoted to his mother and, according to Abby, felt her loss deeply. Both his parents had hoped that he would become a Quaker minister, but he evidently had tuberculosis, for now he went into a decline, as it was put in that time, and died just a year after his mother. His loss was almost too much for his father to bear. Abby grieved over Isaac, and worried over her father.[45]

Death was a not uncommon event in the families of that period. Summer after summer, yellow fever took its toll of the inhabitants of Philadelphia, New York, and Baltimore. Because of poor sanitary conditions there were also many deaths from dysentery; tuberculosis was rampant and cancer, untreatable at that period, took a heavy toll. However, it cannot be assumed that the sense of loss was less numbing then than in a time of more longevity. Abby Hopper's whole life was to be shadowed by the loss of family members. Her ability to come to terms with death and to sublimate her grief in acts of philanthropy was her outstanding characteristic, according to her admirers. During the Civil War, her capacity to comfort and support dying soldiers on the battlefield, as well as to aid their grieving parents, stemmed, it was said, from her own experiences with death. One lesson she learned early was that keeping busy was a great antidote to grief.

Among the frequent visitors to the Hopper household at the time of Sarah's illness and death had been a younger woman, an Irish Quaker, Hannah Attmore. Although younger than Sarah Hopper, Hannah had developed a friendship with her and had often assisted her in the household. She was a favorite with the children and, although considerably younger than Isaac, was a quiet, sedate person and a suitable companion for him. Isaac began to walk to meeting with Hannah and to discuss his worries about his children. In turn, she consulted him when her mother died and she had to settle her estate, including some lands in Ireland. One day Isaac asked her if she would like to become a member of his household. "Oh, I would like nothing better," she replied. Then suddenly realizing his true meaning, she blushed deeply. In February 1824 they were married under the care of the Pine Street Meeting.[46]

Before the marriage, Isaac consulted his older children and gained their approval. In later life, Abby Hopper always referred to Hannah as "mother" and was concerned about her welfare. When yet more Hopper children were born to this second marriage (Isaac in 1824, Mary in 1826, Thomas in 1828, and Hannah in 1831), Abby became attached to them and concerned with their care. Yet in her letters to her sister, Abby frequently wrote of the merits of her real mother. Once, forty-five years later, writing of a child who was being taken to witness the remarriage of her father, she said, "It is a mistake. Having known the experience I am qualified to speak."[47]

Whatever her feelings, Abby Hopper remained a member of her father's household for another five years, keeping her school, helping with the babies, visiting among her friends. She was always active; her quieter sister Rachel once complained that she was everlastingly on the go. "I'm sure I don't visit much," Abby wrote her sister Sarah, "but as I do all the visiting that is done, and all the errands, shopping etc. I must go out occasionally. She hates to see my bonnet go on, even for meeting."[48]

Among Abby's friends were young men as well as young women. She attended social events with Thomas Fisher, Dillwyn Parrish, and Edward Townsend. One family legend was that she went with a young man to visit a glass works. To their surprise they found there was a fifty-cent admission. Abby's escort blanched, but gamely invited Abby to go in nevertheless. Abby mischievously entered, but was careful to leave a fifty-cent piece at his house the next day. Nevertheless, she had no steady beaux.[49]

Little stigma attached to being a single woman in Quaker Philadelphia at the time. Quakerism, with its emphasis on gender equality, encouraged women to believe that they could live happily independent of men. In the seventeenth and eighteenth centuries many Quaker women were travelling lay ministers; in the nineteenth century they kept shops, taught school, and began to enter the professions. In the nation at large, fewer women were marrying, some 7.3 percent remaining single at the time. Many of these single women were becoming schoolmarms or working in the textile mills that were just being established in New England. Busy with her school and her life in her father's family, Abby Hopper appeared to be settled into a comfortable routine by the time she was twenty-eight. She told her friend Deborah Wharton that she had resolved to live a life of single blessedness.[50]

Abby Hopper spent the first thirty-one years of her life in Quaker Philadelphia. As her father's daughter she shared his many ups and downs with Quakerism and eventually left the Society. Yet its stamp remained with her. She continued to wear Quaker clothes and use Quaker language. In her nineties she was described by the New York politicians she lobbied as "that little Quaker lady."

2

The Abolitionist/Feminists

A long with escaping slaves and ex-prisoners, trouble was a constant visitor to the Hopper household. No sooner Isaac Hopper been reinstated in Quaker meeting and married his second wife than the whole family was embroiled in a major controversy. This was the split between the Orthodox and Hicksite Friends, which occurred in Philadelphia Yearly Meeting in 1827 and spread throughout American Quakerism in the next few years.[1]

The Hicksites were named for Elias Hicks, a Long Island farmer and Quaker minister of the old school. Hicks believed in the authority of the Inner Teacher or Inward Light to interpret Scripture and to understand the meaning of the historical Jesus. He loved liberty and was opposed to all pomp and outward authority. He felt wealth and power were incompatible with the Religious Society of Friends and longed to see Quakers return to a more simple way of living. He was strongly antislavery and preached against the keeping of slaves; he went to great lengths not to use products of slave labor in his clothes or his household. Travelling as a Quaker minister in the Philadelphia area, he urged Quakers to use Free Produce and criticized wealthy Quakers who did not participate in the boycott of slave products.[2]

These views upset many prominent Quakers of the day. There had been an evangelical revival among British Friends, which had spread across the ocean and was affecting primarily the more cosmopolitan American Friends with ties across the seas. Emphasis was now being placed on redemption from sin through the crucifixion of Jesus Christ, on the necessity of faith in salvation, and on the authority of the scriptures. The lay ministry in meeting for worship was being examined for its compatibility with these beliefs; those who did not measure up were being criticized by a

17

committee of the meeting and told to confine their ministry to what were now considered correct beliefs. Hicks was so criticized, or "eldered," to use the Quaker term, when he spoke in the Philadelphia area in 1819. He and his friends objected to the eldering, claiming that it stemmed from a misuse of ecclesiastical authority. The controversy stirred up many hidden conflicts, particularly those between the plain-living, rural Friends and their more sophisticated urban counterparts; between those who were strongly antislavery and those who believed the subject of slavery was too controversial to bring up in meeting; between those who regarded themselves as reformers, wanting to rid the Society of the trappings of wealth and power, and those who felt there was need for centralized control. Class, in other words, played an important role in the controversy. Families became split over the issue, and old friendships cooled.[3]

Isaac Hopper had met Elias Hicks when he came to the Philadelphia area in 1819, and became a strong partisan. The two had much in common; a simple farm background, a dislike for pomp and authority, an identification with the poor, a fighting spirit. Isaac admired Elias's courage in preaching against slavery in the South and in standing up to the weighty Friends of Philadelphia Yearly Meeting. The two corresponded about the growing tensions, and Isaac Hopper attached himself to the group in Philadelphia Yearly Meeting that objected to Elias Hicks's being eldered, even if some did not subscribe to all his views. Abby Hopper's advocacy of her father and her own dislike of arbitrary authority made her an early follower of Hicks.[4]

Lines were already tightly drawn in 1823, when Mary Waln Wistar organized Philadelphia Quaker women to visit women prisoners in the Walnut Street jail. Wistar belonged to the Quaker establishment, and it was from these circles that she drew her colleagues. She had been inspired by the work of Elizabeth Gurney Fry, an upper-class English Friend, in visiting women prisoners in Newgate prison, beginning in 1816. Born into one wealthy family and married into another, Fry invited Quaker women from prominent families to join her Ladies Association for the Improvement of Female Prisoners at Newgate. We do not know whether Abby Hopper evinced interest in prison reform in her early twenties. We can however surmise that she would not have been asked to join the Wistar group.[5]

In 1827 the smoldering fires of ecclesiastical debate finally burst into open flame at the Philadelphia Yearly Meeting. Under the leadership of a Quaker educator, John Comly, a majority group tried to oust the conservative clerk, and when this proved impossible, decided upon "a quiet re-

treat from the scene of confusion." A schism resulted, with bitter arguments over meeting houses and school properties. Some meetings were
primarily Hicksite and disowned or expelled the Orthodox from membership. Others were Orthodox and disowned the Hicksites.[6]

The Pine Street Meeting, to which Abby Hopper and her family belonged, was one of the latter, and once more Isaac Hopper faced disownment at the hands of the elders, who could not refrain from
mentioning his previous sin of "departing from the truth." This time,
however, Isaac was able to argue that being disowned was the work of
partisanship. He and his family moved their membership to a Hicksite
meeting in Darby, and Isaac entered zestfully into the bitter conflict between the two branches.[7]

Strongly partisan, Abby Hopper took the Hicksite side of the argument and enjoyed poking fun at some of the stuffy Orthodox. Yet there
was some sadness too. Her favorite uncle, Josiah Tatum, remained
Orthodox, and relations with him became strained.[8]

Many of the customers who had frequented Isaac Hopper's tailoring
shop were wealthy city Quakers, who joined the Orthodox party. After
the split, they withdrew their patronage, and business languished. Isaac
Hopper had never been devoted to the tailoring trade anyway, and when
a new opportunity arose to manage a bookstore devoted to the printing
and sale of Quaker books, he was intrigued. The controversy within
Quakerism had produced a thirst for Quaker books, and a New York
friend of the Friends, Marcus Gould, interested in publishing, decided to
start a store and to edit a new Hicksite paper, *The Friend, or the
Advocate of Truth*. He needed a well-known Friend to head up the project, and who better than Isaac T. Hopper?[9]

The only drawback was that the job demanded a move to New York
City. The Hoppers had deep roots in Philadelphia. The oldest daughter,
Sarah, was married and settled there, and Abby was happily ensconced in
her school. Isaac discussed the offer with Hannah, and they decided reluctantly that for the sake of their large family of children they must make
the move. Accordingly, they packed up in the summer of 1829 and moved
to a rented house in downtown New York City.[10]

Because of her school, Abby Hopper stayed behind and lived with her
married sister, Sarah Palmer, and her family. She was twenty-eight years
old, but being away from her family, and especially her beloved father,
was very hard. She looked forward to his letters eagerly and shared them
with Philadelphia friends and relations. "My dear father cannot imagine
what a rich present his letter was. It raised my spirits to the 99th degree

and I feel 'great spirits' to answer it," she wrote. The Palmers and she had attended a Quarterly Meeting, at which Exeter Meeting had asked to join the Hicksite branch, and Sarah Hopper Palmer had been named clerk for the coming year. "The *elevation* does not set remarkably well on Sarah, but no doubt her father will be proud she is so well thought of," Abby Hopper commented, with some apparent jealousy. James and Lucretia Mott had spent an evening with them, reading the letter from Isaac Hopper and talking about how well things were going for him. In April Isaac Hopper wrote to Abby that they were moving, and that she should not go to the expense of dismissing her school for the sake of helping with the move, although they would be pleased to see her. He also asked for news of the Orthodox Yearly Meeting and of further details of the split. Abby's longing for her family evidently did not diminish and, finally, in the summer of 1830 she moved to join her father's family at the house at 122 Allen Street and to take charge of a Quaker school for girls nearby.[11]

Abby Hopper's devotion to her family of origin sounds out of character for her sturdy sense of self, but it simply reflects a theme that runs through many of the letters of women of this period. Only a comparative handful were venturing to teach or work in the mills in the early years of the nineteenth century. Home remained a major focus of their lives.[12]

New York City, to which Abby Hopper moved in 1832, was still confined to the lower tip of Manhattan Island, although beginning to grow rapidly. The harbor bristled with ships from all parts of the world, and New Yorkers liked to stroll in Castle Garden at the Battery and survey the docks. Fulton Street market offered every form of seafood as well as fruits and vegetables from nearby farms. Wall Street was becoming a commercial center, and the new city hall was everyone's pride. The Hoppers lived in a quiet downtown section of small individual homes with backyard gardens.[13]

Abby Hopper enjoyed exploring the noisy, bustling city but missed Philadelphia and its inhabitants. During the winter she had spent with the Palmers, she had often been in the company of a young man who was a partner of Jonathan Palmer, her brother-in-law. James Sloan Gibbons was a member of a distinguished Quaker family with pre-Revolutionary roots in Chester County, owning property, which they sold at a modest price to the committee planning to build Westtown Boarding school in 1799. James's father, William Gibbons, a physician, had moved to Wilmington, Delaware, and here he and his wife, Rebecca Donaldson Gibbons, had had fourteen children and raised all but one. Dr. Gibbons was a strong supporter of Elias Hicks and edited a newspaper for a time supporting the reformers' cause.[14] His son James S. Gibbons was tall, handsome, high-spirited, and compatible, but he was too young for Abby Hopper, she thought, being nine years her junior. It may be that one of her reasons for leaving Philadelphia was to get away from an attachment she thought could go nowhere. In September the Palmers visited in New York, and on their return she wrote jestingly to them about *Jim:*

> Jonathan, I can *easily* guess who helped thee from the boat with the children. It was *Jim* without a doubt. Just like one of his kind acts—tell me *one* good trait that fellow doesn't possess—can't name *one*. Sarah, thee is right; *"he is a none-such of the present age"*—of *every age.* If I were only a few years younger and there were not so many nice girls flocking round him *on the spot,* I'd *set my cap. . . .*[15]

During her first several years in New York, Abby Hopper was preoccupied with running a girls' school for the New York Monthly Meeting (Hicksite) the forerunner of the present Friends Seminary. The school was located in a building on Elizabeth Street, connected by an iron bridge to the Hester Street Meeting, not far from the Hopper home. Unlike her school in Philadelphia, of which she was the proprietor, Abby's new school was under the care of a committee of the monthly meeting. Isaac wrote to Sarah to say that the committee was very attentive and kind to Abby, reported an obvious improvement in the school, and was well satisfied. But Abby was enough her father's daughter to resent authority, especially when it exceeded reasonable limits. She set out to accept the supervision, but after the first year she found it as galling as her friends in Philadelphia had expected, knowing the independence of her mind. She wrote to her friends William and Deborah Wharton about it:

> My present occupation is, on some accounts, desirable; it affords a better opportunity than I have hitherto experienced, of increasing my store of knowledge, which has always been very limited. Yet the circumstance that I am under the *direction of those in authority,* is not exactly in accordance with my views of independence. A declaration of my freedom has remedied some difficulties, and under the *present* regulation, I am tolerably content. . . .

I made a proposition a few days since to have my room enlarged
four feet, which will take in the unoccupied space in the larger
apartment. The only argument against the alteration is that it
will detroy the *uniformity* which is certainly of little account in
the consideration of the health of a large number of children (60)
and my own . . . . Classes in succession from nine to three, with
half an hour's intermission at noon.[16]

At noon there was a recess and Abby Hopper hurried home to a quick
lunch prepared by Hannah Hopper, and then raced back to be ready for her
12:30 P.M. grammar class. Later, she often had to spend her lunch hour getting ready for a sewing class which some of the parents insisted upon.
Arithmetic came in the afternoon, and she had to deal with her scholars in
two separate classes. From nine to five, she wrote a friend, she often had no
time to herself. Despite the strenuous schedule, she loved the job but continued to feel rebellious about the supervision of the committee. Her good
friend Mary Thomas wrote from Philadelphia to urge her to accept the
overseers, since they would not give up the right to visit, but to "stick to thy
bows—do not be wheeled out of those necessary articles while thy own
mind is easy with their presence. Thy concerned friends must find out, what
we in Philadelphia know, that thou art an independent character."[17]

Meanwhile, she took her place once more in her father's household,
helping her stepmother and sister Rachel do the washing for the large
household whenever there was fresh rainwater in the cistern, supervising
the white-washing of kitchen, cellar, vault, and pantries, and gathering
grapes from the vines in their backyard. Hannah had a new baby and was
frequently confined to her bedroom, but Isaac was in good form, and entertained the whole family at suppertime with his adventures of the day.

Isaac Hopper was preparing to take a trip to Ireland to look into
Hannah's affairs and collect some money owed her. He was still in some
financial difficulties and had borrowed money from his employer, Marcus
Gould, to pay off his debts and to finance the trip. He left in September,
his children John, Josiah, and Abby accompanying him by boat to the
ship that was to take him abroad. Abby wrote a glowing account of his
sailing quarters to her sister Sarah, describing how she was able to hold
back the tears until he was out of sight.

There, my dear sister, I think I have been in a good degree *fa-
vored* as Friends say. Our dear father has left us, and to give thee
an idea of my feelings on the occasion would be utterly impossi-

ble—though no one *knew,* as I manifested not the least emotion, in the presence of any, until I bade him "Farewell" in his own little lodging room on board the vessel. . . . Kept my eye on father until I could distinguish him no longer. The Captain of the Boat then handed me his *glass* and said, "you feel very badly parting with your father. Here, look at the old gentleman as long as you *can.*" I *did* until I saw the young Irishman take him by the hand to assist him in descending, and then the tears came in torrents— not quite enough to float a vessel—but the thought I would not see him for *months,* was quite as much as I could bear.[18]

Edward Hopper, now twenty-one, was left to manage the bookstore while he continued his study of the law. Josiah, eighteen, and beginning to study medicine, also helped. But the two had problems in the absence of their father. An overzealous member of New York Monthly Meeting complained to Abby Hopper that the brothers had placed an engraving of a cat next to one of Elias Hicks and thought it was supposed to symbolize the Orthodox cat that bit Elias Hicks, a reference to the recent schism between Orthodox and Hicksite Friends in New York. Abby Hopper had to explain that the picture of the cat had no such meaning, and had been placed there at random. More seriously, Edward had trouble keeping the account books up to date. Marcus Gould, stopping by to make a routine inspection, discovered the accounting lag and jumped to the conclusion that Isaac Hopper had no intention of repaying the debt.

Isaac Hopper spent most of his time abroad travelling in Ireland, where he encountered a great deal of prejudice against the Hicksites, which he boasted he was able to overcome by careful explanations and by publication of a small pamphlet explaining the separation. He left, having made many new friends, and went on to England, where he visited Jordans Meeting House, the burial place of William Penn, and other Quaker historical sites before sailing for home. His arrival at the house on Allen Street in May 1831 was the cause of rejoicing.

Unfortunately, Marcus Gould was awaiting the return of the traveller with somewhat less enthusiasm. The two had words, but were influenced by fellow Friends to sit down to arbitrate their differences. At this meeting Isaac Hopper paid Marcus Gould $1,200 still owing on his debt, signing over to him two checks made out to Isaac in the total amount of $850 and the rest in cash, and Marcus signed a paper saying that he was entirely satisfied. But one of the checks that had been written to Isaac Hopper failed to clear the bank, and Marcus Gould again began to be afraid that Isaac was trying to defraud him. He published a paper outlining his grievances, and Isaac responded with a pamphlet stating his side of the argument. Having made good the bounced check, Isaac Hopper felt he had repaid Gould honorably and decided to leave his employ and set up his own book shop at 326 Pearl Street.[19]

Isaac Hopper was always stretched financially to the limit and, though he appears to have paid his debts eventually, was sometimes late. This sort of financial juggling was frowned upon by the Quakers. It had caused him to be disowned in Philadelphia, and it now created a shadow around his name among New York Friends.

While her father was still abroad, Abby Hopper had paid a visit to Philadelphia in May, having arranged for a substitute to take her school. (Her pupils complained that the substitute only smiled once during Abby Hopper's absence.) She was evidently seen in the company of James Gibbons during this visit, for one of her Philadelphia correspondents wrote archly, "I often laugh when I hear anything said like James S. Gibbons and Abby Hopper making a match of it."[20] During a second visit in the fall of 1831 James must have proposed, for in November he wrote to Isaac Hopper, asking for his consent to a marriage between him and Abby. They had been on close terms for some time, James wrote, and only "the circumstances of my situation in regard to pecuniary prospects" had delayed their engagement.[21]

Isaac Hopper wrote back agreeing to the match. "My daughter's comfort and welfare is very nearly allied to my own, and although I feel much in the prospect of her leaving my family, I believe it right to say that I find no cause to put any obstacle in the way of your proceeding as thou hast proposed." Sister Sarah Palmer also wrote approvingly of the engagement, saying she considered James the only man who would ever suit Abby, but chastising her for keeping the romance a secret for so long. Abby's good friend Deborah Wharton wrote as well to congratulate the young couple and express her approval, especially since it meant that Abby would be living in Philadelphia again.[22]

Abby's was not the only engagement in the Hopper family. Rachel, the quiet second sister, had become engaged a few months earlier to Samuel Brown, a staid New York Quaker who became the teacher for the boy's school under the care of the monthly meeting. Abby was busy throughout the fall sewing for her sister's wedding, but soon the whole household became involved in preparing for Abby's own nuptials as well. When Edward Hopper announced his engagement to Anna Mott, oldest daughter of James and Lucretia Mott, there was general rejoicing.

But the Hopper family was never long without trouble. Into the happy prenuptial bustle came tragedy. In early February 1832, both Abby and Hannah came down with scarlet fever, and the disease spread to the two youngest members of the family, Thomas, aged three, and Hannah, aged one. Little Hannah had been sickly all her life, and quickly succumbed. Tommy, however, was a robust child, and it was hoped he would survive. Abby was especially devoted to him, describing him as having blond, curly hair, big blue eyes, and winning ways. Rachel could not bear to watch the suffering of her little half-brother and stayed away as much as possible, but Abby moved her bed into his room and nursed him, holding him and singing him nursery songs until he died.

"My dear brothers and sister can have some idea of our exceeding sorrow at parting with our beautiful idol, " Abby wrote to the group in Philadelphia. "We all loved him too much, and I have made up my mind never to allow myself to become so devotedly attached to any child. . . . I believe I have learned with *thee,* my dear sister, to be reconciled to these changes—and on such occasions, to be, in some measure, composed—in the late affliction, I found it *necessary,* for the comfort of those around me. Employment has had the effect to alleviate my sorrow. We feel very solitary—but eleven left, including our domestics, one of which we shall soon part with."[23]

James Gibbons came to visit during this trying time and was a gentle, considerate nurse, according to Abby. Both her parents became devoted to him, and she found parting with him hard when he had to return to Philadelphia.

Gradually the household recovered from these deaths, although Hannah Hopper was not herself until summer. Rachel Hopper and Samuel Brown were married at the Hester Street Meeting house on August 9, 1832, with all the Hoppers in attendance, and James Gibbons present to accompany Abby.

By late fall, Abby and James had set a date for their wedding, and were busy buying furniture. They bought half a dozen straight chairs with rush seats, a rocking chair with arms, a cherry bedstead, and a carpet of two shades of green, James's favorite color. Abby was thrifty, but treated herself as well to some gold banded cups and saucers, to entertain her bridesmaids.[24]

The wedding took place at Hester Street Meeting house on February 14, 1833. Isaac and Hannah Hopper, Rachel and Samuel Brown, brother John Hopper, and sisters Susanna and Elizabeth Hopper attended the wedding, as well as Abby's half brother Isaac, aged nine, and half sister

Mary, aged seven. Mary remembered the wedding well, and described Abby's costume in later life:

> Abby's wedding dress was what was called in the old days "tea-colored" Turk satin. It was made with a surplice waist gathered in at the belt front and back; was plain on the shoulders, high neck, had small leg o' mutton sleeves, with a thin, silky material in the neck and at the wrists. She wore a white camel's hair shawl and white kid gloves. Her bonnet was of the finest split straw, of the shape called "cottage," with white ribbon strings coming from the sides halfway from the top, and having a white silk cape at the back.[25]

The dress had been given Abby Hopper by Elizabeth Hicks, the companion to whom Abby had lent her best dress when the two were travelling together. Abby had put it carefully away at the time and wore it for the first time on her wedding day.

James Gibbons was still a partner of Jonathan Palmer's in Philadelphia, and the young couple set up housekeeping in the Palmers' house on Ninth Street. For a honeymoon they visited James's large family in Wilmington, Abby Gibbons meeting her twelve new brothers and sisters-in-law, ranging in age from twenty-seven to two, for the first time. The younger children stared at her so intently that she was amused, but the senior Gibbonses made her feel at home. The second day of the visit they went to meeting twice by sleigh, since there was snow on the ground. James must have become chilled, for returning to Philadelphia he developed a bad cold, and Abby nursed him for several days while his doctor father came up from Wilmington to see how ill his son was.

Despite this unfortunate beginning, it was apparently a good marriage, especially in the early years. Writing to her sister Rachel, Abby boasted of her new husband:

> I might say my husband is, (as I have before asserted), just such an one as few possess and *all* may envy. No wish is left ungratified. Unsolicited, *every* want is abundantly supplied; and if I am not the happiest of wives, it is not *his* fault. I cannot but wish that our dear father and family, including you, were so near us that we might exchange visits of an evening. This, added to our countless enjoyments, would complete our paradise.[26]

James's early letters to Abby were full of affection and admonition. Although Abby was a strong-willed woman, and nine years his senior, James from the first assumed a husbandly, even a fatherly tone, urging Abby to be very careful and not put her head out of the window when she travelled in the railroad cars, and chiding her when he believed that she shared their private letters too indiscriminately among her family. He expected to be treated as the head of the family, and Abby apparently so treated him. But hers was the stronger personality, and he was often swept up in her concerns. In later years, she may have come to resent this.[27]

Isaac and Hannah Hopper planned to pay a visit to their Philadelphia daughters during the summer of 1833. Isaac was following with a great deal of interest the trial in Trenton in which Orthodox Friends were suing the Hicksites for some of the property that the Hicksites had occupied after the separation. "It will be gratifying once more to see my Orthodox Friends, and particularly so if they should be disappointed in their naughty attempt to wrest the property from its rightful owners," he wrote gleefully. He was also eager to catch up on antislavery affairs. James Gibbons had attended the convention of blacks held in Philadelphia earlier to discuss the antislavery crusade.[28]

That crusade was gaining in vigor. A young man, William Lloyd Garrison, had begun to publish a newspaper, *The Liberator,* in Boston in January 1831, and to travel about the country arguing against the colonization scheme, in which blacks would be sent back to Africa, and preaching a far more aggressive attack on slavery than the Pennsylvania Abolition Society promoted. He often visited Philadelphia, staying with James and Lucretia Mott or Robert and Harriet Forten Purvis, wealthy African American abolitionists. In December 1833 he returned to that city to organize the American Anti-Slavery Society, which agitated tirelessly for the immediate abolition of slavery. Four days later Lucretia Mott, her daughter, Anna Mott Hopper, her mother, Anna Coffin, some additional Quakers, and some Unitarians including Abba Alcott, mother of Louisa May Alcott, met and organized the Philadelphia Female Anti-Slavery Society, a launching pad for women's political action and agitation for women's rights. A number of African American women, including Grace Douglass, Charlotte, Margaretta, and Sarah Forten, and Harriet Forten Purvis, were among the founding members, giving this group from the start a different caste from many Protestant do-good organizations of women of the period.[29]

From the first, Isaac Hopper and his children were supporters of Garrison. They read *The Liberator* and joined the various antislavery societies he organized. Thus, Isaac Hopper was a founding member of the New-York City Anti-Slavery Society, organized in 1833, and was chosen as a manager of that body, while Sarah Hopper Palmer became active in the Philadelphia Female Anti-Slavery Society.[30]

Early in the summer of 1833 Abby Gibbons discovered she was pregnant, and she and James began to plan for a home of their own. This meant a great deal of hemming of linens and tablecloths. Abby was glad to have a visit from a Gibbons cousin who helped her to quilt four comforters for the beds, and from little Mary Hopper, who hemmed handkerchiefs and ran errands. In November James and Abby moved into a house at 31 New Street, Philadelphia, and here, on January 16, 1834, their first child, William Gibbons, was born.[31]

"For three days, Abby seemed to take no great notice of it. She vexed me, for thee knows I can't bear *rational* mothers," Sarah Palmer wrote to sister Rachel Brown, who had also just had a baby boy. "She now seems very proud of it, and likes to have it noticed; which reformation is very pleasing." Abby's early letters about Willie however were reserved; she kept to her usual ironic tone in describing the bewilderment of the neighbors because a variety of doctors came to the house to take care of some postpartum symptoms of hers and to vaccinate "the boy."[32]

Willie thrived, but business did not. In April the firm of Gibbons and Palmer was faced with bankruptcy, and the Gibbonses found it necessary to give up their home on New Street and share a household with the Palmers again. Abby wrote her sister Rachel and her husband that she was taking the move in her stride.

> I cannot see why people should be unhappy because they have an occasional *up and down* in the world. Some wonder that James and I should be so *cheerful.* James says, did he give up to despair, it would disqualify him for paying his debts; and should *I* fret myself to fiddlestrings, *my milk would dry up* and I should have to *buy* for our boy, and that expense we can't so well afford just now. Add to this, a Doctor's bill might be to pay, and perhaps an *undertaker's* follow. So we have resolved to enjoy all there *is* to enjoy, and endure cheerfully what *must* be endured.[33]

The summer was difficult to endure. In Philadelphia there was cholera, and Abby took her new baby to Wilmington to visit her in-laws. In New York the local antislavery society attempted to hold a meeting on July 4, with both blacks and whites present. Sentiment against antislavery agitation, and against blacks and whites mingling, was beginning to build in northern cities as white working-class men were told that free blacks would take their jobs. Resentment against middle-class abolitionists who meddled with relations with the South was also growing. Interrupted by an angry mob, the gathering was postponed until July 7, when it was again forced to disband. On July 9 yet another attempt to hold the meeting was made, this time in the Chatham Street Chapel. Inflamed by a newspaper article, a mob gathered, burst into the chapel and continued rioting for three days, damaging the property of abolitionists Arthur and Lewis Tappan, and threatening Isaac Hopper's bookstore on Pearl Street, before turning their full fury on the black community.[34]

In the fall Abby Gibbons paid a visit to her father's family in New York, with her baby Willie, and there discussed the possibility of moving back to the city and rejoining her father's household. James hated to be so far from his own family in Wilmington, but knew it would mean a lot to Abby to be with her beloved father. There seemed to be no particular job future for him in Philadelphia, and New York offered more prospects. Abby returned to Philadelphia in late November, in time to attend a Pennsylvania Anti-Slavery Society meeting with James at which Robert Purvis spoke of his recent trip to England and the continent. The couple moved to New York early in 1835. Here James continued to search for permanent employment. In the summer of 1836 he was offered a job as first teller in a bank in Chicago at the handsome salary of $1,000 a year but turned it down because he was sure Abby would not want to move that far away from her family. Finally, in 1837, he started work as a teller for the bank of the state of New York. Abby regarded him as a great success and wrote her sister that she hoped that she would not be too proud of him.[35]

By this time, two more children had been born to Abby and James Gibbons, Sarah Hopper on September 9, 1835, and Julia on June 21, 1837. Abby was an industrious housewife, busy keeping her growing brood in clothes. "Re-tailing shirts, corking knees, toeing hose and other not less important calls from the frail tabernacle, have occupied my time," Abby wrote Sarah. Nevertheless, she still found time to join her father in antislavery concerns.

Isaac was now sufficiently famous for his underground railroad activities that his reputation was known in the South. Early in 1836 John Hopper, twenty-one, now a lawyer, traveled to Charleston, South Carolina, on business. Here he was recognized as a son of the infamous abolitionist and attacked by an angry, drunken mob. His trunks were

searched for abolitionist literature and an ancient pamphlet on colonization, given to him by a Charleston antiquarian as a gift to his father, was
taken as proof of his membership in the antislavery movement. The hotel-
keeper, though unfriendly to abolitionists, sent for the mayor of the city,
who locked John Hopper in the jail overnight, then the next morning
managed to smuggle him on a vessel bound for the north. Abby Gibbons
and her brothers and sisters were all shocked by this narrow escape of
their young brother, and Abby was confirmed in her antislavery beliefs.[36]

In May 1837, shortly before giving birth to her third child, Abby
Gibbons attended the first Anti-Slavery Convention of American Women,
held in the Third Free Church, Houston and Thompson Streets, New
York City. Present also were such famous women abolitionists as Lucretia
Mott, Angelina and Sarah Grimké, two sisters from a South Carolina
slave owning family, who were making a name for themselves as anti-
slavery lecturers, Lydia Maria Child, an author, Mary Grew and Sarah
Pugh, Philadelphia school teachers, Anne Warren Weston and Maria
Chapman, Bostonian abolitionists. Abby Gibbons's sister-in-law, Anna
Mott Hopper, was there with her mother, Lucretia Mott. Grace Douglass,
a founding black member of the Philadelphia Female Anti-Slavery Society
was fifty-two, the oldest woman present, accompanied by her school
teacher daughter, Sarah Douglass. Maria W. Stewart, a member of the
New York Colored Ladies Literacy Society, and Julia Williams, a black
teacher from Boston were delegates. Warned that the Ladies New York
Anti-Slavery Society had no black members, the Grimke sisters had written to the integrated Philadelphia and Boston societies urging them to
send black delegates and had informed New York black groups, such as
the Ladies Literary Society, of the meetings. As a result, one of every ten
delegates at this opening convention was a black woman, and Grace
Douglass was chosen vice president by unanimous vote.[37]

Abby Gibbons was accustomed to a certain degree of integration. In
her father's home, black colleagues as well as black clients of benevolence
were often entertained. The Philadelphia Female Anti-Slavery Society had
a number of active black members, including women belonging to the
prominent Forten and Purvis families; and Lucretia Mott and Anna Mott
Hopper made it a practice to invite black friends to their homes. This,
however, was running contrary to generally accepted practice. Even
among abolitionists, the concept of doing something for blacks did not
include working with blacks on an equal footing. In New York City,
where the movement was dominated by conventional clergymen, this was
especially true.[38]

The Convention went on record as approving the immediate abolition of slavery, the use of Free Produce, and the end of social discrimination on the basis of skin color. The women pledged themselves to gather one million names for a petition calling on Congress to abolish slavery in the District of Columbia.[39]

For many women, the convention was the first call for women's rights. Angelina Grimké offered a resolution calling for women to move beyond their accustomed sphere:

RESOLVED, That as certain rights and duties are common to all moral beings, the time has come for woman to move in that sphere which Providence has assigned her, and no longer be satisfied in the circumscribed limits with which corrupt custom and a perverted application of Scripture have encircled her; therefore it is the duty of woman, and the providence of woman, to plead the cause of the oppressed in our land, and to do all that she can by her voice, her pen, and her purse, and the influence of her example, to overthrow the horrible system of American slavery.[40]

The women also debated whether they should use appellations such as Miss or Mrs. with their names. Quakers had always refused to do so, stating their name plainly as Margaret Fell or William Penn. Some of the early abolitionist/feminists were questioning the use of Mrs. as placing woman in a subordinate position. It was decided that each woman should choose how she was to be recorded. Many of the delegates who were not members of the Society of Friends chose not to use the titles. Abby Gibbons, like her former teacher Lucretia Mott, was recorded according to Quaker style.[41]

A second meeting of the Anti-Slavery Convention of American Women was planned for 1838 in Philadelphia, and Abby Gibbons was again present, having come to stay with her sister, Sarah Palmer. The abolitionists in the City of Brotherly Love had been having such difficulty in procuring a place to meet that they had raised funds to build a new structure, Pennsylvania Hall, dedicated to that purpose. In addition to the antislavery women, other reform groups were holding meetings in the new hall at the same time. Opened with ceremonies on May 13, Pennsylvania Hall was surrounded by an angry mob throughout the four days of the meetings. Public prejudice against the antislavery activists, already at an all-time high, was further enflamed by the sight of black and white delegates mingling freely. The sight of Robert Purvis, who was of very light complexion, handing his darker wife, Harriet, down from a carriage was brought up in a later court hearing as one of the episodes that incited the riot.[42]

The antislavery women's groups could not agree on allowing women to speak to mixed or "promiscuous" audiences, so on the third night an informal mixed meeting was held at which women spoke, among them Angelina Grimké and Abby Kelley of Lynn, Massachusetts. This further incensed the angry crowd, which frequently burst into the hall to interrupt the speeches. On the fourth day the manager of the hall requested the women to leave early and turned over the key of the hall to the mayor of the city, who shortly left the scene. At his departure the mob burst into the hall, turned up the gas jets, and set the hall on fire. They then threatened the Mott home, before turning their attention to the black community and to Mother Bethel Church and the Shelter for Colored Orphans. Horrified by the ravages of the mob, but themselves unperturbed, the women held a meeting the following morning at Sarah Pugh's school house, at which Lucretia Mott spoke and Anna Mott Hopper was elected to the business committee. The women pledged themselves to increase, not decrease their contacts with their "colored" sisters.[43]

A third meeting of the Anti-Slavery Convention of American Women was held in 1839 in Philadelphia, in a riding academy because no church, meeting house, or public hall would take the risk of holding such a convention. Abby Gibbons was unable to attend this third convention, but Sarah Hopper Palmer was present, and Anna Mott Hopper served as secretary pro tem and a member of the committee of publications. The mayor this time had offered police protection if the women would avoid "unnecessary walking with colored delegates." The women indignantly refused. "We passed a flaming resolution at our antislavery society. We mean to be independent and have as many sable sisters as will meet with us," Sarah Palmer wrote Abby.[44]

The more the antislavery women struggled to raise money, to hire halls, to support newspapers, and to petition the government, the more impatient they grew with the restrictions placed on them in society as women. The prohibition against speaking to mixed audiences of men and women, "promiscuous" audiences as they were called, was first challenged by Angelina and Sarah Grimké, who lectured in New York as agents of the American Anti-Slavery Society. At first they spoke only to female audiences, but soon, drawn by reports of Angelina's oratory, men began to slip into the meetings, and they became, in the language of the day, "promiscuous." Later, the two sisters travelled through New England speaking to male and female audiences, to the despair of the clergy, many of whom were members of the American Anti-Slavery Society. Another early challenger was Abby Kelley, a handsome young school teacher of Irish Quaker background from Worchester, Massachusetts, who began her speaking career the night that Pennsylvania Hall was burned. So impassioned did Abby Kelley become that she wrote to Lucretia Mott before the 1839 convention of anti-slavery women to question the advisability of holding any more women's conventions unless with open doors, since it seemed to her to be an acceptance of the ban against promiscuous audiences. "Aunt Lucretia doesn't know how to answer her," Sarah Palmer wrote to Abby Gibbons. Lucretia Mott finally did write a reasoned letter, defending separate women's meetings as a way of increasing women's strength until true equality could be achieved.[45]

In 1839 both the New England and the Pennsylvania Anti-Slavery Society decided to accept women on an equal footing. The American Anti-Slavery Society, however, was deeply split between a conservative wing, led by a number of clerics who accepted St. Paul's injunction against women speaking in public, and a more liberal wing, led by Garrison and his followers. A conflict was at hand.[46]

The Ladies New York Anti-Slavery Society sided with the conservatives and did not admit black members. Abby Gibbons, therefore, did not join this group, and was not involved in these initial battles. In 1841, she joined the Manhattan Anti-Slavery Society, composed almost entirely of blacks, which was of brief duration. Most of the time she worked with men, especially her own father and husband, in the antislavery enterprise. While other women, including her own sister Sarah Palmer in Philadelphia, were establishing deep ties with other women, and with them experiencing the frustrations of gender restrictions against women's becoming active politically, Abby Gibbons participated at a distance and did not form the bonds that others experienced. When, ten years later, she began to establish a network, it was among more conservative women interested in prison reform and other charities. This may have been a factor in the peripheral role she played in the women's rights struggle that grew out of the antislavery movement in the 1840s.[47]

3

The Woman Question

In addition to their troubles over the admission of women, there were growing tensions within the American Anti-Slavery Society over a number of issues: the concept of nonresistance to evil advocated by some its members, differing views on the importance of political action for the abolition of slavery, the extremism some of the more conservative members saw in the leadership of William Lloyd Garrison. In 1840 these issues came to a head in the annual meeting of the Society, held in New York. When Abby Kelley was nominated to the business committee, the Garrisonians, including James Gibbons, voted for her, while the more conservative group, called the clerical wing because so many of its members were clergy, were opposed. When she won election, the conservatives withdrew to form the American and Foreign Anti-Slavery Society.[1] Edward Hopper, who had just seen his parents-in-law, Lucretia and James Mott, off to England to attend the World Anti-Slavery Convention (where Lucretia was not seated because of her gender) wrote to Abby Gibbons to express his hopes that this would be the end of the feuding.

> The separation in the Anti-Slavery ranks was not surprising to us. I hope good may come out of it. I often think separation in large bodies proves beneficial to all. I hope now the respective parties may agree to disagree, and henceforth, not be picking each other to pieces. I fear abolition of Slavery is little thought of when party blood is excited, and I think it is quite time that each should work in his own harness.[2]

William Lloyd Garrison was staying with the Gibbonses at the time of the split and wrote his wife, Helen, that there was a lively discussion going on about the future of the Society in the Gibbonses' parlors, with Cyrus Burleigh, Abby Kelley, and Nathaniel Rogers all joining in. James Gibbons was the only member of the executive committee of the American Anti-Slavery Society who did not resign at the time of the crisis. Instead, he became head of a newly constituted executive committee, which included blacks and women, Robert Purvis, Lucretia Mott, Maria Child, and Maria Chapman among them. The Old Organization, as the remnant was called, was smaller and more cohesive, but it was in desperate financial straits. Prior to the final split, the conservatives on the executive committee had turned over its paper, the *Emancipator*, to the conservative New York Anti-Slavery Society, giving away not only subscription lists but even files and office furniture. Remaining funds had been transferred to a member of the New Organization, so the treasury was empty.[3]

With high hopes, the stripped down American Anti-Slavery Society decided to publish its own newspaper, *The National Anti-Slavery Standard*. From the beginning, the paper was constantly in debt and James Gibbons, who played the role of business manager, often reached into his own pocket to pay creditors. The Gibbonses were still quite poor at this time, and James risked his family's well-being several times by going into debt for the sake of the paper. As the only New York member of the executive committee in the beginning (later his wife, Abby Gibbons, his father-in-law, Isaac Hopper, and others were added), he was also obliged, from time to time, to travel to Boston to meet with other members of the executive committee. In the summer of 1840, he stayed with Henry and Maria Chapman, the gracious Boston abolitionist, and met her young sister, Caroline Weston. He also called on Ellis Loring. In Northampton he stayed with David and Maria Child. David was a journalist, involved in an experiment in manufacturing sugar from beets. Maria was a well-known popular author, whose *Appeal in Favor of That Class of Americans Called Africans* had brought her to the attention of the antislavery movement, and led to her further writing on the subject of slavery. James Gibbons's first reaction to all these New England abolitionists was favorable. "It would be delightful to have you here," he wrote Abby. "I should feel as though we were all elevated into a higher heaven than New York can be with its selfish pro-slavery spirit."[4]

Since the old New York Anti-Slavery Society had been under the influence of the clerical wing and became part of the new organization, it was necessary for the Hoppers and Gibbonses and others of like mind to form a new group. Both Abby and James Gibbons, as well as Isaac and John

Hopper, were present in September 1840 when the Manhattan Anti-Slavery Society was organized, under the presidency of a black abolitionist, Thomas Van Rensselaer, to include many blacks, men and women. At Christmastime Abby Gibbons went to Boston to help put on the annual Anti-Slavery Fair, and in March she wrote to the Weston sisters, Anne and Deborah, urging them to come to New York to help organize the Anti-Slavery Fair to occur in May 1841 during the meetings of the American Anti-Slavery Society. They would be more than welcome to stay with the Gibbonses while they did so. Her letter reveals that, despite the principles instilled in her by her father, she still harbored a certain degree of unthinking race prejudice.

> We are now in a dilemma having issued a call for a Fair, and having so few come to aid us save our Boston friends, who, I believe, intend it. Philadelphians say they have enough to do to help themselves. *Here* I am the only *white* female member of the Manhattan Anti-Slavery Society, and the *colour* inefficient. All our children have the measles, two of them severely, and the baby has been so indisposed since as to occupy my close attention. Thus we are progressing, or rather not progressing at all.[5]

Race prejudice was by no means rare among abolitionists. The concept of blacks as backward and childlike, needing the supervision and help of their white antislavery colleagues, surfaced time and again in antislavery circles. The Pennsylvania Anti-Slavery Society and the Philadelphia Female Anti-Slavery Society had a sprinkling of middle-class black members, including members of the wealthy and aristocratic Purvis and Forten families, but in New York there had been far fewer black members, the Ladies New York Anti-Slavery Society having discouraged any black women from joining. In time, black abolitionists themselves split between integrationists, who continued to work with the white abolitionists, and separatists, who believed they were experiencing condescension from their white colleagues. Abby Gibbons continued to be an advocate for black equality, but unlike her sister, Sarah Palmer, had no close black friends.[6]

The antislavery fairs, held principally in Philadelphia and Boston, were a chief means of raising money for the antislavery cause. Anna Mott Hopper and Harriet Forten Purvis were often chief organizers of the Philadelphia event. In both Philadelphia and Boston the antislavery women worked throughout the year preparing articles to sell at the fair, including many handkerchiefs, aprons, and "pockets," (bags which women wore around their waists, the forerunner of pocketbooks). Many of these items were decorated with a kneeling slave and the legend, "Am I not a Woman and a Sister?" The women also sold stationery and an antislavery medal with the same message. James Gibbons wrote to Sarah Palmer to propose that the medal be promoted as a gum-cutter or teething ring for teething babies.[7]

Babies were much on James Gibbons's mind. Lucy, their fourth child, had been born on October 30, 1839, and in 1841 Abby Gibbons was pregnant once more. Because so much of the family income went into the antislavery coffers, Abby Gibbons managed with minimum household help. Habits of thrift, economy, and orderliness, which she had learned from her own hard-pressed mother, helped her to run the household, while she gave an increasing amount of her time to public ventures.[8]

While her own family increased, Abby Gibbons kept a close watch on her father's family affairs. Business in the bookstore on Pearl Street was slowing down considerably. At first, following the separation between the Hicksite and Orthodox branches of the Society of Friends, there was a great demand for Quaker books, as both sides searched early Quaker writings for justification for their positions. But as the excitement died down, the demand grew less. Isaac had originally augmented his income from the bookstore by publishing a newspaper, *The Friend, or Advocate of Truth*. After the break with Marcus Gould he continued to write for this paper until its demise, then, in 1838, he launched a new publication, the *Friends Intelligencer*. Family correspondence of the period was full of efforts to sell subscriptions, but despite the best combined efforts of all the Hoppers this paper too did not survive. (It was resurrected five years later in Philadelphia and was published for more than one hundred years.)

Finally, in 1840, following the split in the antislavery movement, Isaac became the treasurer and book agent of the executive committee of the newly re-organized American Anti-Slavery Society, at a salary of $600 a year, and moved to an office at 143 Nassau Street, where the new publication, the *National Anti-Slavery Standard*, was edited by Nathaniel Rogers. Isaac had always been interested in publishing and began to write a series of articles for the *Standard* on the many escaping slaves he had met through his work with the Pennsylvania Abolition Society, the prisoners he had aided for the Pennsylvania Prison Society, and the "fallen women" he had helped to a new way of life. He had continued with all these philanthropic enterprises after he moved to New York. After publishing several of these accounts, the editor began to schedule them reguarly under the heading, "Tales of Oppression."[9]

One such tale was that of an escaped slave, Thomas Hughes, who came to Hopper's door one night and asked for shelter. He said that he was the son of a wealthy planter in Virginia, who sold his mother with himself and his twin sister when they were eleven years old. His mother and sister were subsequently sold a second time, and he was shipped to Louisiana in a coffle of five hundred slaves. Here he was again sold, this time to a man called John P. Darg, who brought him to New York. He had run off, he said, with the hope of reaching Canada.[10]

Hopper accepted this story, as he had many others, and found the escaping slave safe lodging with an elderly Quaker woman. However, the next day he read an article in the *Sun* offering a reward for a man who had stolen $8,000 from a house on Varick Street. Isaac suspected that this was his runaway and later confronted him. Hughes confessed to taking the money in the hopes of using it to bargain with his master for freedom. He had divided the money into smaller sums and placed it at the homes of New York blacks for safekeeping. After Isaac Hopper remonstrated with him, he agreed that Isaac and another New York Quaker, Barney Corse, could collect the money from the black caretakers, and return it to its owner in return for a promise of manumission.[11]

Hopper and Corse, therefore, set about collecting the money and were able to recall most of it and present it to the owner, only to be charged by John Darg with having conspired with the escaping slave to steal the money. The slave himself was imprisoned and the two Quakers indicted by the Grand Jury. The case against them was flimsy, however, and they were never brought to trial. Meanwhile the slave was sentenced to two years at Sing Sing. When his time was up, Isaac visited him and told him that he was now a free man and could stay in the North. His former master, however, also visited, and promised that he could return home as a free man and be united with his wife. This Hughes eventually agreed to do. The pro-slavery newspaper made a great deal of the case, attempting to prove that Hopper and Corse had used unscrupulous methods, and using Hughes as an example of the so-called fact that the average slave might prefer slavery to freedom.[12]

In becoming thus publicly visible in the antislavery cause, Isaac Hopper knew he was risking the displeasure of the Religious Society of Friends. That society did not approve of the participation of its members in antislavery associations, believing that Quakers should not mingle in ecumenical reform movements but work against slavery within the

Quaker fold. Friends were beginning to object that antislavery activities were involving the Society in mingling "with the world's people," in controversy in the meetings, and in a political debate that was enflaming the public and might lead in time to bloodshed.

These objections had first surfaced in the Orthodox wing of the Quakers, and Elias Hicks's antislavery sentiments had been one reason for the separation. Following that separation in 1827, however, the Hicksite or liberal wing of the Society of Friends had itself been troubled with differences between its more conservative and more liberal members. The conservatives were shocked by the fact that London Yearly Meeting, which tended to regard itself as the parent body of Quakerism, refused to recognize the Hicksites, considering them not to be Christians. In an effort to refute this charge, the Hicksite conservatives became themselves concerned that only orthodox theology be preached in their meetings, and thus began to censure their own members as they themselves had once been censured.

One aspect of the new wave of Hicksite orthodoxy was to move away from the strong antislavery sentiments that had motivated Elias Hicks, Lucretia and James Mott, and other leaders. The Hicksites began to feel that abolition should no longer be preached in their meetings because of its tendency to disrupt the membership. In 1839, when Lucretia Mott sought a hall in which to hold the Third Annual Convention of Anti-Slavery Women in Philadelphia, her own Cherry Street Meeting denied her the use of the building. She was unable to find any site except that of a small Universalist Church, and was forced to use a riding hall. Later, Mott herself was often criticized for bringing such causes as antislavery and women's rights into meeting for worship, and ultimately she was denied a minute that endorsed her right to visit other Quaker meetings as a travelling minister.[13]

Trying to satisfy the objection of New York Hicksite Friends to antislavery activity, Isaac Hopper organized in 1839 the New York Association of Friends for the Relief of those held in Slavery and the Improvement of Free People of Color. This wholly Quaker group published pamphlets on the foreign slave trade, prepared arguments for the antislavery cause, and established a school for African American adults, male and female. The association was from the first integrated by gender and Abby Gibbons was glad to join her father, husband, and brother in membership, and to take several major responsibilities. When a meeting place was sought for the new school, she offered a room in the Gibbons house at 31 Rivington Street, into which they had moved in 1840. The school met four times a week for two hours, and the scholars were charged fifty cents a quarter. It had an enrollment of thirty-six and an average attendance of twenty. Abby Gibbons and Isaac managed to procure desks for the scholars at fifty cents each. The scholars learned fundamental skills but also listened to lectures, such as one on astronomy in May 1841.[14]

Although the school moved to other quarters in a year's time, it set a precedent for Abby Hopper Gibbons. From then on, there was often a school of some sort in her home, run by herself and later by her daughters. Teaching was a part of domestic life to her, like mending or cooking. Wherever the Gibbonses moved, the selection of one room as the schoolroom was the first decision made.

Despite its peaceful agenda and good works, the New York Association was constantly in disfavor with an influential faction of local Friends, who were at that time much under the influence of George White, a flamboyant evangelical minister who was a member of Rose Street Meeting. White was a New York businessman who had been dismissed, or to use the Quaker term, "disowned" by the Friends for bankruptcy in 1820 and restored to membership in 1832. Despite his orthodox theology and his strongly evangelical views, he reapplied and was admitted to the Hicksite branch. His Christ-centered message made him immediately popular among the more conservative Hicksites, and he began to travel in the ministry up and down the East Coast. He was so persuasive that at first even Isaac Hopper responded to his enthusiasm. When George White applied to the meeting for a minute to travel in the ministry among New England Friends, Isaac Hopper offered to go along as his travelling companion. "Not withstanding he and I differ widely on some points, I love the man, and have nearer unity with his spirit than almost any other friend in the city," he wrote Sarah Palmer in June 1839.[15]

But as George White grew in popularity he began to attack abolitionists and to make it his personal crusade to rid the Society of antislavery Friends and those advocating women's rights. In a sermon at the Cherry Street Meeting house in Philadelphia he expressed these views:

No matter into what vice you have gone, join not these associations. I tell you that I preach Christ, the wisdom of God, and the power of God. There is no name under heaven by which we can be saved but by His. Depend not, then, I say, upon the Temperance Society, or the Abolition Society, or the Tract Society, or the Mission Society, or the Bible Society, which rely upon the strength of man, and not upon God. I say thus in the face of heaven, these are abominations in the sight of God, and in the presence of the angels. Such of you as have fallen into such infirmity, come and bow at the feet of Jesus, to whom all power has been given to heal every affliction.[16]

As White grew more confident, his epithets for the reformers grew wilder. He called them, "howling wolves, too famished to bite," "contemptible reptiles," "household vermin," and men "too lazy to work, ashamed to beg, and some of them ashamed to steal." Worst of all were advocates for women's rights. "What did woman want in the name of rights, but liberty to roam over the country from Dan to Beersheba, spurning the protection of man," he preached. He himself would fall over the whole earth before "he would submit to the dictates of an imperious woman." He made several trips to Philadelphia, in an apparent effort to persuade the Friends there to disown Lucretia Mott. In New York he began to attack Isaac Hopper and the Friends Association. For a while he had little success, for Isaac had many friends in both New York and Philadelphia.[17]

Both Mott and Hopper fought back. In May 1840, Isaac attended the Philadelphia Yearly Meeting, and there spoke persuasively for the reformers, according to his son Edward:

He spoke admirably on the subject of dealing with offenders, Slavery and the Indians. His remarks were close to the point, well delivered, and well received. Many have expressed great satisfaction with the decided and manly character of his views.[18]

But White's passion was persuasive, and slowly the elders of Rose Street Meeting in New York swung around to his point of view. The Friends Association was forbidden to use the meeting house, and on one occasion was actually locked out of it. When they protested, they were asked to answer a series of objections to its existence, promulgated by White.

Shortly after this, in March 1841, George White finally found the weapon he needed to attempt the unseating of Isaac Hopper. It came in the form of an article published in the March 25 issue of the *National Anti-Slavery Standard*, called "Rare Specimen of a Quaker Preacher." Its author, Oliver Johnson, was a frequent contributor to the paper and an antislavery lecturer, who had stayed at the Hoppers' home for several months and attended meeting with the family, though he himself was not a Quaker. In November 1840, he had heard a fellow abolitionist speak at Rose Street Meeting, only to be drowned out by a shuffling of feet. The next week Johnson had gone again to Rose Street, and had heard George White's preaching.

> George F. White delivered a discourse (if we may call it by that name) which, for incoherence of argument, misrepresentation and caricature of the sentiments of others, abusiveness of style and passionate ferocity of manner exceeded anything we ever hear from a man professing to be a minister of the gospel. . . . But for the outward peculiarities of a Quaker assembly, which we saw about us, we should have been ready to conclude that we had missed our way and gone to a political caucus, and that we were listening to the harangue of some unscrupulous demagogue, who supposed his only chance for preferment depending on the facility with which he could blacken the reputation of his neighbors. The expression "hireling lecturers, "hireling editors," "hireling printers and book agents," "Servants of the devil," "emissaries of Satan," "hypocrites," "blasphemers," "hypocritical workers of poplar righteousness," "coming out of the bottomless pit," etc. were used in an indiscriminate manner no less shocking to a charitable mind than to a refined taste.[19]

Later in the same meeting White charged that he had knowledge of the fact that a group that claimed to practice nonresistance had plotted to take control of the meeting house by force. This was an obvious reference to the efforts of the New York Association of Friends to hold a meeting in the Rose Street Meeting house. Johnson did not contradict this statement, but he wrote White a letter, remonstrating.[20]

At the next meeting, with Johnson again present, White claimed that the abolitionists had said that "the hope of the slave was not in God, nor in the truth, but in the themselves." Johnson rose in meeting and refuted this statement. White spoke a second time and said he had proof, which he would willingly show to anyone who came to his house. Johnson and James Gibbons accordingly went to see him. He refused to show Johnson anything, and produced for James only a statement of the Junior Anti-Slavery Society of Philadelphia which had little relevance to the point under discussion.

By this time White and Johnson were engaged in an epistolary battle. Johnson published their correspondence in a pamphlet that was widely

circulated, and this further inflamed White. His denunciations of abolitionists at Rose Street Meeting grew wilder. He called them "wolves,"
"reptiles," and "household vermin." Referring to the Thomas Hughes
case, he said the ex-slave had made the right decision. "I had a thousand
times rather be a slave, and spend my days with slaveholders, than to
dwell in companionship with the abolitionists."

Johnson's article in the *National Anti-Slavery Standard* repeated the
history of this conflict and made no exaggerated charges. But to the many
conservative New York Friends who were deeply attached to White, it
seemed like an attack, and they responded by holding their members to
blame. Four days after the offending article appeared, Isaac Hopper, James
Gibbons, and Charles Marriott, an elderly Friend, were requested to meet
that night with the elders of Hester Street Meeting. Here they were questioned about their membership on the executive committee of the
American Anti-Slavery Society and their relationship to the *National Anti-
Slavery Standard*. Two days later they were formally charged by their
monthly meeting with "being concerned in the support and publication of
a paper which has a tendency to excite discord and disunity among us."

Neither James Gibbons nor Isaac Hopper had read the article by
Johnson. The editor of the *Standard*, Nathaniel Rogers, made his own decisions, and the executive committee did not exercise the role of censors.
Nevertheless, the three men agreed in general with Johnson and were not
prepared to disown the article and make an apology to the meeting.

As a result, the monthly meeting began dismissal or disownment proceedings against all three men. Ever the fighter, Isaac Hopper determined
to oppose this injustice and appealed the case first to the Quarterly, then
to the Yearly Meeting level. The resulting controversy soon spread to the
other Hicksite yearly meetings and began to affect Quakers in Ireland and
Great Britain. Letters supporting the three abolitionists poured in from all
quarters. Henry Gibbons, James's brother, wrote an article attacking
George White in the *Temperance Standard*. The elders of the monthly
meeting felt themselves under attack and published "An Explanation," in
which they went beyond the article in the *Standard*, and brought up the
grand jury charges against Hopper in the Darg case, making it appear
that Hopper had a cloud hanging over his head for possibly having conspired with Hughes to influence the latter to steal the money.

The case resulted in a storm of controversy. Both the Quarterly and
Yearly Meetings became bitterly divided; in the end the Yearly Meeting
was forced to abandon its Quakerly practice of waiting for unity and

took a vote on the case. Eighteen were in favor of disownment, fifteen opposed, and three abstained. Ordinarily such a narrow margin would have prevented the Yearly Meeting from taking action; but the circumstances were not normal, and the three men were formally disowned.[21]

Isaac Hopper's children were appalled at the action against their father and angered when Friends argued that there was fault on both sides and that Isaac Hopper should make some form of apology. Sarah Palmer argued vigorously with members of her own Cherry Street Monthly Meeting who made these suggestions or defended George White, and had a stormy session with Mary Hallett, a member of New York Monthly Meeting who came to call upon her in an evident effort to promote a reconciliation. "I've married Freedom," she declared, "and declare to love it all the days of my life." The case only deepened her commitment to antislavery and to the religious principles of Friends. She was encouraged by Lucretia Mott, who objected to the action against Isaac Hopper, and preached about it in Cherry Street Meeting.[22]

Abby Gibbons at first believed that New York Meeting would withdraw its charges. Visiting Sarah in Philadelphia in June, she wrote to her father that local Friends believed New York Friends had concluded to remain quiet. But by threatening to resign, George White was able to persuade the Hester Street Meeting to go ahead with the disownment proceedings. Abby then supported both her father and her husband, James, in carrying the case to the Quarterly Meeting and wrote Sarah to describe George White's attacking sermons and the timidity of former friends. Phoebe Post Willis, once Lucretia Mott's travelling companion, had asked to be excused as clerk of the women's business meeting rather than sign the documents, Abby Gibbons complained, writing that she was ashamed of Willis.[23]

In October, when the Quarterly Meeting failed to uphold the Hopper-Gibbons-Marriott appeal, James Gibbons decided he had no desire to carry the case forward. Isaac Hopper and Charles Marriott, however, appealed to the Yearly Meeting, and Abby Gibbons continued to support her father. After the New York Yearly Meeting met in May, and, following a three-day struggle, rendered its negative verdict in her father's case, she determined to resign from Hester Street. On the day of the Monthly Meeting, she tied on her bonnet, marched into the meeting, sat in the fourth row from the front, facing the clerks, and after the minutes of the preceding meeting were read, stood and read her statement in a clear, loud voice.

New York, 6 mo. 1st, 1842

To the Monthly Meeting of New York:

I request that my name, and the names of my children, William, Sarah Hopper, Julia and Lucy, may be erased from your list of members, and from this date, I consider the connection which has hitherto existed between us, to be entirely dissolved. The principal reasons which induce me to take this step are:

1. The Monthly Meeting publicly denies the leading principles and testimonies of the Society of Friends; particularly, it rejects the testimony of truth against the great evils of Slavery and Intemperance.

2. It imposes restrictions on the freedom of conscience, which are inconsistent with the requirements of Christian duty, and disowns those of its members who refuse to conform to such restrictions.

3. It has disowned my husband and father, because they conscientiously engaged in promoting the testimony of the Society against Slavery, and has been guilty of the plainest violations of its own Discipline, to procure the confirmation of their decision by the Quarterly and Yearly Meetings. Its Overseers, Elders and principal Ministers, to secure the same end, engaged for many months in the defamation of moral character, in a most invidious and disgraceful manner.

4. Its Ministers and Elders have introduced a proposition to recommend, as a minister of the Society, a man who stands in the relation of landlord to grogshops, thus affording practical proof that it rejects the testimony of truth against the Sin of Intemperance.[24]

"Thou wilt like to know *how* I behaved myself," Abby wrote to her sister Sarah. "Mary Hallett says, 'better than she thought I *knew how*.'" Other friends told her she remained calm, despite one woman shouting, when she first began speaking, that the meeting was being imposed upon. In theory Abby should have given her paper to the clerk to read, but as she wrote Sarah, she was sure that this would not happen, and she wanted Friends to hear what she had to say.[25]

Following her lead, her brothers John and Josiah resigned from New York Monthly Meeting, and her brother Edward from the Cherry Street

Meeting in Philadelphia, although his wife, Anna Mott Hopper, remained an engaged member. Sarah, Elizabeth, Susan, and Rachel also remained Friends. Isaac Hopper himself refused to acknowledge the disownment, and continued to attend meeting and sit in his accustomed seat. "The Society of Friends may have disowned me, but I have not disowned the Society of Friends," he stated.[26]

Many people remained angry about the disownment. "You will see by the 'Anti-Slavery Standard,' how the N. Y. pseudo-Quakers are conducting toward Isaac Hopper, James S. Gibbons, and Charles Marriott," Lucretia Mott wrote friends. "I bear my testimony against their intolerance in every circle." George White was the object of a lot of the anger, and though he had won the battle, he evidently lost heart, and declined rapidly in importance in the Society of Friends, until he became remembered only as the man who had once opposed Isaac Hopper.[27]

Abby Gibbons and her brothers were not alone in their decision to resign from the Society of Friends at that period. Abby's colleague in the antislavery struggle, Abby Kelley of Worcester, Massachusetts had written a letter disowning the Uxbridge Monthly Meeting of the Society of Friends in March of 1841. Elizabeth Buffum Chace, also a Garrisonian abolitionist and, after the Civil War, a prison reformer, followed suit in 1843. There were a handful of others who despaired of influencing the Quakers to take a more radical position. But each decision was an intensely personal one to the Quaker involved, brought up to feel the Society of Friends to be a part of his/her extended family.[28]

Abby Gibbons did not return to membership in the Society of Friends, although she kept to Quaker dress and Quaker speech all her life and insisted that her children maintain these habits. She also remained true to Quaker principles in regard to racial equality, to truth telling, to social concerns such as prison reform—all testimonies she had learned from her father. In other matters she drifted away from her strict Quaker background, attending the theater, reading novels, and eventually departing from Quaker pacifism. In the 1850s she began attending the church of Octavius Brooks Frothingham, a liberal Unitarian minister, although she never joined. As she explained to a daughter.

> Some like to join the church and others do not. I find it safe and satisfactory outside of it all. I read the Bible, especially the Book of Ecclesiasties which I like and do not care to have it explained, having my own version. . . . I read chapters of my life and try to profit thereby.[29]

Isaac Hopper did not remonstrate with Abby Gibbons, or John, Josiah, or Edward Hopper for resigning from the Society for his sake, but he was pleased with those that remained. Writing to his daughter Susan in 1844, he spoke of his hope that she would remain a Friend:

> There is nothing that gives me more comfort than to see my children attached to the principles in which they were educated. These principles have done much for the world and they will sustain and support all who adhere to them through every storm and tempest with which they may be assailed. Mayest thou, dear Susan, never suffer thy mind to become soured, or thy affections alienated from the Society of Friends, for although there are many in the Society who have nothing but the name to recommend them, yet there are many others who are the salt of the earth.[30]

Her father's disownment brought forward Abby Gibbons's protective instincts. When the American Anti-Slavery Society, in financial straits, decided to reduce his already small income just at the time of the disownment, she wrote a forthright letter to Ellis Gray Loring, saying that she considered the letter that James had written to the Massachusetts Society on the same topic, "exceedingly tame," admitting that she was too sensitive where her father was concerned. She suggested that it would have been better to reduce the salary of J. A. Collins, "who was the means of bringing the Society in debt pretty extensively." She also deplored the idea of the executive committee being moved to Boston. Agents hired by Boston for the New York office had all proved unsatisfactory, she complained. James had never known half the "losses and crosses" that Abby had experienced and was thus too placid in accepting the decisions of the executive committee, although he was "spirit crushed."[31]

Also supporting James Gibbons against the arbitrary edicts of the Boston clique at this time was Lydia Maria Child. "James S. Gibbons has for two years worked like a cart horse for nothing. You talk about sending S. J. May to man the breach if Hopper and Gibbons cannot do it. I know of no breach to man," she wrote indignantly to Maria Chapman in May 1842. In October she complained to Ellis Loring about the lack of financial support from Boston. "James S. Gibbons drew his own salary a month ahead. He makes $1500 a year and has five children to support, besides keeping a necessary for all traveling abolitionists."[32]

Maria Child had come to New York in May 1841 to become editor of the *National Anti-Slavery Standard* and to board at the home of Isaac

Hopper. The American Anti-Slavery Society had first asked David Child to be the editor, but David was still trying to extract sugar out of beets and didn't want to be away from his Massachusetts farm. Maria, who had been writing and publishing since 1824, was by far the more accomplished of the two, but even the liberals of the day automatically thought that a man would make the best editor.

Maria Child was a cosmopolitan woman with a love of music, the theater, and art, none of them prized in the quiet Quaker home of the Hoppers. But she stimulated them with her appreciation of literature and of intellectual debate, while she was moved by the kindness and goodness she perceived in Isaac and in Hannah. She wrote a friend that at the house on Eldridge Street she was settled in a large, sunny front room and was "as comfortable as a poodle on a Wilton rug." "If I must be away from him," she wrote in another letter, speaking of her separation from David, "I could not be more happily situated than in Friend Hopper's family. They treat me the same as a daughter and a sister."[33]

The Hopper household had recently shrunk. Susan had moved to Philadelphia to live and work with a Friends family; Josiah, now a doctor, had just married a New York Friend, Martha Comstock. Only Elizabeth, John, Mary, and Isaac shared the parental roof. John, at twenty-four, was restless. He had been developing more worldly tastes than his family and several years before had confessed to his father that, far from obeying the Quaker prohibition against attending the theater, he had been to see the actress Fanny Kemble sixty-seven times. He himself loved to act, to tell jokes, to make merry. The arrival of the glamorous and sparkling woman author Maria Child was a diversion for him, and he became her constant companion in delightful rambles to the Battery, to the Palisades, even to Brooklyn. He brought her fruit and flowers and sought out her company on every occasion. It was apparently an innocent relationship but a close one. Maria, who was thirty-nine, fifteen years his senior, told her nephew that she thought of him as the son she might have had. Later, when John fell in love with a beautiful young woman, a singer, and the daughter of a wealthy family, Maria was delighted when they eloped. She dedicated a book to him, wrote about him to his sisters, and mourned him when he died.

Abby Gibbons and Maria Child became good friends. Maria admired Abby extravagantly, as she did Isaac. She wrote to her in 1842, saying that she would, if she could, give her a golden palace, "but you would take down your walls, piece by piece, to feed the hungry and clothe the naked, and leave yourself no roof." Abby's goodness was not lost on her, she said, but was a daily refreshment and a stimulating example. She thanked her for her goodness to herself, to her father, and "unremitting kindness and sisterly love to John," and said that whatever her destiny was to be, Abby Gibbons would always be a dearly cherished sister. She wrote about the same time to Ellis Loring, "I do love Abby, almost as much as John, she has a noble, unselfish nature."[34]

As editor of the *National Anti-Slavery Standard*, Maria wrote editorials praising Isaac Hopper and denouncing his detractors. Writing about the disownment of the three she commented, "A Society has need to be very rich in moral excellence, that can afford to throw away three such members." She also encouraged Isaac to continue to write his "Tales of Oppression."

In the fall of 1841, just as the disownment proceedings were going to the Quarterly Meeting, Abby Gibbons gave birth to her fifth child and second son, Isaac T. Hopper Gibbons. She had to give up the evening school for blacks for the time being, but she continued with her other duties with the Friends Association and the antislavery fairs. With much of the household money going to support the *Standard*, she could not spend a lot on household help and had to content herself with a nineteen-year-old immigrant German girl. The children were often sick, and she was anxious about them. She was soon pregnant again, and on November 17, 1843, her last child, James, was born. She was forty-two and tired after the long string of pregnancies. The baby apparently thrived at first, but caught whooping cough from his older brothers and sisters when he was a year old and became very ill. Abby Gibbons's stepmother, Hannah Hopper, spent long days at his bedside. Maria Child took a turn and other relatives and friends sat with him, but neither James nor Abby Gibbons were willing to leave him, and they became worn out with the long struggle. On November 26 Isaac wrote to his daughter Susan in Philadelphia that he had pretty much resigned himself to the death of this youngest grandchild, but that his parents could not let him go. The next day he appeared much better, and Abby and James managed a night's sleep, but the improvement was not to last. The battle went on until December 15, 1844 when at ten minutes past twelve the baby James breathed his last.[35]

When her little half brother Tommy had died in 1832, Abby Gibbons had suffered so much that she had resolved never to become deeply attached to another child. But despite the ironic tone she cultivated in her letters, she was an emotionally involved mother, and the loss of this child threw her into a period of despair. "This terrible affliction overwhelms us with grief," James wrote in his journal. The Gibbonses buried their child in Greenwood cemetery in Brooklyn, rather than the Quaker burial ground, and mourned him for many months.

4

Our Imprisoned Sisters

Abby Gibbons's formula for getting over grief was always to keep busy. Just as her son James died, she was offered an opportunity to work side by side with her father in the field of prison reform, a cause that was to shape the rest of her life.

Isaac Hopper had continued his interest in prisoners after his move to New York. He visited prisoners in the Tombs, the city jail in downtown New York, so nicknamed for its Egyptian style of architecture, and in Sing Sing, the penitentiary up the Hudson River. He often befriended ex-prisoners who sought him out. Several of these he took home to live with him and Hannah at the house on Eldridge Street they now occupied, where, according to his biographer, there was always room for one more.[1]

This lifelong interest led him to become part of a group that met in December 1844 and established the New York Prison Association, at the request of the Inspectors of the Penitentiary at Sing Sing, with the purpose of aiding ex- prisoners in their reentry into society. Since his job with the American Anti-Slavery Society had just been ended as the result of budgetary constraints, he was free to take a position as agent of the new society, at $300 a year, and to establish an office for the association at 13 Pine Street.At the age of seventy-four he launched into still another career.[2]

Isaac Hopper's work as agent of the Prison Association included lobbying for its incorporation under New York State law. At first the legislators were opposed, for there was public fear of coddling prisoners and concern that the new society might somehow interfere with the authority of the State over prisons. Isaac Hopper made numerous trips to Albany for the Prison Society, and finally spoke before the legislature. According to one witness, he carried the day with his eloquence.[3]

At the new office, Hopper became a one-person social service department, looking for job opportunities for newly released prisoners or encouraging them to get vocational training. As his reputation spread, more and more families of prisoners or ex-prisoners themselves came to his office. Among the ex-prisoners were women. Isaac had always been gifted at working with women, and he helped several to rehabilitate themselves after prison and find employment. But it was clear that a number of women ex-prisoners needed a place to stay under supervision while they prepared to reenter society. At his urging, the Prison Association organized a Female Department, which first met in January 1845, with Abby Hopper Gibbons a member of the executive committee.[4]

Abby Gibbons was entering a relatively new field. Work by women among women prisoners had been given its initial impetus in 1813, when Elizabeth Fry of England began her visits and reforming efforts at Newgate Prison. In 1823 a Philadelphia Quaker, Mary Waln Wistar, inspired by Fry, organized the Female Prison Association of Friends in Philadelphia and began to pay regular visits to the Arch Street Prison. Later this group established a house of refuge for juvenile offenders, arranged for a matron to care for the women in the Arch Street prison, and lobbied for a separate facility for women prisoners. In 1853 they developed a halfway house, the Howard Institution.[5]

Abby Gibbons had, of course, read about the work of Fry in England, and she may have known about Wistar in Philadelphia, although since the group of women there were made up of Orthodox Friends she would not have been in touch with them. With little in the way of models to work from, she and her colleagues spent the first six months visiting women at the Tombs and on Blackwell Island. The prisons they saw were dark, dirty, and unsanitary. Waste was collected in buckets, which were seldom emptied. Food was poor and discipline severe. In the Tombs, there were only forty-two cells for women and never less than seventy inmates. Separation between male and female convicts was lax; not infrequently women became pregnant during incarceration.[6]

Treatment of women prisoners throughout the nation at this time was dismal. There were far fewer women than men prisoners and arrangements for them were haphazard and often inadequate. In addition, the public was more strongly prejudiced against women felons than their male counterparts. According to Victorian notions, women were expected to exert a pure and moral influence over society. When women failed to live up to this impossible standard, they were regarded as especially depraved, and therefore less deserving.[7]

In the early nineteenth century, states began to build penitentiaries based on the concept of reforming prisoners. In New York, Auburn Penitentiary was built in 1816 and occupied in 1821; in Pennsylvania, the Eastern State Penitentiary was built in 1823. The two followed competing systems. The New York Commissioners were devoted to a method called the silent system, which emphasized hard work, isolation, and silence. Under this regime, inmates were not allowed to talk to one another, even when they sat together at table or worked together in prison industries. Pennsylvania, on the other hand, used a system of separate confinement, which kept prisoners rigorously apart, but attempted to avoid isolation through a continuous flow of prison visitors. Each system had its enthusiastic proponents.[8]

Harriet Martineau, a British author and reformer, was an advocate of the silent system. In 1838, she visited Auburn and wrote about the women prisoners:

The arrangements for the women were extremely bad . . . . The women were all in one large room, sewing. The attempt to enforce silence was soon given up as hopeless: and the gabble of tongues among the few who were there was enough to paralyze any matron. . . . There was an engine in sight which made me doubt the evidence of my own eyes: Stocks, of a terrible construction; a chair, with a fastening for the head and all the limbs. The governor [warden] liked it no better than we; but he pleaded that it was his only means of keeping his refractory female prisoners quiet while he was allowed only one room to put them all into.[9]

In 1839 the New York prison officials had opened a woman's penitentiary at Ossining, near Sing Sing, called, ironically, Mt. Pleasant. Here the rule of silence was enforced until 1844, when a daring and imaginative matron, Eliza Wood Farnham, was hired. Farnham, a Quaker, had previously worked as a teacher and had written a book about her adventures in the West called *Life in Prairie Land*. She was interested in phrenology and had edited a book by Marmaduke Sampson, *The Rationale of Crime*, which attributed criminal traits to the development of certain sections of the brain, but emphasized that the prisoner could be reformed by treatment and education that developed more positive attributes.[10]

On becoming matron of Mt. Pleasant, Farnham hired four assistant matrons. One of these, Georgiana Bruce (later Kirby), subsequently wrote about her experiences at Mt. Pleasant in a book of memoirs, *Years of*

Experience. She described how Farnham relaxed the rule of silence, allowing prisoners to talk to each other in low voices for half an hour each afternoon. Farnham also introduced novels to the prison library, allowing inmates to take books to their cells at night, and improving lighting so that it was possible for them to read. When the women sewed it had been customary to read the Bible aloud: instead, Farnham read *Oliver Twist.* She attempted to make the prison less gloomy by introducing flowers, curtains at the windows, and a piano. One difficult inmate was given a rag doll to play with at night. For inmates with children, a nursery was provided, perhaps the first in women's prison history.[11]

Visiting Mt. Pleasant in 1845, reformer Dorothea Dix described it as "under the direction of a matron, who, with her assistants, are much interested in the improvement of those under their charge." Another visitor was Margaret Fuller, a transcendentalist, an editor of the New York *Tribune*, and a feminist, who followed her visit with a series of articles defending the "fallen woman." Such a woman was a victim of circumstance, she said, and needed the help of her sisters to overcome the obstacles that had forced her to crime.[12]

Meanwhile, Farnham's innovations had shocked the conservative members of the Board that administered both Sing Sing and Mt. Pleasant. Farnham was criticized, particularly for relaxing the rule of silence, about which the male board members were fanatical. She fought back, but with a change of administration she was forced to resign in 1847.[13]

Against this background, members of the newly created Female Department of the New York Prison Association continued to visit women in the city prisons. Their studies soon taught them that the majority of the women in prison were there for short terms, and their crimes were often alcohol related. Some were prostitutes, some were charged with larceny, a few with aborting a baby. Most, they believed, wanted to reform. The women of the Female Department attempted to find shelter and employment for many who were being released, some members taking former inmates into their homes. But the need to provide housing for the flow of released prisoners soon outran their capabilities.[14]

Abby Gibbons and her colleagues therefore decided to rent a house where discharged female prisoners could stay while they readjusted to life on the outside, and while the women of the Society sought placements for them in homes or factories. In the early spring of 1845, they began to raise money, helped by Margaret Fuller's articles in the *Tribune*, and in June they rented a three-story house at 191 Tenth Avenue. They employed two women as matrons, and on June 12 formally opened the Home for Discharged Female Convicts.To the delight of the executive committee, they were soon informed that they were the first such halfway house in the world. In England a wealthy woman had established a residence for teenage young women before they were sent to Australia, and in France a clergyman had established a farm where he took a small number of discharged female prisoners. But the Home, which housed as many as thirty women at a time and averaged 150 tenants a year, was unique, and prison officials all over the world wrote to inquire about their methods.[15]

A stay at the Home was completely voluntary. Residents could leave if they wished, but if they chose to stay they had to abide by house rules, which included getting permission to leave for short outings. If they came home drunk from such outings, they were instantly discharged. Under the care of two matrons, the home was kept to a strict schedule: up at 5:30 A.M., worship at 6, breakfast at 6:30, then on to a schedule of classes in reading, writing, arithmetic, and a period of sewing, during which someone read aloud. The members of the executive committee procured sewing orders for their charges, and the residents earned money, which was supposed to go to the Home for their keep. There was a strict 9 P.M. bedtime. The Bible was read daily and on Sunday evenings city missionaries came and preached to the little flock. Unfortunately, they were Protestant, while the majority of the residents of the Home were Catholic. At this time, many working-class women in New York and Philadelphia were newly arrived Irish immigrants, fleeing the potato famine, who came to the shores of the United States full of hope and naivete. Too often they were taken advantage of by unscrupulous employers, badly underpaid, or, failing to find any work at all, turned to or were lured into prostitution. Naturally, these women resented the slurs that Protestant ministers often made against Catholic priests.[16]

James Gibbons, who took a slightly ironic view of the Home, wrote to Caroline Weston about it:

> Two or three months ago, one of the City missionaries went there and preached against the Catholics, stating some facts relative to the easy terms upon which the priests promise to get sinners into Heaven's gates. There were twenty-eight women of the "working classes" present, twenty-two of whom were Catholics, and they justly esteemed it an insult to religion as well as to themselves. One of them interrupted the brother by saying very

deliberately, "You *lie*, Sir. Hoary headed man as you are you *lie*, Sir . . . "

The "brother" was requested by the lady managers . . . to cease his visits, as they were no longer acceptable—a just concession to the spirit of Freedom which shines through Vice brightly enough to eclipse and put to shame the tallow-candleism of the Church.

The "brother" had sense enough to see his mistake, and re-quested permission to be allowed the privilege of speaking again to the women. Permission was granted, and he made an apology for what he had said.[17]

Abby Gibbons was appointed to the first committee set up to oversee this Home, and she continued to work at it until she reached the age of ninety-two. She attended board meetings, of which she was often presi-dent, and visited female prisoners in the Tombs, where she became a close friend and admirer of Flora Foster, the matron. Foster later became a board member of the Home. Abby Gibbons also spent one day a week as a volunteer at the Home and sought and found jobs for her charges when they were ready to leave. Since many of the inmates of the Home in the early days were alcoholic, it seemed important to her to try to find them places in the country, where they might be out of temptation's way. She placed quite a few women from the Home in a paper mill in Herkimer, New York, and others with friends in rural settings, such as the home of the Weston sisters in Weymouth, Massachusetts. She herself always had a woman from the Home in her own house.

One long-time member of the Gibbons household was a young woman who had been imprisoned in the Tombs for the crime of infanticide, al-though she claimed to be innocent. On release, she was pursued by the madam of a house of prostitution and, having no other place to go to es-cape, asked to be readmitted to prison. Here she was visited by Abby Gibbons, who saw to it that she was assigned to the Home on her release, and later hired her as a nurse in the Gibbons household. She subsequently married and had a family of her own, but often visited both the Hopper and Gibbons households.[18]

Sometimes the women whom Abby Gibbons thus employed went on sprees. One woman worked industriously all week in the Gibbons home, but on Sundays the old longing for alcohol returned, and she would of-ten take something of little value from the Gibbonses' house on her way out, then, overcome by remorse, find a boy to return the purloined goods. After a year of this, Abby Gibbons found her a place in a rural area of Connecticut where she outgrew her problems, married, and employed servants of her own, often sending a generous contribution back to the Home.[19]

From the beginning, Abby Gibbons was successful in attracting a community of middle-class women with progressive views to serve on the board that managed the Home. Caroline Stansbury Kirkland, a native New Yorker, educator, and author, joined the committee at its inception. Following a career in teaching, Caroline Stansbury married William Kirkland, and with him managed a girls' school in Geneva, New York. In 1836 the couple and their children moved to Livingston County, Michigan, then a frontier community. Bored and lonely, Caroline Kirkland began to write and publish sketches of frontier life, launching a successful literary career. In 1843 the Kirklands moved back to New York and careers in journalism, and Caroline joined the Female Department of the New York Prison Association. In 1853 she published a book, *The Helping Hand,* on early years of the Home.[20]

Another deeply involved woman was Catharine Sedgwick, also an author, who lived in her family home in Lenox, Massachusetts, in the summers and New York City in the winters. Her novels of early New England won her popularity and fame. Although she had many liberal ideas, the only concern she was attracted to was prison reform. She became "First Directress" of the Home in 1848 and held that post until ill health forced her to resign in 1863, often writing articles about the needs of discharged prisoners.[21]

There were many others. Sarah Doremus, a wealthy New York philanthropist who helped to found several social service institutions in the city, was a founding member of the Female Department and spent a great deal of volunteer time at the Home. She became "Second Directress" under Sedgwick, and "First Directress" when Sedgwick resigned because of ill health in 1863.[22]

Antoinette Blackwell Brown, the first American woman to be ordained a minister, visited the Tombs with Abby Gibbons in 1855, as well as accompanying her on missions to the slums, to the institutions on Randall's Island, and to the city hospital. Later, her sisters-in-law, Elizabeth Blackwell, the first woman physician in the United States, and Emily Blackwell, also a pioneering woman doctor, were drawn into Abby Gibbons's circle, while Gibbons expanded her interest into hospitals serving women and children. Phoebe and Alice Carey, two women authors, moved to New York in the early 1850s and became close friends of Abby Gibbons and supporters of the Home.[23]

These women formed the core of the Female Department of the New York Prison Association and, later, of other charities and reform movements that evolved from it. They grew together as they learned more about the women under their care, as well as some of the matrons they met in the prisons. They supported each other in times of personal trial and formed deep and abiding friendships, which lasted a lifetime in many cases. Margaret Fuller lived near the Gibbonses while in New York and spent her last night in the United States, before sailing for Italy in August 1846, in Abby Gibbons's home.

In defending the rights of women prisoners, these pioneers came up against public prejudice against "fallen women." In the Victorian era, with its concept of pure womanhood, the woman who had sinned was regarded as beyond redemption, whereas a man who committed the same crime might be rehabilitated. A double standard, under which woman's sexual license was not tolerated but that of her seducer regarded as a natural expression of the male nature, played into this prejudice. Directors of the Home were told that they were coddling the women prisoners and perhaps recruiting them to a life of crime, that it was distasteful to refined tastes to contemplate aiding these fallen women, that they had after all chosen their own fate, and that there were better objects of public philanthropy.

In response, the women argued that no woman at the Home had ever chosen imprisonment in order to be rehabilitated, that they who worked daily with the fallen women were willing to continue to do so, in fact felt they gained from the experience, and that nine out of ten of the women they aided had been forced into crime, usually by some man, and had never made the choice themselves. Moreover, there were strong arguments for women coming to the aid of other women. Drawing from the vocabulary of the recently launched women's rights movement, Caroline Kirkland wrote in *The Helping Hand*:

Woman is the natural and God-appointed aid of woman in her needs; the woman that feels not this, has yet to learn her mission aright. Among the most precious of Woman's Rights is the right to do good to her own sex. . . . It is time that women—excused from many of the severer duties assumed by the other sex—should consider themselves as a community, having special common needs and common obligations, which it is a shame to them to turn aside from, under the pleas of inability or distaste. *Every woman in misfortune or disgrace is the proper object of care to the happier and safer part of her sex.*[24]

To those who questioned their ability to rehabilitate women, the managers of the Home replied, come and see. According to statistics they kept from 1845 to 1851, the Home admitted a total of 877 women, placed 312 in situations, settled another 172 with their families or in hospitals, alms houses, etc., and listed only 158 as returned to "evil ways," or discharged for improper conduct. Another 211 were unaccounted for. By 1864 the number of residents had risen to 2,941, of whom 1,083 were considered rehabilitated, and only 480 as "hopeless." A number of women who had once been residents at the home became respectable middle-class women, and, in turn, donated time and money to the agency.[25]

Along with the help they offered, these nineteenth-century reforming women were not free from condescending to their clients. Their ideal was the pure middle-class woman whom they themselves strove to be, and only those inmates of the Home who came to emulate this ideal were considered to have achieved a worthwhile goal. While their understanding of the double standard that produced the "fallen woman" was in advance of their time and of many of their contemporaries, they had little concept of poverty and class differences as systemic in nineteenth-century American society. Hard work and regular habits would be rewarded, they believed, just as they had been rewarded in the lives of their fathers and husbands. It awaited another generation of reformers, active in the settlement house movement in the late years of the century, to begin to make the connections between wealth and poverty.[26]

These mid-nineteenth-century philanthropists were blinded by their own immersion in the Victorian ethos to the gender bias which was embedded in some of their reforming work. Believing that women should be returned to a state of "pure womanhood," they proposed to treat offenders as wayward girls who needed guidance. This led to the introduction of a differential between the treatment of men and women. Later in the century, when many of these same women began to work for women's reformatories, they proposed that for the same crimes women were to be engaged in longer periods of rehabilitation than men were subjected to. In addition, some women who might have been quickly released were to be exposed to a long period of questionable "rehabilitation."[27]

Nevertheless, Abby Gibbons sometimes expressed an understanding of the situation of poor women. Writing to her daughter Sarah some years later, she talked of all she had learned from working at the Home:

> As for the "Home," people do not have faith in "sinners" (so called). I am thankful to have known them so long and so well, that I want to stand by them as long as I live. Maria Lowell said our family had "a natural love of sinners." They are so sinned against, that with their limited opportunities, I often wonder they come out so well, when we see the mighty wrongs among professional saints (so considered by a benighted people,) and how all this is overlooked, while the poor world must suffer even from *their* shortcomings.[28]

As early as 1852, Abby Gibbons and her friends were having difficulties with the all-male New York Prison Association, which had firm ideas of how to manage the Home. They felt that the men were not as concerned as they were to raise money for the Home, and they objected to the men's insistence that all residents must be convicts, rather than women who had simply been arrested for vagrancy or drunkenness and then released. In 1854 a committee of the New York Prison Association attended one of the meetings of the Female Department with some further suggestions for how the Home was to be conducted. The Female Department was but a department of the Prison Society, the men stated.[29]

Some of the women present disliked this assertion of male authority and decided to form an independent association, the Women's Prison Association and Home. The legislators in Albany opposed the idea of a separate women's society and Abby Gibbons and her colleagues had their first experience in lobbying. They soon learned the importance of having letters from prominent citizens and the power of the press on their side. The friendship between the Gibbonses and Horace Greeley, editor of the *Tribune*, was helpful. In May 1854, the Women's Prison Association and Home was incorporated, with Catharine M. Sedgwick as "First Directress," and the refuge named "The Isaac Hopper Home."[30]

The incorporation experience launched Abby Gibbons on what was to be the main focus of her career, speaking up for women prisoners and other objects of her charity. Her direct manner and her obvious sincerity had an impact on legislators, and her absolute belief in the rightness of her cause made her an effective spokesperson.

The house on Tenth Avenue was adequate, but the Women's Prison Association [WPA] looked forward to the day when it might need more room and could own property. On May 3, 1856, Abby wrote to her daughter Sarah, "Yesterday, to visit five Councilmen. Obtained their votes in favor of giving 'The Home' four lots for building, and agreed to meet committee, at City Hall on Second day. I am now sure of success, as I am sure the Mayor will sign the Bill."[31]

The struggle to establish the WPA as independent sharpened Abby Gibbons's ideas about woman's position in society. In May 1854, shortly after the dispute reached its climax, she wrote to her son Willie about it:

> If we could give you men the beginning of an idea of the drudgery to which women are obliged to give themselves up, you would know why it is that we are not fit companions for you; who may well be called "the stronger sex," for everything tends to make you so.

> "In all my wanderings through the world of care"—my world, which lies chiefly among the poor, oppressed women and children—I find great misery growing out of the low estimate in which woman is held. She marries; her husband thinks she was made to get his dinner and patch his shirts; she passes her days and nights in "work, work, work"; and he comes fretting home to the fireside, after smoking and drinking; with no words of sympathy, no appreciation of the ills which encompass her, and really believing that he, alone, has aught to complain of.[32]

Several months later she voiced some of the same sentiments to her sister, Sarah Palmer, as she talked about her daughters' future prospects:

> Alas for woman! Every day I see how I must submit to hear them talk and do as other Mothers' daughters are obliged to, while my husband and son have greatly the advantage; for their intercourse with the intelligent world gives them opportunities to see, hear and learn, which our everyday life does not and cannot afford us.[33]

She was often disappointed, however, in the performance of some of the women she recruited for her charities. The board of the Home for Discharged Women Prisoners was far too large, she thought, and there were many duds among the board members. They appeared during the winter months, then flew off with the birds of spring, without accomplishing anything, she complained to Catharine Sedgwick:

> We did, in days gone by, use these now useless ones to visit the prisons. Their sympathies were awakened, and the result was money. They reach a certain class, by their kind manner, and feel that they are doing something.

> Moreover, it takes more than one class of mind—and a force in number, to visit our prisons. An Elizabeth Fry or a Miss Dix, could not begin to do it. It is not to talk with the officers, but patiently to gain the confidence of the prisoner and lead her in the way of a better life. A ward is sufficient work for a day, and a communion of labor alone will accomplish the work. Our Meetings are *talking* Meetings, and when we *leave* them, we feel that nothing is done. A support for the "Home" is not thought of. Peace is death. We are afraid to be outspoken and faithful to each other. We need a "Rights" woman. Let her come! Where is she?[34]

Abby Gibbons, however, was never very active in the organized women's rights movement, just now getting underway under the leadership of her old teacher Lucretia Mott, as well as Elizabeth Cady Stanton, Susan B. Anthony, and others. Most of the women prison reformers with whom she worked were conservative, believing that woman's separate sphere should be maintained in order to rehabilitate their "fallen sisters." She was also learning that she could influence the course of events through lobbying and raising money and came to feel she did not need the vote in order to achieve her objectives, although she would be glad to vote if suffrage were finally won. Because many of the women in the movement were personal friends, she kept in touch with the movement and agreed to serve as vice president when the leaders organized a convention in New York in 1860. Thereafter her name does not appear on women's rights rosters.[35]

Her daughter, Sarah Emerson, believed that Gibbons did not participate fully in the women's rights movement because of her practical nature. She preferred to be at work at the Hopper House or elsewhere, rather than engaging in philosophical discussions on the nature of woman. This may be true. But Emerson may also have been reflecting her own conservative views. Abby Gibbons's letters reflect far more interest in the issues of women's rights than her daughter acknowledged.

In addition to operating the Home, the women of the Women's Prison Association made regular visits and reports on conditions in the city prisons and almshouses. The abuses they found, they reported to the city government. Thus began a practice of regular lobbying, both at City Hall in New York and the legislature in Albany, in which Abby Gibbons was often involved.

One such regular inspection was a trip to visit the women prisoners on Blackwell Island. Abby Gibbons and Catharine Sedgwick were on Blackwell Island one day on this errand when they saw the children from the city orphanage at Long Island Farms being moved into a temporary wooden building because their former home had been burned to the ground. "A sadder sight than these blind and crippled children, sick in body,crushed in spirit, my eyes never witnessed," Abby Gibbons wrote. On the spot she and Catharine Sedgwick determined to try to provide some cheer in the children's lives. For several years Abby Gibbons organized a Fourth of July picnic for the children, who were now resettled on Randall's Island. This was an elaborate affair with a parade, flowers, baked goods and toys for sale to visiting benefactors, as well as hampers of picnic food for the children themselves. In 1846 one of the early picnics occurred on a day of wind and rain, according to James Gibbons's journal. In 1850 Julia Gibbons was in charge of a toy table, and "made quite a bit of money," she wrote her brother Willie.[36]

Later, the annual party was shifted to Christmastime, and Abby Gibbons and her circle dressed dolls for the orphans, taking them over to the island to present them to the children. Catharine Sedgwick, Caroline Kirkland, and other women from the Women's Prison Association were regular Christmas visitors to the island. Abby Gibbons frequently recruited influential men to go with her also, such as U.S. Senator John P. Hale. She lobbied to improve conditions for the orphans and later, after the Civil War, became a board member of a private New York orphanage.

Following up on her campaign to interest influential men in her causes, she took the wife of the senator, Mrs. John P. Hale, to call on a young couple about whom she was concerned. The wife had consumption, the husband suffered from rheumatism and "a serious malady (from which he will never recover) *utter shiftlessness.*" While her husband rested she had worked all winter making men's shirts. Now she was dying, and Abby Gibbons arranged to send her food packages and to call as often as she could.[37]

Yet another concern into which she brought her influential friends was the Industrial School for German Girls, which she helped to found after she noticed the plight of some homeless German children in her neighborhood. The school, on Avenue C, was under the general auspices of the Children's Aid Society of New York and came to educate as many as two hundred children. As president, Abby Gibbons influenced several wealthy men to raise money for the school. She remained in the post for twelve years, taking an active part in its management. As a result of this involvement, Gibbons became interested in all the industrial schools in the city and served for a time on the board which oversaw them.[38]

Neither the Isaac Hopper Home, nor Randall's Island, nor the German School caused Abby Gibbons to forsake her interest in antislavery work. She was, according to Lori Ginzberg, unusual among her sister nineteenth-century reformers in keeping in contact with both abolitionist and women's rights circles after turning to institution building. Each May, when the American Anti-Slavery Society held its meetings, she entertained as many visiting abolitionists as she could crowd into her house, doubling up the children and occasionally the guests as well. Sometimes she asked black and white to sleep together, quite an unusual occurrence in those days. Among her guests were many of the great names of the antislavery movement; William Lloyd Garrison, who made the Gibbons house his home when he was in New York City, the Grimké sisters, Lydia Maria Child, Abby Kelley, the Weston sisters, Charles Burleigh, Edmund Quincy, and many others. Her brother John, who had married a singer, Rosa DeWolf, in 1847, also entertained antislavery visitors, as did Isaac Hopper himself.[39]

The Manhattan Anti-Slavery Society, organized in 1840, was short-lived, and in June 1853, members of the Hopper family were active in pulling together a new New York Anti-Slavery Society, with Abby Gibbons serving on the executive committee. This group celebrated the anniversary of the abolition of slavery in the British islands in August and held a meeting in September, which was interrupted by a Tammany mob under the leadership of a ward leader, Captain Isaiah Rynders.[40]

Tammany, representing the Democratic Party, was strongly opposed to the abolitionists, who were perceived as interfering with business relations with the South, and threatening northern labor with the competition of free blacks. Rynders had earlier interrupted a meeting of the American Anti-Slavery Society in 1850, with the cooperation of the New York City police, according to William Lloyd Garrison. In the late summer of 1853, the mob also broke up a series of reform conferences including that of the World Temperance Society, the American Antislavery Society, and a Woman's Rights convention. Garrison, who was staying with the Gibbonses, was shouted down at the women's meeting.[41]

Undeterred, the New York Society organized a lecture series at Broadway Tabernacle in the late winter and early spring of 1854, with such speakers as William Lloyd Garrison, Charles Lenox Remond, Henry Ward Beecher, Horace Greeley, and Lucy Stone. The society continued until the Civil War, with Abby Gibbons serving on the executive committee. She wanted the group to hold an annual Anti-Slavery Fair but felt she needed support from the executive committee of the American Anti-Slavery Society in doing so. This long-standing complaint was never fully resolved.[42]

Thus, Abby Gibbons,in her early fifties, had begun to make the transition from the radical causes of her youth to the involvement in institution building and concurrent political action typical of the women reformers of the nineteenth century. She was becoming aware of her own power to influence legislators and wealthy men to support the concerns to which she was devoted. Yet because of the influence of her father and of her mentor, Lucretia Mott, and her close friendship with the Grimké sisters, she did not cut her ties with her radical past.[43]

5

"Losses and Crosses"

Like many of the Victorian philanthropists, Abby Gibbons continued to make her home and family the center of her emotional life. And in common with many of them, as well as countless other women of the period, she suffered a series of losses that refuelled her involvement in her causes.

Her pride in her children was immense. In November 1845, Abby Gibbons wrote to her sister Susan in Philadelphia describing her five children:

> Willie, Sallie and Lucy have gone to a party at Dr. Beales'. I was proud of the trio, as I beheld them (as *I* think) tastefully, yet simply clad. Willie, in a suit of black, an elegant shirt, made by Caroline, and one of my best white handkerchiefs. Sally, in plain delaine—brown, white and blue plaid, inch and a half square, lace round the neck—gold heart and cross and plenty of petticoats—hair braided and tied with white satin ribbon—two "birds' nests." Lucy, the veriest pink in all creation, a *Venus*, with her fair hair and pink complexion, graceful as a fawn, and voice like a bird's. Dressed in pure white and coral necklace—a perfect beauty, unadorned, bewitching to all.

> And here sits Julia by my side, writing a letter—would not go to the party, because it would be out of character and she has no taste for it. Her father seemed to insist, as *he* said, that she might learn how to behave herself; but *she* being the daughter, and *I* the mother, he was over-ruled. It is not trouble to me, if she occasionally sits on one foot, or speaks at the top of her voice, or

Gibbons Family, 1854. Standing: William, Sarah, and Julia; seated: Lucy, Abby, and James Gibbons. Courtesy of Friends Historical Library, Swarthmore College.

spreads out full length; she has goodness of heart, with other rare qualities—enough to outweigh all deficiencies; and I would rather have her *Nature's* own child, than with all the airs and graces to be acquired at a tea party.

Isaac is decidedly his own master and has himself under admirable control. Mrs. Hatch was here today and said she would give a fortune for such a boy . . .[1]

The reference to Julia's being raised as nature's child reflects Abby Gibbons's philosophy of parenting, which was one of little discipline, at least during the early years. Isaac Hopper used to refer to his Gibbons grandchildren as "the Ranters,"(a sect in seventeenth-century England who believed that all strong emotion was from God and should be acted upon) because of the amount of liberty he felt their parents gave them. Abby Gibbons allowed them to use the parlor furniture for games and encouraged them all to draw or paint, with the result that one of them, Lucy, became an artist. On the other hand, as they grew older, Gibbons had strong expectations of how they ought to behave and regarded it as a matter of course they would support her in her opinions and endeavors. In common with many of her contemporaries, she was a dominating mother.[2]

Rather than enrolling her children in local schools, Abby Gibbons usually arranged for someone to live in and tutor them. For a number of years the tutor was her own younger half sister, Mary Hopper, who lived in the Gibbons household. In addition, Abby Gibbons entertained the children of her brother Edward Hopper from Philadelphia, inviting them to spend months with her. And there was very frequently a stray child or two whom she had found in the prisons or the orphanage who seemed especially in need of motherly care.

But tragedy struck yet again at the Gibbons family. In March 1847, Isaac, at five and a half years, became ill with a severe case of croup and, after ten days, died of the disease. This second loss in a little over two years depressed Abby Gibbons's spirits more than she liked to admit. Friends commented that it was three years until she was entirely herself. While she endeavored to remain calm in public, to her sister Sarah she admitted the depth of her pain:

> The blow *stunned* me. I cannot yet realize the mournful fact that our angel boy, our life's sunlight, is no more round about us. I listen for his sweet voice by day and hear him breathe through all the night. I believe I appear as usual, for I have desired that ourselves alone should bear the weight of this terrible calamity. Sometimes I am overwhelmed, as is the case tonight. Such utter desolation comes over us![3]

For solace she turned to a closer relationship with Willie, her oldest and now only son. Born in 1834, Willie was thirteen when Isaac died. Having completed schooling in New York, he spent his summers with Wilmington relatives and his winters in New York, assisting his father in the importing business at Ocean Bank. While he was away, Abby Gibbons wrote him many letters, praising him for being a dutiful son and urging him to avoid all temptation, such as "sangarees and other drinks and preparations where wine is used, even though there be but a *drop*." She urged him to cultivate patience and tolerance of the foibles of others, particularly his relatives, and to make himself useful.[4]

> Every human being ought to be useful in the world. We have various gifts, and should contribute to the comfort of one another. Uncle John laughs at thy mother's gift, but she is *able* to be laughed at, and feels *better* when she has taken an old hag from the gutter, and put her in circumstances to become a woman, and enjoy some of life's little flowers.[5]

When he finally left the employ of the American Anti-Slavery Society, James Gibbons reentered the field of banking and shortly began to do well. He was soon regarded as "a man of consequence," according to his brother-in-law John. Like many New York families, the Gibbonses had moved frequently from rented house to rented house, from 150 Eldridge to 31 Rivington Street to 27 Seventh Avenue, all in the downtown section. In 1846 they moved uptown to West 14th street, then regarded as the northern edge of the city. In the spring of 1851 they were prosperous enough to buy a large house at 19 Lamartine Place, off 19th Street. William Lloyd Garrison, visiting them in their new house, reported to his wife that they were now "more than two miles uptown." Here they were to live for many years. Abby Gibbons bought new furniture and rugs for the new house and was worried that her father would consider her a spendthrift. He tolerated the new stair carpet but called the plush rug in the parlor "extravagant." "I had an eye to pleasing husband and children and repented too late," Abby Gibbons wrote to Sarah. "I like the peculiarity of plainness, because everything else is common."[6]

She was, however, very proud of her new house and invited her brothers and sisters to visit. The opening of the New York's first World's Fair, in the summer of 1852, brought flocks of Philadelphia visitors. Many came to see the Crystal Palace, a block-long structure of glass and steel patterned after its original in London, which was situated between Forty-first and Forty-second streets east of Sixth Avenue, in Bryant Park. Inside were industrial exhibitions from all over the world, including such curiosities as a new foot-pedal sewing machine. Next to the Palace a cylinder glass tower served as an observatory in which visitors were carried skyward in a steam-driven elevator. From the tower you could see the whole city, to its northern boundaries at Fiftieth Street and its southern terminus in the green of Castle Garden at the Battery.[7]

Abby Gibbons's chief concentration remained her children. Willie by this time had begun studying law in New York. "I do believe he will be A. No. 1," she confided in her sister. "He is caressed, and I hope will not be spoiled. He is very popular with the young ladies, and has more invitations than he is allowed to accept."[8]

In the fall of 1851, Abby Gibbons enrolled Sarah and Julia in a school in Lenox, Massachusetts, run by Elizabeth Dwight Sedgwick, the wife of Charles Sedgwick, Catharine Sedgwick's younger brother. The school accepted a limited number of young ladies to live with the family and taught deportment as well as literature and penmanship. Among the pupils were young women from prominent New England homes. Ellen Emerson, daughter of Ralph Waldo Emerson, was a pupil, and in time became a close friend of Sarah Gibbons, introducing her to her cousin William Emerson from Staten Island.

At first the Gibbons girls, aged sixteen and fourteen, were homesick and their parents wrote to them exhorting them to be brave. "Almost before this ink is dry, you will have letters which show you how near home you are," James wrote. "When you get interested in your studies, you will feel better." Abby Gibbons urged them not to spend so much time writing letters home and to be "womanly," promising them, if they were good, that Willie would visit them at Christmas time. She herself was planning a Christmas visit to Randall's Island, and suggested that her daughters make doll clothes out of calico, since she intended to supply the sick children with dolls and toys as long as she lived. She was also planning, after Christmas, to raise money for Lajos Kossuth, a Hungarian freedom fighter who was touring the United States at the time, and was pleased to hear that her daughters were similarly engaged in Lenox.[9]

In December Isaac T. Hopper caught cold on one of his excursions to see a discharged prisoner. The cold spread to his chest and by January he was very ill, attended daily by his physician, Dr. Beales. He rallied some in February, but became so ill in March that the family decided to move him to the Gibbons house, with the hope that the change of scene and air would help. Abby Gibbons attended him personally and kept him company; whenever she was long from his room he asked where she was. His wife, Hannah, took her meals in his room, and Rachel Brown was often in attendance. He wrote his daughter Mary that he had the best nurses in the world, her mother and sisters. Nevertheless, he did not improve and on May 7, 1852, he died.

In the course of the winter, Lydia Maria Child had written to Isaac Hopper asking his permission to write his biography. He had agreed, and when he was dying James Gibbons had sent for her. She arrived on May 5, and was with him when he was so weak he could only whisper. After saying goodbye to each of his children he asked for her and breathed out a last message which she understood to be directed to the Society of Friends. "Tell them I love them-though I felt called to resist— some who claimed to be rulers of Israel—I never meant—Tell them I love them *all*."[10]

Several days after his death a delegation from the Hester Street Meeting arrived at the house with the invitation that Isaac Hopper be buried in the Friends burial ground. Perhaps Hopper himself might have accepted, but his children could not bring themselves to permit it. He was buried instead at Greenwood Cemetery, accompanied by his family, a few friends, and Lucretia Mott. "It is fitting," she said, "that he should not be buried within the walls of sectarian prejudice." Abby Gibbons spoke at her father's grave, saying, "He has finished his work, and it is meet that he should have rest."

Abby Gibbons's life had for so long revolved around her father that his loss was a heavy blow, even though she knew that, at eighty-one, he had lived a rich life. "He has helped the poor, and has worked for the needy all his life, and when his work is done we must let him go cheerfully," she had written her daughters some months earlier. Nevertheless, she mourned her father deeply. An officer of the New York Prison Association wrote to Abby Gibbons urging her to come to the office, although he said he understood the feelings which kept her away. "I have found it to my comfort to change the furniture of the office so that it might not appear so lonely without your dear, venerated Father."[11]

One of Abby Gibbons's mournful duties after her father's death was to try to notify her brother Josiah Hopper, now a ship's doctor on board a vessel called *The New Orleans*. She was unable to reach him before he read a newspaper account of Isaac Hopper's death, and according to witness, "became insensible and moaned for a week." Several years later she learned that he was very ill and coming home to die. She prepared a bedroom in the house on Lamartine Place, "where the sun shines in, and he can see the first spring flowers." Unfortunately, he died in Panama and was brought home for burial in Greenwood, causing Abby Gibbons and her sisters fresh cause for mourning. It was in this period of her life that Gibbons began to speak of the "losses and crosses" one must bear.[12]

In 1853 Lydia Maria Child's biography of Isaac T. Hopper was published. Much of the book consisted of stories of Isaac's clients, from the records of the Pennsylvania Prison Society, the New York Prison Association, or the Pennsylvania Abolition Society. Many of them Isaac Hopper had published as "Tales of Oppression" in the *National Antislavery Standard*. There were also liberal quotations from favorable editorials and letters. Catharine Sedgwick wrote Abby Gibbons to say that she was sorry that Maria Child had not put more of her skill into the book, made it more a biography and less a compilation, "but perhaps, as it is, it is more level to the mass of readers, and we should remember that 'the greatest happiness to the greatest number' was the rule of your father's life."[13]

On the whole, Abby Gibbons and her brothers and sisters were pleased with the book and gave copies away liberally. Catherine Beecher, the author and advocate of education for women, was one of the celebrities to whom Gibbons sent a copy. Another was Fredrika Bremer, the Swedish author, who had become a friend of the family when visiting the United States.

"You are reading, I suppose, the biography," Abby wrote Julia at Mrs. Sedgwick's. "I have just finished it and am satisfied for the most part. It seemed to bring dear grandfather very near, though he has not seemed far away since he left us."[14]

William Lloyd Garrison had been fond of Isaac Hopper and missed his cheerful and sympathetic presence. But staying with the Gibbonses was the next best thing, he wrote in an open letter to the *Liberator*. "Next to seeing that departed venerable friend of humanity Isaac Hopper is seeing Mrs. Gibbons, his daughter, who in all sympathetic and benevolent qualities of her mind clearly resembles her father, as well as in some of her features." In February 1854, Garrison was staying at Lamartine Place when Abby Gibbons invited friends to gather for a seance where a medium, Mrs. Leah Brown, attempted to contact the spirit of Isaac Hopper as well as that of Jesse Hutchinson, one of the Hutchinson singers. There were strange rappings and drummings but no definitive appearances, according to Garrison.[15]

Following her father's death, Abby Gibbons's affections seemed to turn even more strongly to her children, now adolescents. She regretted having them away from her while at school and looked forward to their return to the parental home. "My spirit droops often when I think that for all the live-long year we must dwell apart," she confessed to Julia when she sent Lucy also to the Sedgwick School. She did not seem to face the fact that her daughters might ever move away, either for marriage or career. Yet she wanted them to enjoy the best possible education and thought she had found it for them in Lenox. She also may have remembered her own disappointment in not having been sent to Westtown as a young girl. Thanks to James's prospering career, she did not need to stint at her children's expense.

Abby's only son, Willie Gibbons, had been studying law in a law office in New York and decided he needed more formal training. In the spring of 1854 he therefore entered Cambridge Law School, a precursor of the Harvard Law School. Abby's pride knew no bounds. She wrote to him frequently, mingling expressions of her favoritism with motherly admonitions:

> The question arises, to whom shall I write? Witness answereth, to my only and well-beloved son. I love all my children alike, though Willie is a little closer to my heart, for his path has been strewed with roses, and as he grows older he must expect to meet briers and thorns. . . . When I read the list of thy wants, I was somewhat horrified, and found myself sighing to think there was no end to imaginary needs. How could thee ask for the old settee thy father rests upon, that is endeared to us by a thousand memories? It has been stage-coach, railroad car, baggage wagon, *everything* to our dear children now in Heaven. We could sooner part with any piece of furniture of modern date. And the desk, that has furnished our rooms ever since we were lovers! Time will teach thee what thou canst not now know.[16]

A few weeks later she wrote again to caution him against his habit of exaggerating and his fondness for argument. "Dear me, do not disappoint me, for I have set my heart upon thy being a model for the race of young men to succeed thee." She ended by urging him not to go too often to Boston and to avoid varioloid and girls.[17]

James Gibbons wrote frequently to Willie also. In the spring of 1855, he reported to his son on the Anti-Slavery Anniversary meetings, where the topic of Kansas was uppermost, and also to tell Willie about a friend, William Thayer, who was involved in a military adventure in Nicaragua led by William Walker, a man who appeared to James to be exploiting a civil war there to his own ends and might set up a dictatorship:

We have had the best Anniversary Week in Anti-Slavery history. [Charles] Sumner was the star. It needs only a judicious course by the true friend of freedom to confirm our Northern public sentiment finally in its favor. One of the most unfortunate misfortunes of the Anti-Slavery agitation has always been the ascription of too much influence to persons, and too little to events. It will be a high wisdom to make the most of these latter; though I do not detract from the just merit of the former. The Kansas outrage, on top of the repeal of the Missouri Compromise, is the chestnut burr under the horse's saddle, and our Northern horse kicks and rears tremendously, and will pitch his rider inevitably. . . .

We had a [William]Thayer dinner last evening. He is going out to Nicaragua with Filibuster Kinney, to start a "commercial colony," and is entirely persuaded that this is the object and total aim of the expedition. I think, however, that he is mistaken. There is, at least, a reservation as to what shall be done when they get there. Powder and ball, no women and children, swords and Saxonism, a rich country with no government, and a weak scattered population—and anyone can guess the rest. Kinney is now detained by government legal process. I suspect the concern to be devilish and piratical, and that they will introduce slavery into their Colony, if they succeed in establishing one.[18]

After several months at Cambridge, Will Gibbons discovered, that if he were to compete with the other prospective lawyers with whom he was studying, he needed a more liberal education. He therefore asked his parents' permission to enroll in Harvard College. Abby was reluctant to face his being far from home for so long, but knew it was for his own good and therefore consented. In the fall of 1855, Willie enrolled in the sophomore class and moved into rooms at Stoughton. Abby helped to get him settled, bought him a teapot, and cautioned him to wait before following up on a summer romance with Hetty Wharton.

Her three daughters were home that fall, Sarah attending the New York School of Design, Julia going to Miss Howland's, and Lucy at home for a year, at the suggestion of James. Abby said that she would have decided otherwise, but was planning to send her to visit her Philadelphia relatives and would enter her next year in a school for young ladies. Nevertheless, Abby continued to feel lonely for Willie. She wrote him a string of letters telling him of her outings and advising him against accepting an editorship of a student paper, which she feared would distract him from his studies. He listened to her advice, but took the editorship anyway. When he wrote urging her to come to Boston to visit him at Christmastime she said she felt she could not forego her trip to Randall's Island and disappoint the "300 sick children who depend on my baskets of dolls and toys." But she might make a quick trip if there was a strong wish on his part to see her.[19]

On the night of Saturday, December 15, Willie spent the evening with friends in Boston. Crossing the bridge to Cambridge on his way home he stumbled and fell over some construction materials. He was apparently unhurt and seemed fine the next morning, but later in the day experienced sharp pains, giddiness, and nausea. He did not think it was serious, but on Monday he allowed his friends to persuade him to see a doctor. Someone suggested that he wire his mother, but he was afraid it would worry her, and the doctor seemed to think he would soon be better. However, he grew alarmingly weaker, and in the middle of the afternoon the doctor sent a telegram to Abby. When he learned of this he said he was sorry, and a few minutes later, "O, I hope I won't die; it would kill mother." Shortly after this he lapsed into unconsciousness, grew weaker, and in a short time, died.

Abby and James Gibbons received the first telegram in the early evening and sent another back, asking for details. In a few hours came the terrible second message, saying it was too late. His death was ascribed to a blood vessel, broken when he fell. Abby had had a premonition that he ought not to cross that bridge, but had put it out of her mind as foolish. Now, in the midst of her shock and grief, she felt guilt that she had not warned him.[20]

Three college classmates accompanied his remains to New York, where a funeral service was held in the Gibbons home, in silence, after the manner of Friends. Then he was buried in Greenwood Cemetery with his two brothers and his grandfather. Sadly, Abby and James Gibbons made the journey to Cambridge to bring his things home and to visit his closest friends.[21]

In death, William Gibbons achieved a fame that seemed to outrun his brief life. The students of Harvard held a memorial service for him, the president, Dr. James Walker, preached a sermon about his life and death, friends from far and near wrote tributes. His faults were forgotten, his youth and promise and graciousness of manner remembered. The list of those who wrote to console the Gibbonses reads like a roster of the reformers of the period: William Lloyd Garrison, Lydia Maria Child, Theodore Parker, Theodore Weld, Caroline Kirkland, Moncure Conway, Sarah Grimké, Catharine Sedgwick, Fredrika Bremer, Joseph Choate, William Chandler, John P. Hale, Elizabeth H. Schuyler, Henry Foote.

For Abby Gibbons, it was as though a black hole had opened at her feet, swallowing up all her hopes and joys. She stumbled through her days, and nights were a torment. She regretted bitterly not having gone to Cambridge to see him before Christmas. "The house is like a tomb," she wrote a friend a few months later. "Dear Willie was so in my heart that it would be strange indeed if I were not left desolate. I ought not to hurt myself to take up the pen, for I am not in a state of mind to write. Dear idolized child, as ever lived . . ."[22]

James Gibbons too was devastated. He had to take an extended business trip in March and wrote his brother-in-law that his travels were "as agreeable as possible to a man with the heaviest weight on the heart that mortals ever carry. I am all the time waking up to the dreadful reality that makes it become more dreadful."[23]

Abby Gibbons's brother Edward and sister-in-law Anna Hopper also lost a beloved child, George, in January, and the two sets of bereaved parents consoled each other. "How little those know who have never lost a dear child—it is vain to speak or write," Abby wrote to the Hoppers. "She (a friend) asked me why I did not cry more. I could have told her that the tears that used to come to my eyes now go to my heart."[24]

After a few months of this, Abby Gibbons began to fear that she was losing her mind. Even in her depressed state she knew she must not yield to this and decided to try to distract herself by getting busy. As the story was told later, she put on her bonnet and went to see the mayor of New York to ask for financial support for the Isaac T. Hopper Home. To her surprise, she was successful. This led her gradually to take up again her other charities. She wrote to her daughter Sarah about it:

> I have been busy at home, doing many things in all my spare moments and seeing many people, and but for the constant employment what should we all do, and this is work in which dear Willie sympathized, he never spoke lightly of it but always encouraged me and how many times he helped me. When a very little boy in 14th Street I remember well how our poor neighbors

loved him and kind and loving he was to poor children . . . never shunning any, however tattered their garments.[25]

Talking with Willie's friends and admirers in Cambridge was also a balm. Abby Gibbons went to Cambridge the spring after the funeral to visit Willie's room, and stayed with Harvard President Dr. James Walker and his wife. Here she met many of Willie's former classmates and friends. There was solace in imagining him in his old haunts and hearing him praised, and Abby formed the habit of making a regular visit to Cambridge each fall, sometimes staying with the Walkers, and meeting Willie's classmates, some of whom became close family friends. She also regularly visited the Sedgwicks in Lenox and Maria and David Child in Wayland. Other friends of Willie's came to the house at 19 Lamartine Place. Among these were James and William Thayer, William Emerson, Christopher Langdell, Charles Elliott, James C. Carter, George O. Shattuck, Robert Rantoul. Most of them were lawyers, many to make a mark in American history.

Abby's brother, John Hopper, commissioned a marble bust of Willie, and this was set up in the parlor, along with some of his most cherished belongings. Abby always kept a vase of fresh flowers before the bust, and the room became a sacred spot. She expected her daughters to share completely in her idolization of the lost Willie and to devote their lives to his memory, as she intended to devote hers. This worked for Sarah and Julia, but ultimately not for Lucy, who rebelled.

James Gibbons, for his part, immersed himself in literary work, which had always been a major interest. He wrote a book, *The Banks of New-York, Their Dealers, the Clearing House, and the Panic of 1857*, which was regarded as clear and readable explanation of contemporary banking practice. In March 1860, he undertook publishing a magazine, *The Century*, which had been started by Thomas M'Elrath in 1858, and which he continued to put out until December, employing Lucy to help him read proof and perform other editing chores. The magazine covered a wide range of topics, but was devoted to the cause of abolition. James had developed the habit of taking several careful meteorological readings a day, and these were published in *The Century* during James's term as publisher.[26]

Abby Gibbons sometimes resented James's preoccupation and thought that even when she travelled he did not always know she was gone.

Your father's thoughts are doubtless running upon a book or a periodical, and I am not certain he is aware of my being away, save when he sits down to table, *'Spose* he does not imagine me there, if he imagines anything of a domestic character, but *I* imagine, being as I'm a woman, and have travelled some way *into* life, that I shall be about to travel *out*, as well.[27]

The loss of Willie may have begun the gradual development of a distance between Abby and James Gibbons. With trips to Cambridge, and summer vacations in the Berkshires and elsewhere, Abby travelled frequently without James in the years after Willie's death. The changes of scene helped some. Yet for another five years at least, she managed only to go through the motions of living. Abby wrote her brother Edward about her feelings, since he too was still mourning a son:

Time does very little for us, nor do I depend upon the lapse of years to wear away the aching and loneliness of my desolate heart. Those around me need help and I dispense what I can and while I may seem to my friends a brave and cheerful spirit, they know not, and never will, how all the while my very soul mourns that the light of my life is gone. Strange if I should ever become reconciled to such a separation.[28]

In the fall of 1861, a former teacher of Willie's, Theodore Tebbets, published a slim memorial volume on Willie's life, which further added to his fame in death. Abby Gibbons loved it and sent it to everyone she knew. Although it reopened old wounds, it was also part of the healing process. After the book was out she seemed more inclined to go forward with her life, and to concern herself with her three remaining children.

6

"The Calls of Humanity"

By the mid-1850s, the antislavery movement, in which Abby Gibbons had been involved most of her life, was in some disarray. The use of nonresistance or moral force as a method to protect escaping slaves and ultimately to end slavery had been a tenet of the Garrisonians since 1833. Now it was coming more and more into question as black abolitionists turned against it following the passage of the Fugitive Slave Law of 1850, and white abolitionists began to question its usefulness in their efforts to protect escaping slaves from recapture. While some antislavery activists, including Parker Pillsbury, Stephen S. Foster, and Garrison himself, insisted that they were able to carry on the struggle with moral weapons alone, others began to question this practice.[1]

In 1854 the U.S. Congress passed the Kansas-Nebraska Act, specifying that Kansas could decide whether to be open to slavery by the will of the majority of settlers. As a result, proslavery advocates gave financial support to proslavery settlers, while the abolitionists raised money for the antislavery settlers. In addition, the Kansas crisis caused some antislavery activists to question their former tactics and to turn to political action. A new Republican Party was organized in 1856 (James Gibbons's brother, Charles Gibbons, of Pennsylvania, was one of the founders) and backed John Fremont in the 1856 presidential race.

The inevitable result of the rush to settle Kansas with rival groups was an outbreak of hostilities between the two factions. News from "bloody Kansas" motivated many of the Garrisonian abolitionists to repudiate nonviolence and purchase arms for the antislavery settlers. Thomas Wentworth Higginson led armed men into the territory, and Henry Ward Beecher's congregation gave each settler's family a Bible and a breech loading rifle, which came to be known as "Beecher's Bibles."[2]

Lydia Maria Child was inspired by the situation to write a novel, *The Kansas Emigrants*. Her nephew, George Luther Stearns, a well-to-do Boston philanthropist, organized the national Kansas Aid Society, and helped to start satellite societies in cities all over the northeast. When he first went to New York City to talk about Kansas aid he had the assistance of both Abby Gibbons and Henry Ward Beecher in calling the first meeting. Gibbons subsequently served for a time as president of the local society.[3]

One of the Kansas settlers to be armed with Beecher's Bibles was John Brown, who had settled in the Ossawatomie colony, with five of his sons, and was made head of the local militia. In May 1856, Kansas proslavery forces, joined by "Border Ruffians" from Missouri, attacked the town of Lawrence, burning down the hotel and pillaging many homes as well as destroying the presses publishing the antislavery newspapers, *The Herald of Freedom* and *The Kansas Free State*. Outraged, Brown, with four of his sons and two others, carried out a midnight execution of five proslavery colonists at Ossawatomie Creek. This was the beginning of a civil war that raged in Kansas until September. It was claimed by George Stearns's biographer that Stearns had no knowledge of the massacre at Ossawatomie and was under the impression that the rifles were being supplied to Brown for defensive purposes only. "Don't shoot unless attacked," he frequently commanded. But using weapons, even defensively, violated the principles of nonresistance, and caused many abolitionists to reexamine their attitudes toward armed struggle.[4]

In May 1856, Charles Sumner, senator from Massachusetts, gave a spirited speech in the Senate concerning the situation in Kansas. A Southern Congressman, Representative Preston Brooks of South Carolina, was so angered by this speech that he beat Sumner with a cane on the floor of the Senate, injuring him so seriously that Sumner was unable to return to the Senate for more than three years. John Hopper, Abby Gibbons's brother and a friend of Sumner's, was responsible for finding a place for him to stay at Cape May, where he could recuperate, while still threatened with total paralysis, out of the reach of the press and politicians. This brutal attack on one of their number also caused many abolitionists to waver in regard to nonresistance.[5]

Deeply religious Quakers, such as James and Lucretia Mott, continued to be sure that slavery could be defeated by moral force alone. Abby Kelley Foster, who had grown up as a Quaker, but like, Abby Hopper Gibbons, left the Society because of what she regarded as its timid attitude about opposing slavery, was also strong in her adherence to nonresistance, as were many others. Had Isaac Hopper lived, he would likely have been one of that number. But to Abby Gibbons and her brothers and sisters, it began to seem that the only answer to the slavery question lay in armed resistance.[6]

Just when Gibbons changed her mind it is difficult to say. In May 1857, George Stearns wrote to her to tell her about current plans. There was need for money for the relief of families who had lost their homes as a result of the fighting and the inroads of the Border Ruffians, he said. But there was also a fund being raised to organize a secret force, under the control of John Brown, to repel the attacks of the proslavery forces and to defend the Free State. This would be purely defensive warfare, he argued, and he hoped that Abby Gibbons, who was president of the Kansas Aid, might be able to support the effort. If not, the money could be used for relief. According to her memory at age eighty-one, it was sent to Brown.[7]

Years later she recalled that John Brown had spent a morning with her in October 1859, a few weeks before his strike at Harper's Ferry. He told her of his plans, and she told him that she sympathized with his objective, but did not believe his scheme practical. In fact, she recalled, she did not dream that he would accomplish it. She also asked how he intended to avoid harming women and children in his raid. "I won't hurt a hair of their heads," he told her.[8]

Yet Abby Gibbons remained close to William Lloyd Garrison, who still supported nonresistance, and she enjoyed entertaining his son Wendell when he visited New York. Other antislavery colleagues visited too, including Sarah Grimke and Angelina Grimké Weld. In 1838 Angelina had married Theodore Weld, and with him and Sarah had run a community and a school at Eagleswood, New Jersey. The two sisters had taken up wearing the bloomer costume, a loose-fitting tunic over bloomers, which some of the abolitionist/feminists wore as a protest against the tightlaced and unwieldy women's clothing of the day. Abby Gibbons thought it made them look ridiculous:

> They are people of great and singular gifts, insane on the subject of Woman's Rights—wearing bloomer dresses,—and so plain as to prevent (certainly, stand in the way of) any form of dress they may choose to adopt. Neat in all their ways, youthful in feeling, but oh! so appearing, that a sight of them would make anyone laugh the livelong day,—while all respect and love them. She (Sarah Grimké) bored Sarah and Julia to death on the "Rights,"

and did not convert them. . . . It is well their father and mother have faith in the same direction.[9]

Abby Gibbons remained deeply interested in women's rights herself and was delighted when her friend Catharine Sedgwick wrote a novel, *Married or Single?* suggesting that a woman might be as happy in one state as the other. Abby advised Sally, Julia, and Lucy to read the book and to take up professional work after their finishing school years. "It is the wish of my heart that thou and thy sisters may think seriously what there is in this ever busy world to demand your interest," she wrote Julia, admonishing her at that same time to keep to the Quaker habits of speech. "Let it [your life] not be spent in heaping comforts upon those who were never needy but seek out or rather lend a hand to such as happen in your way." Julia became a teacher, Lucy taught piano lessons and illustrated children's books, Sarah tutored private students, translated stories and articles from German, and helped her mother at the Home. Abby Gibbons herself left home to fill in for Elizabeth Sedgwick at the school in Lenox while the latter recovered her health. She could afford to be away from home, she wrote, because she had such efficient daughters.[10]

In 1858 Sarah became engaged to William Emerson, a cousin of Ellen Emerson and a nephew of Ralph Waldo Emerson. William was suffering with the malady that carried off many Emersons, tuberculosis, and until he regained his health there were no immediate prospects of a wedding. Abby Gibbons was pleased with the young man, but eager that Sarah not attempt to immerse her life in his. At the same time a friend of her daughters' from the Sedgwick School, Addy Drury, announced her engagement, and Abby Gibbons thought she was handling it well:

> There is a great need that every engaged girl should preserve with tenderest care, all her near family relations, which she can never afford to lose, however she may deceive herself into the romantic and false idea that she must narrow the sphere of her affections and interests to the selfishness of one individual, who never possesses all the elements required to secure such happiness as mortal woman stands in need of. Let her nature enlarge that there may be room for all.
>
> I am greatly pleased with Addy's perfectly natural way of touching upon her present course as if she had a voice and a will and a way, as a woman should and an independence to speak without

liberty from any, and with a frankness and honesty that does honor to her womanhood. They are both individuals to be led by their own individual convictions, a course tending to the benefit of each. I never yet found a man right in all things, neither a woman. My words are for the thought of my dear unmarried daughters who have come up their own way pretty much and I am jealous that their lovers might mislead them.[11]

At about the same time, John and Rosa Hopper's only son, William DeWolf Hopper, was born. Named for Willie, this Willie Hopper became close to Abby Gibbons's heart. (In later life he changed his name to DeWolf Hopper, was a famous actor, and the father of Hedda Hopper, the Hollywood columnist.) Willie's birth was hard, and Rosa's mother was so upset she wanted to leave the bedchamber, but Abby Gibbons, who wept privately but kept her voice cheerful, insisted that Mrs. DeWolf stay, persuading her by observing that John would be proud of his mother-in-law if she did so. Her expectations of the strength she expected to find in other women were expanding.[12]

The outbreak of the Civil War in April 1861 was greeted by the abolitionists with mixed feelings. If they could believe that the war was being fought to end slavery, and not merely to preserve the Union, they could rejoice, but there were many aspects of the government's action, such as the recognition of slavery in the border states, that were deeply troubling. For those abolitionists who had continued to support nonresistance, a time of testing was at hand.

Many Quakers were torn between their loyalty to the antislavery cause and to their historic pacifism. This was especially true among the Hicksites, who had been, as a group, more active in the antislavery cause. Families were split over the issue. Lucretia Mott, as has been said, remained a pacifist, claiming that the resort to arms was a tragic breakdown in a long process of ending slavery through moral force. Her son-in-law, Edward M. Davis, however, chose to fight and was given the rank of captain. He also leased his farm in Chelten Hills to the U.S. Army for the training of the first federal black troops, at a camp named, rather incongruously, Camp William Penn. Mott therefore had black soldiers as neighbors. She baked pies and turkeys for them and preached to them while still opposing the war as such.[13]

Because of the nature of the war some young Quaker men enlisted. Most were expelled or disowned from their local meetings for engaging in war, but those who sought to rejoin Friends after the war were generally forgiven. Other Quakers, male and female, found service as teachers to the "contraband," as the slaves who flocked around Union army camps were called, or went south to work among the newly freed slaves on the Sea Islands. Quaker women packed boxes of clothing for the contraband and raised money for the new schools established behind Union lines for the freed slaves. Lucretia Mott participated in this activity. A number of Quaker women became Civil War nurses; of these, Cornelia Hancock, who served after the battle of Gettysburg, is the best known. Elizabeth Comstock of Michigan, a noted prison visitor, and Sarah Smith of Indiana, who was to become matron of one of the first reformatories for women prisoners, visited army hospitals and nursed the sick and dying.[14]

But still other Friends found any participation at all against their consciences. When the draft came, some young men refused on conscientious principles to hire a substitute, and were drafted into the army and tortured when they refused to hold a rifle or drill. And Quaker manufacturers refused to supply the army with necessities, such as blankets.

The Hopper men, John and Edward, had both resigned from the Society of Friends at the time of their father's disownment and had no problems of conscience about supporting the war effort. Sarah Palmer, who had remained a Friend but was often highly critical of the Quakers, wrote to Abby Gibbons about the reaction of some in Quaker Philadelphia:

> Quakers are drilling, contrary to all the peace principles of the Sect; indeed, from all appearances we may suppose their hopes are based on war. I'm opposed to war—to cutting down men like grass—but if ever war was holy, this one, in favor of the most oppressed, the most forbearing, most afflicted, down-trodden, insulted part of humanity, is a holy war. But I am hoping that the weak, presumptuous, sickly, clamorous, selfish, traitorous South will be frightened (as I think they are now, in a measure) into subjection.[15]

For the women of benevolence with whom Abby Gibbons was associated, the coming of the war meant a sea change in their attitudes. Many of them had been abolitionists and had begun their careers deeply distrustful of a government that enforced slavery, and of many of the institutions of society that supported it. Now, suddenly, the government seemed to be supporting their own cause. What was needed now, they believed, was not radical enthusiasm but discipline and organization to achieve the goals toward which they had been working.[16]

For Abby Gibbons's daughters and other young women who came of age at this time, the war offered their first opportunity to become involved together in the causes that had attracted their mothers and shaped their growing up. Ellen Wright, Lucretia Mott's niece, and Lucy McKim, daughter of Sarah and Miller McKim, had been to school together at Eagleswood, the school run by the Grimké-Weld household, and were close friends. They viewed the conflict optimistically and were eager to be involved. In New York, Abby Gibbons had worked with Eliza Schuyler in the Women's Prison Association and Sarah Shaw in the abolition movement. The daughters of these two, Louisa Lee Schuyler and Josephine Shaw, both threw themselves into war service. Sarah, Julia, and Lucy Gibbons were also excited about participating in the war. None of these younger women retained the nonresistance sentiments of the older generation, nor the deep distrust of government which had been part of the movement. The war seemed a noble enterprise to them.[17]

In April, shortly after war was declared, doctors Elizabeth and Emily Blackwell called together a meeting of women at Cooper Institute to discuss war service. Some two or three thousand women attended and founded the Woman's Central Association of Relief. This group, with offices in downtown Manhattan, became a branch of the U.S. Sanitary Commission. Abby Gibbons and her daughters were involved from the first, along with Josephine Shaw, Louisa Lee Schuyler, and her friend Ellen Collins, a young Quaker philanthropist.[18]

Through the Woman's Central Association, Abby Gibbons met many women who were going south to volunteer their services, and in the fall she thought it would be well for her to go also, to see how the supplies she was soliciting and packing were being used. To respond to the needs of wounded soldiers was to answer "humanity's call," Abby Gibbons believed. With her daughter Sarah she went to Washington in late November 1861. Here they spent their first days visiting hospitals, including the School House Hospital, the Patent Office Hospital, and various regimental hospitals. As they went from bedside to bedside, they distributed stockings and homemade cake.[19]

At the hospital for the New York Fiftieth Regiment they found thirty men crowded into an old building, with no sheets and no women to nurse them or wash their clothing. Abby Gibbons and Sarah stayed as long as they could, providing each patient with his own cake and stockings, and buying milk for some who could not afford to purchase it from the women who came around daily with cans of milk for sale.[20]

"We value the great amount of good done by the Sanitary Commission," Abby Gibbons wrote in her journal. "If all were such men as Dr. J. H. Douglas, the good would be incalculable. He knows how to approach men and women, is a good worker, and commands the respect of all with whom he is associated."[21]

When she wasn't nursing, Abby Gibbons took time to see the sights of Washington. She found the city "the dirtiest, most God-forsaken hole in the universe," but was interested to attend sittings of both the Senate and the House. Her abolitionist connections put her in touch with members of the Republican Party, of which her brother-in-law, Charles Gibbons, had been a founder. With letters of introduction from him and others, she was presented in short order to many Washington notables, including George E. Baker, treasurer of the National Freedmen's Relief Association, and his wife, Florence, with both of whom she soon became fast friends. She and Sarah stayed with Judge Chipman and his wife, and there met such notables as Secretary of Treasury Salmon Chase and his daughter Kate, as well as General Walter Sprague, Kate's finance. Abby Gibbons was charmed also to meet Dr. Mary Walker, "a very thin little woman in bloomer costume, very short, presides over the Indiana Hospital. She is so little as to make it seem really funny but she is a triumph. She has a keen eye and a competent manner and the patients like her."[22]

Early in December, Abby Gibbons was invited by New York friends to drive out to Hunter's Point, Munson's Hill, and Falls Church in Virginia. At Falls Church they found a schoolhouse utilized as a hospital, full of men dying of fever. One very young soldier begged Abby Gibbons to stay and take care of him. Her motherly heart was touched, and she sought out the surgeon on duty to ask if she might help. "You can if you will," he replied. Abby found lodging for herself and Sarah in an adjoining saloon, where a Rebel family reluctantly gave them a drafty attic.[23]

The next day, the two women undertook a thorough cleaning of the ward, and baths for as many of the patients as could be moved. As often as possible, they asked convalescent soldiers to do the bathing. Then they undertook to prepare nutritious soups and jellies for the patients too ill to deal with the coarse fare of the army. Their first day was so successful that they stayed for some weeks. So popular did their food become that the wounded soldiers themselves took up a collection to buy them a proper cook stove and pans, so that they need not keep running to the regular army mess to prepare food. Sarah, in addition, did a great deal of reading to the soldiers, wrote letters for them to their sweethearts and mothers, and sewed scarfs for their necks. Although there were six dead bodies in the schoolhouse when Abby Gibbons and Sarah took over the nursing, the rest of the patients all recovered, thanks, they said, to the extra care they received.[24]

Many of the soldiers who fought in the Civil War on both sides were very young, some only fourteen or fifteen. These youthful soldiers, far from home, were lonely for their mothers, especially when they lay deathly ill in the crude army hospitals. The presence of motherly women, such as Abby Gibbons, was as good for their souls as their stomachs. The fact that Abby, her daughter, and others like her, had no previous training in nursing was balanced by the fact that they supplied the sort of individual attention that was totally lacking otherwise. In addition, in the middle of the nineteenth century, most women had done enough home nursing to qualify themselves for the simpler medicine of the day.[25]

To understand the role of volunteer nurses such as Abby and Sarah Gibbons in the Civil War, it is necessary to picture the extremely primitive state of medical care in the army of the period. At the beginning of the war there were only twenty-seven surgeons and twelve assistant surgeons in the Union forces. There were no general hospitals, only regimental hospitals consisting of three hospital tents and certain medicines and surgical supplies. Each regiment was assigned one surgeon and two assistant surgeons. There were no trained ambulance workers, and most ambulances were ungainly two wheeled oxcarts. There were no disinfectants; no drugs other than quinine and morphine. There was no anesthesia, and soldiers facing amputation were given whiskey or literally asked to bite the bullet. Surgery was often performed by men with little training and poor instruments, including hacksaws. As a result of lack of antiseptic conditions, 90 percent of all soldiers suffering from stomach wounds and 62 percent of other wounds died. In addition, diarrhea and other infections killed many others. More soldiers died of infection than of wounds.[26]

Under these crude circumstances, the baths and nourishing meals that women such as Abby Gibbons were able to provide afforded some slight relief to the intolerable suffering of the soldiers, while their presence and obvious concern were an invaluable lift to their spirits.

In order to prepare special foods for their invalids, Abby and Sarah Gibbons and other volunteer nurses depended upon supplies sent to them by Northern friends and sympathizers. Army rations were crude and inadequate; without extra supplies there was no hope of preparing the eggnogs, beef teas, and wine jellies that Abby Gibbons used to nourish her patients. Barrels and boxes of supplies were shipped to her regularly from the Woman's Central Association and from friends in New York. Stimulants were regarded as essential for battlefield nursing, and even the most conservative Quakers contributed spirits to these shipments. Abby Gibbons wrote home after the arrival of one of many such shipments:

> We have been very busy using the contents of your great box. How kind of Robert and George Haydock to send such valuable stores! I hope thou wilt drop in and tell them how useful we have found all the good things. The gin was a perfect blessing and flavors our gelatin, serving at the same time as a valuable stimulant.[27]

As Abby Gibbons demonstrated her ability with the patients, some of the doctors turned to her for help with critical patients. This was the case with Dr. Alvis Gall who asked her to help build up the strength of one young man because it was going to be necessary to take his arm off at the shoulder. Abby Gibbons fed him her specialties of beef tea, brandy, and eggnog for a week, after which the doctor pronounced him strong enough for the operation. Gibbons was grateful not to be present when this took place, but shortly thereafter was hastily called to tend the young man, who was still on the operating table and dying. She again fed him, this time through a glass tube, until he was strong enough to be moved, and watched over him until his father came to see him and the two could say goodbye.[28]

As army nurses, Abby and Sarah Gibbons were entitled to army pay. But they refused their small salaries, asking that the money be used for medical care for their patients. Instead, Abby Gibbons's brother John Hopper supported them, and sent them supplies. John felt it was his contribution to the war effort, as he wrote his sister Sarah in Philadelphia:

> Sallie reads to them and writes letters to their homes for them and is a great blessing and as for Abby she is mother and sister and friend to everybody there. In fact she is everything to everybody there. Large quantities of things are sent to her from all quarters, the givers reposing such entire confidence in her judgment and taste in such matters. It is hard work and very disagreeable work, but they feel it to be their mission and indeed so it is, a most blessed mission. They receive no compensation and

are to receive none, and it is my special desire to have it so. They are there entirely at my expense and will remain, I suppose, as long as their strength holds out. Everybody is very kind and respectful to them.[29]

After some weeks at Falls Church, and a flying trip home to New York City to celebrate Christmas with her family and take care of business for the Isaac T. Hopper Home, Abby Gibbons received word through Secretary of State William H. Seward that nurses were needed at Winchester, Virginia, where there were many wounded federal troops. Abby and Sarah Gibbons arrived there in early January 1862, and went to work in the Seminary Hospital, nursing men recovering from cruel amputations, as well as some with fever. One soldier had fallen into a fire after being wounded and was so badly burned that, when they first looked at him, Sarah fainted. After poulticing the wounds, Abby Gibbons had to take her back to their quarters. Recovering quickly, Sarah returned to the wards and was able thereafter to deal with whatever sights came her way. Later, Abby and Sarah Gibbons were put in charge of the most severely wounded men. They also worked at the Union and the Academy hospitals, opened as more patients came in from the battlefield or from campgrounds plagued with fever.[30]

When they first arrived in Winchester they found the nurses and surgeon in a great state of excitement over the arrival of two nurses from New York handpicked by the reformer Dorothea Dix for the job. Dix was well known for her advocacy of the mentally ill and her call for establishing mental hospital facilities, rather than housing "lunatics" in the public prisons. In 1845 she had published a book, *Remarks on Prisons and Prison Discipline in the United States*, which Abby Gibbons admired. At the outbreak of the Civil War, Dix, now fifty-nine, had volunteered her services to the army to recruit nurses and was in the process of being appointed superintendent of nurses. This was to be a highly controversial period in Dix's life. She chose to bar from her service all nuns and members of other religious sisterhoods and stipulated that the others be "plain-looking, over thirty, and competent," rules that created considerable controversy among doctors, soldiers, and many of the women themselves. She also proved a poor administrator, and was constantly embroiled in controversy with the medical service, with doctors, and with other freelance nurses, who, like Abby Gibbons, simply decided to come on their own and volunteer. Dr. Emily Blackwell commented that she was "deficient in organization and had no idea of the details of hospital management." Clara Barton, a volunteer nurse who was to found the American Red Cross, stayed clear of her, and Louisa May Alcott, who served under her, thought she was "a kind old soul, but queer and arbitrary."[31]

Dorothy Dix's preference for "older and plain-looking" nurses was undoubtedly based on a sensible wish to avoid romantic entanglements between nurses and patients. But she was so open about it that she left herself vulnerable to a great deal of ridicule. The very young soldiers of the Civil War preferred nurses who were either motherly, like Abby, or nearer their own age, reminding them of their sisters or sweethearts, and objected on principle to the "Dixies." More unfortunate was Dix's attitude toward the Catholic nuns, present at the battlefield in great numbers. Her refusal to use them led to a great deal of conflict with the doctors, who found the nuns very helpful.

Dix was not alone in her anti-Catholic prejudice. Protestant America was strongly anti-Catholic in this era, and liberals like the Gibbonses who struggled for racial justice, thought nothing of expressing anti-Catholic views. Many of the inmates of the Isaac Hopper Home were Catholic, and Abby Gibbons's attitude was somewhat softened by this fact, but James Gibbons was anti-Catholic and became more so with the years. Abby Gibbons herself came to share Dorothea Dix's prejudice against the nuns on the battlefield, but this did not soften her attitude toward Dix herself.

Winchester was Abby Gibbons's first introduction to the "Dixies." She found the two who came to work there to be "great talkers, and had stirred up envy, jealousy, and all manner of evil." Abby and Sarah hurried away, determined not to be caught up in anyone else's quarrels.

> Of Miss Dix's lack of taste I will say more when I see you. If she loved power less, humility more, and was possessed of a little tact she might accomplish her work in a far more acceptable way. In the evening two of her nurses sent by Mrs. Griffith of Woman's Central, came round to see us for the relief of their minds. We heard them out, treated them kindly, and promised to look in on their ward.[32]

If the Dix nurses were a disappointment, the Winchester Society of Friends was not. Abby Gibbons made the acquaintance of members of the local Friends Meeting and came to respect the Virginia Friends. "I find *Friends* are the only people here who sympathize with the colored people, and Friends are the only people in whom the colored people have perfect trust." She even went to meeting for the first time since 1842, when she had disowned the Society of Friends. She also met a number of blacks, some slave and some free. She was impressed, she wrote home, with their spirit. "They are a wide-awake people, and I think they will make their way anyway. I see fewer difficulties in the way since I came, than before." She wrote home rejoicing in the creation of the National Freedmen's Association. Abby and Sarah Gibbons attended the local black church services, and much to Sarah's astonishment Abby Gibbons rose and gave a short sermon, just as her mother, Sarah Hopper, might have done.[33]

One service Abby Gibbons was able to render at the hospitals was to comfort the despairing parents who came to the visit dying sons or to claim the remains of those who had died. It was now that her experience in losing three sons of her own proved a way in which she could help others face the pain. Both during and after the war Abby Gibbons received many letters from bereaved parents, thanking her for being with their dying sons and writing to them words of comfort.

Most of the young men dying on the battlefield were contemporaries of Willie's; some, his friends. Jimmy Lowell, of Cambridge, was shot at Richmond. "How heavily that family are losing!" Abby Gibbons wrote her family. "Few young men now stand where Putnam and Lowell once stood—the good and beautiful to look upon—the men that made their mark—and of such promise. Jimmy Lowell was Willie's classmate at Harvard. We knew him well; admired and loved him." Abby Gibbons was human enough to be helped by knowing that other families were now suffering as she had.[34]

As she grew more accustomed to the work, Abby Gibbons became more critical of the medical treatment her charges received. There were some good surgeons. One was a Dr. J. Burd Peale, a son of Reuben Peale, the artist, of Philadelphia. But another surgeon so badly mangled the patients he operated upon that he was to be court martialled.[35]

Gradually the patients from the last battle were recovering. Grace Sedgwick, the daughter of Elizabeth Sedgwick who ran the school at Lenox, had joined Abby and Sarah Gibbons, and the three were prepared to move on to Strasburg. Here, General Nathaniel E. Banks had recently retreated from Harrisonburg and was dug in. The medical director at Winchester said that there were a thousand sick at Strasburg, and the suffering was terrible. On May 19, 1862, they were told that it was not safe to go, but on the May 20 this warning was dismissed as rumor, and the three nurses travelled the nineteen miles in an ambulance, and found quarters with an unwilling Rebel landlady. They had scarcely taken up their new duties, however, when, on the 24th, word came that the Rebels, under Stonewall Jackson, had taken Front Royal and completely cut off the federal troops who would have to retreat, taking their wounded with them. Abby Gibbons was awakened by a doctor, who told her he was responsible for seeing her and Sarah safely out of harm's way, but they must hurry. Abby filled a bag with provisions for the wounded, including port wine, brandy, and brown stout.[36]

> At three A.M. we were seated in a strong ambulance with four horses, making the best of our way in the direction of Winchester. Doctor Blake was much exhausted, having been on the run for several hours, removing the sick from the hospitals to army wagons; and he was the more excited, owing to a recent illness and knowing more of the impending danger than we did; although we were no means insensible to our perilous condition.[37]

Grace Sedgwick, who was staying elsewhere, did not get off in time and hid a number of Union flags, swords, and letters under the mattress of her bed. When the Texas Rangers arrived and asked if there were any damned Yankees around, she said, "Yes, I am a Yankee, but not a damned one."[38]

Abby and Sarah Gibbons agreed to sit up with the driver, while the exhausted doctor tried to sleep in the body of the wagon. They were fifteen minutes in advance of army wagons laden with the very sick; several times during the nightmarish trip these were fired upon and several sick men wounded. At one point a man seized the horses pulling the ambulance, demanding news. Cavalry rode past them at a run, and soldiers on foot sped by.[39]

Finally, they reached Winchester by 8 A.M. May 25, took time to breakfast and to gather up as much of their precious stores as they were able, then spent the day on the way to Martinsburg, Maryland. Here they spent the night with the officers' wives of the 10th Maine Division at the U.S. Hotel, eight women in one room. In the morning, the town was aroused by the sound of cannons from Winchester, where a pitched battle was in progress, and the medical units decided to retreat still further into the country. Many people were on the road already, including numerous contraband, former slaves who had been freed by federal troops. "A Union flag floated from a high pole in a square facing the hotel, and as the loyal men and panic-stricken fugitives passed under it, they raised their hats and caps in recognition—a touching mark of their loyalty," Abby Gibbons wrote. "It brought tears to our eyes."[40]

Soon Abby Gibbons's party was on the road again in two ambulances. They drove as far as Hagerstown, but hearing that there had been a proslavery riot at the Hotel the night before, decided to go on to Middletown, where they finally deemed it safe to spend the night. "Here we found our port wine useful," Abby wrote. She had a little herself before arranging the sleeping accommodations. She and Sarah ended up in a room with eight men and decided not to undress, but managed nevertheless to sleep. Abby Gibbons was delighted that she had remained tranquil through the whole ordeal. "Whether it was my large hope or my Quaker education I cannot tell, but I had a quiet faith that no harm would come to us."[41]

Next morning contraband from Winchester and Strasburg came flooding into town. Abby Gibbons bought what stores she could from local storekeepers, then asked for donations of milk and cold meat. When the townspeople seemed reluctant to help, she scolded them, telling them that the people must be fed, and those who refused would be remembered and punished. "Your houses shall be marked," she told them, threatening implicitly to expose them to the authorities, and perhaps to the press. "It was not long before a bountiful supply was forthcoming," she commented tersely.[42]

Before the retreat from Strasburg, Abby Gibbons had written a letter intended for publication, describing the inadequate conditions for treating the wounded and the lack of cooperation from the Maryland "secesh." After reaching Maryland she wrote a second letter, retelling the story of the withdrawal. Both were published in the *National Anti-Slavery Standard,* and received wide circulation. Their publication gave credence to Abby Gibbons's implied threat that she would expose the uncooperative.

The episode at Middletown reveals Abby Gibbons's sense of the importance of the work she was doing and the inclination to turn to powerful allies to accomplish her goals, which was to characterize her war service. Her years of lobbying for the Isaac Hopper Home now came into play. Although she was willing to work with such organizations as the Woman's Central Association and the Sanitary Commission, she retained her old distrust of authority from her days as an abolitionist and did not readily yield to the dictates of the U.S. Army or the U.S. government when they ran counter to her own sense of mission. Many who worked with her on the battlefields considered her highhanded; others were full of admiration for her ability to realize her goals.

7

"Take the News to Mother"

After sharing in the retreat of General Banks from Strasburg, Abby and Sarah Gibbons returned to New York for a brief stay. There were always the affairs of the Isaac Hopper Home to be taken care of, as well as the Woman's Central Association for Relief. And they wanted to touch base with the family on Lamartine Place.

James Gibbons and the daughters who remained at home were themselves immersed in war work. Lucy and Julia went to Bedloe Island to nurse wounded soldiers; James was active in such organizations as the Freedman's Association and contributed articles and letters on the war to the New York papers. When Abraham Lincoln called for three hundred thousand new recruits in July 1862, James wrote a poem that was published in the New York *Evening Post* and became immensely popular for its patriotic message and its rhythmic lines:

> We are coming, Father Abraham, three hundred thousand more,
> From Mississippi's winding stream and from New England's shore;
> We leave our ploughs and workshops, our wives and children dear.
> With hearts too full for utterance, but with a silent tear;
> We dare not look behind us, but steadfastly before:
> We are coming, Father Abraham, three hundred thousand more!
> If you look across the hill-tops, that meet the northern sky,
> Long moving lines of rising dust your vision may descry;
> And now the wind, an instant, tears the cloudy veil aside,
> And floats aloft our spangled flag in glory and in pride,
> And bayonets in the sunlight gleam, and bands brave music pour:
> We are coming, Father Abraham, three hundred thousand more!

There were two more verses, equally patriotic. Unfortunately, James Gibbons did not sign his name to it originally, and it was generally credited

97

to William Cullen Bryant. Only many years later did James establish his authorship. Thereafter, although he was the author of four books, it was for this song that he was remembered.

Shortly before James wrote this poem, Abby and Sarah Gibbons set out again for Winchester, where many of Major General John Charles Fremont's men were sick and dying. They visited Edward and Anna Hopper in Philadelphia, spent a night in Baltimore, and stopped in Washington, where Abby Gibbons reported home that President Lincoln was complaining that " General McClellan had lost innumerable men and could not account for one, and called him the last immovable man." (A few days later, Lincoln named Major General Halleck general-in-chief of the Army.) The two then visited Harper's Ferry where they saw the hospital and cemetery and spent the night on the floor. The next day Abby Gibbons arranged with an army major for free transportation of her stores and completed the tiring trip to Winchester, where they were cordially greeted by many old friends and recovering patients.[1]

Abby Gibbons had left provisions behind when she made her hasty retreat from Winchester. Other provisions had been sent ahead to be held for her at the Relief Rooms. To her surprise, she learned, shortly after her arrival, that an prominent citizen of Winchester, a man named Atwell Schell, had taken possession of the supplies and moved them to his own house. Filled with indignation, Abby Gibbons went immediately to the Provost Marshal and asked for help. He gave her two guards; with these in tow she went to Schell's house and asked for her stores. When she was refused she went into action:

> I took command and directed one of the guard to remain with my companions below, while I accompanied the other upstairs; the lady of the house being of the party by invitation, to see that we took our own property, *only*. . . .

> Our goods had been packed with much neatness and care, and covered with their own quilts. Everything was turned out, and package upon package rolled down stairs, until a high stack was formed in the centre of the parlor. There was every variety of garment, bedclothes, delicacies for the sick—such as sugar, tea, chocolate, farina, arrowroot, gelatine, and corn-flour and barley in large packages.[2]

The bottles of stimulants, so important to her larder, were of course empty, *stolen*, Abby Gibbons said. When one young woman of the household commented on Gibbons's "impudence" for breaking in to gather her supplies, Abby told her that in New York they would have been punished as thieves![3]

The story of Abby Gibbons's liberation of the supplies was received by her family and friends with delight, adding to her growing reputation as a forceful woman. Commenting in a letter to Sarah, Rosa Hopper wrote, "was she not the woman and man to do it! She ought to be appointed Major General in the army."[4]

As soon as she had recovered the stolen stores, Abby Gibbons turned them over to the 32nd Ohio Regiment, whose guards had come to the rescue. She and Sarah visited three hospitals and did a little nursing, but the needs in Winchester were diminishing, and they wondered where they might be more useful. Like many abolitionists, they were very partial to Major General John Fremont and had returned to Winchester hoping to nurse his troops, but they learned that Fremont had recently resigned his command; rumor said he had been forced by government officials to do so. Abby Gibbons preferred to suspend judgment and continued to have faith in Lincoln and Seward, but it made the stay at Winchester less comfortable. She decided ultimately to go on to Washington, to find out what was happening and to seek another placement.[5]

It was a task to which she brought her developing skill in the use of influence. She did not go directly to the Surgeon General's office but waited until she had a letter of recommendation. At an evening reception, she met a number of influential men, including Peter H. Watson, Assistant Secretary of War, Senator William Fessenden of Maine, and Senator James Grimes of Iowa. Grimes gave her a letter of introduction to Surgeon General William Hammond, a thirty-three-year-old doctor recently appointed to take the place of regular army doctor, Clement A. Finley, at the suggestion of the United States Sanitary Commission.

Abby Gibbons's initial experience with Hammond was not encouraging. When she called at his office, Hammond would not see her until he had read her letter from Senator Grimes. When she said she wanted to go to Point Lookout along with Miss Dix and her nurses (but not as one of their number), taking along her supplies, and wondered if she would be acceptably received, Hammond said gruffly, "I don't know how they'll receive you. I don't know anything about it." He continued, Abby Gibbons complained to James, to be rude and coarse. She quietly retreated, sought out the two senators who had helped her, and with them went to see the Assistant Secretary of War, Peter Watson, who gave her permission to make the trip to Point Lookout. She was still new to politics and did not realize that going around Hammond in this fashion might ultimately be unwise.[6]

On July 19, 1862, Abby and Sarah Gibbons, along with a friend from New York, Mary Parsons, sailed aboard the ship *Clyde* to Point Lookout, in southern Maryland at the confluence of the Potomac River with Chesapeake Bay. Here the Hammond United States General Hospital was about to be opened to receive federal soldiers who had been prisoners of war in the South. Also sailing on the *Clyde* were Dorothea Dix and a party of nurses, plus William Hammond, the surgeon general himself. Smarting from Abby's having gone directly to Assistant Secretary of War Peter Watson, Hammond did not speak to her throughout the trip south from Washington and invited only Dorothea Dix to join him for dinner at the ship's mess. Since none of her other nurses were invited, Dix declined and shared a cup of tea and some biscuits with Abby and Sarah Gibbons. When the ship finally arrived at the Point at eight in the evening, the nurses, exhausted with hunger and fatigue, went to bed as soon as possible.[7]

The next morning there was scarcely time for breakfast, for the ship *Commodore* had just arrived laden with 250 sick men, transferred from the Southern prison camp at Belle Isle. Abby Gibbons went aboard and found the men with no clothes and suffering from hunger. Eleven had died en route. Abby did not yet have her stock of precious stores, but dispensed whatever she had carried with her and tried to provide comfort. The sickest patients were brought to shore and installed in the new hospital.[8]

After the patients were all settled and the Gibbonses had completed their first day of work, they set up housekeeping in a cottage assigned to them by the army on the edge of the bay. They had a beautiful view, but no privacy in which to enjoy the luxury of sea bathing. They loved hearing "the music of the sea" and discovered that it was cool and peaceful on their cottage steps at night.[9]

Abby and Sarah Gibbons were no sooner settled, however, than they were dismissed from service by the surgeon in charge, Dr. Clinton Wagner. Abby had heard that the black cook had been charged with selling a piece of steak to one of the newly arrived soldiers and was to be flogged in consequence. She had learned in Winchester that many federal officers were sympathetic with the South on the matter of race, and thought this might be especially true in southern Maryland. She regarded it as part of her self-imposed mission to stand up for the blacks, as her father might have done. In this case she asked the cook exactly what happened. The man told her that he had not sold the meat, but that the soldier had asked for it and then pressed a twenty-five cent piece into his hand. A clerk in the surgeon's office, a member of one of the first families of Baltimore, who was never sober (according to Abby Gibbons) reported her interference to Dr. Wagner. When she went for an interview with Dr. Wagner, the clerk was present and charged her with taking a black man's word against a white man's, and putting the two on an equal basis.[10]

"Certainly the color would make no difference. I take the side of justice and humanity," Abby Gibbons answered him loftily.[11]

When Dr. Wagner said he was dismissing her because she had interfered with his order to punish the man, Abby Gibbons asked for the charge in writing and told the officer that she had the ear of many congressmen, of the secretary of war, and of the president himself. "You shall feel this," she told him, once more falling back on the power of influence.[12]

According to Sarah, the officials listened to her threats and feared that she was, as she claimed, a woman of influence. The charge for which Abby Gibbons asked never came. Instead, a peacemaker, Dr. David Lee, called on her and persuaded her that she had transgressed a military rule. Abby Gibbons uncharacteristically used her gender, saying she did not think that women were supposed to know such rules, adding that she had no intention of apologizing. However, she went to see Dr. Wagner the next morning, only to discover, she claimed, that her words had had their effect. He told her that he had dismissed the clerk for intoxication and that the black cook was reinstated. At the end of the interview, he urged her to let her wants be known and promised that, so far as he was able, they would be supplied.[13]

"He knew he had gone too far and was trembling for himself; his position was in peril. He knew I had power and would use it. I put my rule in practice and in the language of conduct, forgave him," Abby Gibbons boasted.[14]

No sooner was this skirmish with authority fought and won than Abby and Sarah Gibbons were plunged into the job of helping to care for another 280 sick and dying men, brought on the *Commodore*. The nurses worked all day trying to attend to their patients' needs, without reaching half of them. Food and stimulants were scarce. Abby took time to write to James to beg that more stores be sent right away. Despite the best efforts of the nurses, an additional thirty-five men died. Almost immediately a second ship, the *John Brooks*, brought another 280 sick men to the landing, and the nurses hurried out with ice water, wine, and bay rum to try to save those with high fevers. The scenario was repeated a few day later, when the *Kennebec* pulled into the landing with 312 sick passengers, transferred from the Richmond prison. Abby Gibbons went below and found 150 men crowded together, few with any clothes, and set to work as before.

As the hospital grew toward its goal of four to five thousand patients, Abby and Sarah Gibbons soon got used to the arrival of shipload after shipload of exchanged prisoners, many of them filthy and covered with vermin, some of them dying from malnutrition and fever. Their condition made Abby angry, and increased her antipathy to the Southern sympathizers with whom she felt herself to be surrounded.

In addition to the condition of the prisoners, Abby Gibbons was often embattled over the situation of the contraband, the escaping slaves who came into the camp for protection from their masters. Slaves from Southern states in rebellion against the United States government were called contraband of war and were kept in army camps to perform menial labor. Often their situation was not much better than that of slavery. Slaves from the border states, of which Maryland was one, could be returned to their owners, if the latter signed an oath of allegiance to the United States. Abby was convinced that many of the Southerners did not mind taking the oath without meaning it, in order to recapture their valuable property. She saw it as her duty to save as many of the contraband as possible from this fate.

By taking on the cause of the contraband, Abby Gibbons antagonized many of the officers and men at Camp Lookout. It must be remembered that only a small minority of Union soldiers felt themselves fighting for freedom for the slaves; most believed they were fighting to save the Union but continued to be angry at the meddling abolitionists. In border states, such as Maryland, many of the soldiers came from the area and shared the Southern view of the blacks. They regarded Abby's interference in the cause of the contraband as highly irksome.

One day she was taken to the guardhouse to see a slave who had been whipped. "He was lashed from neck to heels, so closely the lashes crossed each other, the skin being taken off at every stroke. I bade him take off his shirt that I might know his condition was not exaggerated." After he had taken off the shirt, stiff with blood, she gave him a clean one and a pair of pants and asked the army official if he might be given work on the post. He did work for one day, but on the next his master and mistress came for him, took the oath of allegiance, and went home with their slave. "Hardly a man on the ground whom I would call a loyal citizen of the United States," Abby wrote bitterly to James.[15]

Her interest in the contraband led Abby Gibbons to visit their camp quite regularly. Soon she was being called upon to assist in marriages and the birth of babies as well as to supply clothes, medicine, and sometimes food. Her friends and family in the North were kept busy packing boxes of used clothing for this purpose. She also urged her supporters to take ex-slaves as servants if she could manage to find return passage north for them on the vessels that had arrived from New York, bringing supplies. "I was down to the wharf last night at 10:30 P.M. and waited in the Guard House until two in the morning with two contrabands. The Captain of the steamer was a rebel and refused to take them on board. It was not a government boat, of course, I am holding them over for a chance," Abby Gibbons wrote to James. A few weeks later she described the arrival of a a group of escaping slaves, fourteen men and five women with some small children, who had used the moonlight nights to come by boat from Virginia.[16]

"So much of my time is used in pleading for these poor, despised specimens of humanity, brutally treated and scourged as they are, together with my visits to their camps, that it is with difficulty I can command an hour for writing."[17]

In August a contraband working for the cooks was brutally beaten, according to a letter Abby Gibbons wrote home. James Gibbons sent the letter to the New York *Post*. A few days later she complained that the postmaster was a drunken "Secesh," whom she suspected of interfering with the mail. James Gibbons next wrote a personal letter to the President. Lincoln sent the letter on to Secretary of the War Stanton, who passed it on the Surgeon General Hammond. Abby Gibbons was asked to specify her charges. Evidently her response was accepted, for the postmaster was discharged, and there was a sudden change in the way she was treated at the hospital.[18]

"I can have anything I want," Abby Gibbons boasted in a letter to her daughter Lucy. "No one dares send a fugitive to his master & mistress and instead of incivility, our cottage is called Meade Headquarters." She was given the rank of Major General, and was allowed to lecture the officers on their treatment of the privates without being charged with violating military discipline. Many of the surgeons took to visiting her and Sarah in their cottage in the evenings, and friendships developed, especially with Dr. John Stearns and Dr. Clinton Wagner.[19]

If she had won over the doctors, Gibbons was still having troubles with her fellow nurses. There were many Catholic sisters at work on the wards. She believed that Surgeon General Hammond preferred them to the Protestants because they were docile and never questioned orders, even, she claimed, when their patients' lives were at stake. They were given the largest building and lenient discipline, while the Protestant nurses were challenged at every step. Abby Gibbons thought that the attempt to dismiss her the day after she arrived had been part of that policy. Like many Protestants of the time, she entertained the prejudiced fear that the Catholics were using the helpless condition of their patients to make deathbed conversions, and so charged.[20]

Between herself and Dorothea Dix, an uneasy truce prevailed. Abby Gibbons was determined not to work under Dix's supervision, but she did not make an issue of this at first. Miss Dix was often away, and under the impression that Abby Gibbons was one of her nurses, provided her with food for the prisoners. Sarah Gibbons and Mary Parsons, both young and pretty, often made fun of the Dix nurses. "There are enough homely women here to frighten away any number of rebels," Sarah Gibbons wrote to her father. And again, "How Miss Dix manages to get so many forlornities together I cannot imagine. Her nurses are too old and ugly. The doctors are disgusted with her."[21]

A new army chaplain, Mr. Spooner, arriving in September, drew Abby Gibbons's anger when he passed the plate after services, asking for money to buy a new melodeon. Many of the soldiers had not been paid for six months and hung their heads because they had nothing to contribute, but a few officers placed some money in the plate. After the services, Abby Gibbons protested to one of the officers, saying she thought the money would be better spent on milk and eggs for her convalescents. The chaplain heard about this and called on her a few days later to protest. As a Quaker she was opposed to music, he claimed, and was trying to introduce her beliefs onto the post.

"At this I laughed out, saying 'How absurd! So far from it, I object to *any* sect being introduced into the army.'"[22]

The melodeon was given up, but Abby Gibbons had gained another enemy. Spooner and Dorothea Dix became allies, but were unable to make a difference in Abby Gibbons's growing influence.

Part of that influence resulted from the endless stream of supplies sent her from her colleagues in New York. Sarah Doremus sent boxes; Louisa Lee Schuyler, serving on the committee of correspondence of the Woman's Central Association of Relief, organized many shipments to Abby Gibbons. A friend in Skaneateles, New York, Marian Morgan, kept up a steady stream of boxes. Joseph Choate, a promising New York lawyer and friend of Willie's, sent a barrel of lemons, which were very useful; the New York Quakers continued to forward supplies; John Hopper sent concentrated milk and condensed cream. Sometimes as many as thirty boxes and barrels would arrive for the Gibbonses. Provisioning the hospital was so erratic that sometimes these stores of Abby Gibbons's made the difference as to whether or not her patients were fed.[23]

James Gibbons oversaw the shipping of provisions and accompanied one shipment in person in order to see how his wife and daughter were faring at the army outpost. His position as the homemaker while his wife and eldest daughter were at the front was untraditional; most wives stayed at home while their husbands fought. In his letters to Abby and Sarah Gibbons he did not complain of this role but spoke of his visits to the Woman's Central Committee and the Freedman's Association to facilitate their goods. He also kept up an ongoing summary of the war news.[24]

The war news was not good in the summer of 1862. Thomas "Stonewall" Jackson defeated Nathaniel Banks at Cedar Mountain and James Longstreet won a victory over John Pope at the second battle of Bull Run. Federal troops were badly needed, and many of Abby Gibbons's patients, though in no condition to go, left their sick beds for the battlefield. In September, Lee invaded Maryland, and Point Lookout was full of rumors of the approach of Rebel troops. One night a contraband informed the commander that there were Rebels on the peninsula; a small band set out in pursuit and succeeded in chasing them across the Potomac into Virginia. A gunboat was sent to protect the hospital; Abby Gibbons and her nurses watched anxiously as other boats streamed up the Potomac to the defense of Washington. Harper's Ferry fell to the South, but General McClellan was able to stop Lee's advance at Antietam on September 17. The Gibbonses' joy in this event was tempered by learning that William Sedgwick, the son of their great friend Elizabeth Sedgwick, had died on the battlefield.[25]

Abby Gibbons continued to defend the government from its many Northern detractors and to insist that the Union was going to win, despite the many reverses.

What is the matter with the New Yorkers, that they condemn President Lincoln and Secretary Seward? It would be very wise to wait a little longer. I could not point to a man who has done better than Mr. Seward. What he does is well done, and he does not proclaim on the house-top the private acts of the administration.

The news today is glorious. The surgeon-in-charge has just returned from Washington, and gives us the morning paper. Take
courage! the victory will be ours. It is as clear as the sun at noon-
day. I never, for a moment, indulge in any other thought.[26]

So patriotic had the Gibbons family become by this time that Julia
Gibbons began to worry that, under the militia law enacted by Congress
in July 1862, her cousins, Sam Brown and Wilson Powell, would be exempted as Quakers and conscientious objectors. Ought they not at least
have to pay for a substitute, she wondered? The War Department's call
for an additional 300,000 recruits for nine months was somewhat murky
on this point, and there were many letters to the editor about it. Sydney
Howard Gay, who had served for thirteen years as editor of the *Anti-
Slavery Standard* and was now an editor of the *New York Tribune*, wrote
to Lincoln himself for clarification, and was invited to the White House.
(Ultimately, the draft act, as amended in 1864, permitted conscientious
objectors to serve in noncombatant roles or to pay $300 for a substitute,
which some Quakers felt did not give them an acceptable choice.)[27]

By October Abby Gibbons was wondering if her work at Point
Lookout was done. The position of nurses, she felt, was now well established, as well as the concept of providing appetizing meals for the invalids. Her one big concern continued to be the great numbers of
miserably clothed contrabands, who were pouring in to the base. There
were far too many to be put to work at the base, which meant that they
had to be shipped off to Fortress Monroe. Abby Gibbons could see no
sense at all in sending them south instead of north. "People here need
watching for most of them don't give a pin for the nigger," she complained. She herself never used the pejorative word "nigger," but heard it
from the lips of many of the Southerners with whom she was surrounded.
She had come to respect and admire Dr. Wagner, with whom she had had
so many confrontations in the early days. He was a Southerner from
Baltimore, but himself an abolitionist, she believed, and could be trusted
to keep the best interests of the contraband at heart. Unfortunately, the
care of the contraband fell not to him but to the Quartermaster.[28]

Recognizing that Abby Gibbons was their advocate, the contraband
who were settled in the camp begged her to stay. She was of two minds,
fearing that she was neglecting her two daughters and her husband, yet
wanting to nurse her soldiers and protect the escaped slaves from being
sent back to their masters. She complained that Julia did not keep her informed about the Home, and she was afraid she was needed there, too.

"What is best I scarcely know," she wrote to Julia, from whom she sometimes sought advice. "Point the way and I will walk in it."[29]

In late October she finally left Point Lookout for New York, where she and Sarah joined the other three Gibbonses for a homelike Christmas. Like other abolitionists, they greeted the President's Emancipation Proclamation on New Year's Day, 1863, with great joy, although Abby Gibbons was sorry that the border states were exempted. They decorated their windows with red, white, and blue tissue paper, and in the evening turned on every gas jet in the house. Roving bands of proslavery advocates, of whom there were many in New York at the period, noted the illumination and spread pitch over the pavement, up the steps, and all over the front door while the family was out in the evening. "I am indignant at the perpetrators of the outrage committed on your premises," James Walker wrote to Abby Gibbons, enclosing fifty dollars for her work. "The damage, I suppose is not considerable, and the mortification nothing; but it is a serious thing, considered as revealing the temper of the times. There can no longer be any doubt, that what are called the Loyal States make up a house divided against itself."[30]

Abby Gibbons spent the month of January recruiting nurses to accompany her on her return to Point Lookout. Any lingering doubts as to whether she was needed there were put to rest by a letter from Dr. Wagner urging her to come. The Catholic sisters had all been transferred, he said, and Dorothea Dix's nurses put in charge of the old hospital. They lacked a good head to watch over and manage them. He was counting on Abby Gibbons to do this and said he would welcome any nurses she brought.[31]

On the way south to Point Lookout, Abby Gibbons stopped in Washington to plead for the contraband, to get permission for her goods to be shipped free, and for her nurses to be assigned directly to her own charge, rather than to that of Dorothea Dix. As usual, the Capitol was disappointing, "a mud hole," and full of everlasting red tape and overbearing officials. "Fine women will make manifest the shortcomings of men in high places, then things will become better," she predicted optimistically. Secretary of War Stanton received her ungraciously and told her he could not grant her request. The same evening, however, she dined with Senator Schuyler Colfax of Indiana, Senator Jacob Howard of Michigan, and Senator Henry Wilson of Massachusetts, among others, and told them about the conditions of the contraband. They seemed very interested and urged her to write her observations for the New York *Tribune*. "Men of influence here are strangely ignorant," she observed, rather ingenuously.[32]

While in Washington, Abby Gibbons met with a group of wives of senators and other prominent women eager to establish a home for aged and infirm contraband and for contraband children. They had access to a one-hundred-acre plot of land in the District of Columbia, the confiscated property of a Rebel family that had left, and proposed to make it the site of a National Colored Home. Unfortunately none of these women had had experience in organizing a society, and Abby Gibbons found herself undertaking the work of drawing up articles of incorporation and presenting a bill to Congress. She was aided in this by her old friend, Senator James Grimes of Iowa. "Mr. Grimes has faith in women—sensible man," she noted. She was pleased to be of help, but hoped she would get away soon, since she had enough organizational work at home.[33]

Abby Gibbons's experience, first in the women's business meetings of the Society of Friends, then in the antislavery movement, later with the Women's Prison Association and with the German Industrial School had given her a headstart in the development of organized philanthropies, to which many middle-class women of the Victorian era began to turn at midcentury. The group in Washington was to continue to appeal to her for leadership for many years.

Writing to Julia, Abby attributed the renewed respect she was given this time in Washington to a new cloak Julia had given her for Christmas, but also to the biography of Isaac Hopper, which was being widely read in Washington circles at this time. Everywhere she went, people asked her if she were any relation to Isaac Hopper and when she said "daughter," they were very impressed.

By the end of two weeks in Washington, Abby Gibbons felt she had accomplished all she desired. "It is an immense undertaking to carry a question through—the first step is to find out the relations between the heads of the different departments. This I have done thoroughly, and by management secured the desired end," she wrote Julia.[34]

> The Honorable Peter H. Watson has done splendidly for me, and as for the Surgeon-General, he was ready to get on his bended knees!!! I left my card a few days ago, not finding him; and when he learned through Dr. Douglas whose card it was, he sent me a polite message that he would have seen me, but thought it was *gentleman's* handwriting. He was profoundly gracious.[35]

The desired end for which Abby Gibbons had been working was to be the manager of the hospital instead of Dorothea Dix. Dix heard about the arrangement the night before Abby was to leave for the Point and was very disconcerted, according to Abby. "She said a great deal more than it is worthwhile to repeat. Asked to see our papers, and was very angry. She asked why I had gotten the hospital, and I told her that she selected her nurses from a class who were ignorant and had many infirmities. She expressed holy horror at the youth and beauty of my nurses."[36]

On the morning of February 21, 1863, Abby, Sarah, Grace Sedgwick, and five other nurses went aboard the *Matamora* bound for Point Lookout. In contrast to their first trip in July, they were given both supper and breakfast and treated courteously. At the wharf at Point Lookout, they were met by a large delegation of soldiers and staff and given their choice of quarters. Once settled in temporary rooms, they received calls all day. "Best looking set of nurses I ever had the pleasure of seeing," one patient remarked. It was a triumphant welcome.[37]

Abby Gibbons was soon back into the routine of cooking for sick soldiers and providing nursing care for those in need. Her friends the contraband greeted her warmly. They needed her protection more than ever, since the Emancipation Proclamation had made it clear that slaves were to be returned to their masters in the border states. Abby Gibbons began shipping them north as fast as she was able. She persuaded her brother John to take a runaway couple and sent a carpenter off to her brother Edward in Philadelphia to be sent on to New York. Hearing that Robert Shaw, the son of Sarah and brother of Josephine Shaw, was organizing a black militia, she asked if he could not stop off at the Point for recruits. "Miss Dix might rightfully accuse us of belonging to a contraband society, for they flock round us like 'tomtits on a round of beef' as the soldiers say."[38]

Beside Dorothea Dix, Abby Gibbons still had as an adversary the base chaplain, Mr. Spooner, whom she had originally antagonized over the melodeon incident, and who disliked her advocacy of the contraband. A few weeks after her return, she was approached by a relative of contraband who had recently died and was asked about arrangements for the funeral. Ignoring past hostilities, Abby Gibbons went to the chaplain to ask if he would perform the service.[39]

"When there is a funeral, I generally officiate," the chaplain said icily.[40]

"Well," said Abby Gibbons, "I suppose all that is necessary is to say a few words and sing a hymn," meaning that it would not be necessary to go through the entire lengthy Episcopal service. Mr. Spooner, however, took this amiss, and complained to the authorities that Abby Gibbons had asked him to preach a full sermon for a "colored" woman, a thing he did only for distinguished individuals. He felt Gibbons was far exceeding her authority, trying to run the entire base, and at the graveside he talked to several nurses, saying sarcastically, "We shall have order on the Point now that someone has arrived to take command. A person is here who will keep all our affairs in order, and see that the rights of the contrabands are not wrested away from them. She has authority to act, and she *will* act. I mean Mrs. Gibbons."[41]

Another adversary of Abby Gibbons's was the lighthouse keeper. She had had several run-ins with this man, whom she believed to be a Rebel, over her efforts to get contraband aboard vessels headed north. Once he chased a runaway slave to Abby Gibbons's door. In an anonymous letter, which Sarah believed he wrote, he threatened her:

> Head quarters
> Nigger Brigate
> Mrs. Gibins Serg. in charge,
>
> Dear Sir,
>
> As you have taken charge of this place with out any athority and a gainst the will of all the souldiers I Here by Notify you to leave this point in as short time as possible. I in form you in time for what ever soldiers say they generly do and if you dont leave you must not be suprised to see the roof of your little palace taken off some of these dark kingts.[42]

Abby Gibbons took the antagonism of the chaplain and lighthouse keeper in stride, just as her father had been able to laugh off the fury of the slave owners he frustrated. She did, however, report to her influential friends in Washington that the chaplain had refused to hold services for five months, claiming it was because he did not have a proper church building. And she was worried when a new commander, General Henry Lockwood, took control of the base and promised to return slaves to their masters.[43]

Worse was to follow. In mid-March Dr. Clinton Wagner was removed for some minor infraction of the rules, on complaint of his Southern sympathizing enemies, Abby Gibbons believed. She decided to go back to Washington, sure that she could intervene in his behalf and have him reinstated, leaving Sarah and Grace Sedgwick to run the hospital in her absence. This proved to be a mistake. She was unable to budge Surgeon General Hammond about Wagner and stayed for weeks in a vain attempt to do so, while Sarah and Grace met one crisis after another. The contraband, frightened by the new regulations concerning returning them to their masters, came seeking Abby Gibbons; finding "ole Missis gone," they clustered around the cottage and spent the night with the two young women. While Abby Gibbons was still away, the younger women found it necessary to spirit a contraband off by gunboat.[44]

On her return, Abby Gibbons found a new surgeon, Dr. Anthony Heger, in command. At first she found him quite easy to work with, though she missed Dr. Wagner very much. Shortly after his arrival, she wrote to Washington to report on two contrabands being sent out of the camp, and as usual, was asked to support her charges. She did this carefully, and Dr. Heger backed her up, saying that he thought she had the best of the argument.[45]

It was a very different situation than that which had confronted her the previous year on her arrival. Then, Dr. Wagner had seemed bent on dismissing her; now he was her great friend. He wrote from his new posting to tell her his news and added, "I have often reproached myself for the hasty and ungentlemanly manner in which I acted toward you last summer. A lesson I will not soon forget."[46]

Early in May, Abby Gibbons was incensed to find one of the black cooks tied to a tree in front of the Guard House. She asked the man what his offense was and was told he had been insolent and insubordinate. She thought the punishment was out of all proportion to the crime and sought out the officer of the day, Lieutenant Chance, to upbraid him for his treatment of the black man. As a result, Colonel Robert A. Rogers of the 2nd Maryland Regiment charged her with insubordination, although he hastened to say that he thought she was a good nurse. "If she could be persuaded to confine her energies to her legitimate duties of nursing the sick and wounded, her services would be highly beneficial but I must say that, as Protectress General of all who get themselves into trouble, and censor of affairs military, religious and moral, she goes beyond her proper sphere, and might be disposed of. I am sure her presence adds nothing to the harmony and good discipline of the port, for truly sir, a continual dripping in a very rainy day and a contentious woman are alike."[47]

Abby Gibbons answered these charges in writing in a temperate manner, though she objected to being told that she was out of her sphere. "I have always held it [my sphere] to be wherever there is sickness or suffering in any form."[48]

The chaplain, Mr. Spooner, was being dismissed and Dorothea Dix, still angry at Abby Gibbons, made his cause her own. "Lately she has added Mr. Spooner to her force, which is likely to affect him instead of his victim," Abby Gibbons wrote to James. "This is hardly a time for personalities and I wonder they do not see that there is too much heavy work to regard petty differences of opinion. Why cannot people conduct themselves with each working in their own way?"[49]

Wounded and sick soldiers continued to be brought by the boatload to the hospital at Point Lookout. On June 15 the steamer *Mary Washington* arrived with 320 sick and wounded. Abby Gibbons went aboard and found one man dead and several in pitiable condition. A soldier recognized her from her days at Winchester and said he was glad to come to her again. "It is you I want, not a Doctor; mine is a case wanting time." She bathed every face in bay rum and comforted one man who was crying, not because he was going to die but because he was leaving a young wife and three little children. As usual, Abby Gibbons thought about Willie.[50]

The news of battles was discouraging for the Northern sympathizers. In May 1863, Lee and Jackson managed to defeat General Hooker at Chancellorsville, and Confederate General Richard S. Ewell crushed the Union garrison at Winchester and crossed the Potomac. Abby wrote James to say that the rumor was that Washington was threatened. By late June the Confederates were in Pennsylvania. "Dear A. and S.," James wrote. "If Meade has genius Lee will never get back to Virginia. Keep your eyes open and if communication is broken get on a vessel for NY."[51]

As Lee penetrated ever deeper into the North, anxiety grew. Lincoln's call for 100,000 volunteers for six months' service brought a ready response. General Hooker resigned and was replaced by General George Meade, who finally engaged the enemy in a little-known town in Pennsylvania called Gettysburg. Abby and Sarah Gibbons waited breathlessly for news of the great battle that ensued. Their friend Dr. Wagner was with the Union forces there, and they were prepared to go and join him if called.[52]

8

The Draft Riots

In New York City, the Draft Act, passed in March 1863, was just coming into action, and was creating tensions. The fact that men with money were able to pay three hundred dollars and escape the draft, while the working man had no such choice, inflamed tempers. The Democratic Party was not sympathetic to the war, and daily the Democratic newspapers hammered at the theme that the draft would force white working men to fight for the freedom of blacks who would then come north and take away their jobs. To the Irish immigrants, crammed into inadequate housing and paid low wages, the thought of fighting a war supported largely by the upper-class Protestants who employed them had no appeal. Most of their Protestant employers were safe from both draft and job loss. The working men's anger at being condescended to by these moralizing do-gooders spilled over into action.[1]

When draft officers began drawing names on Saturday, July 11, the city was relatively quiet, but on Sunday men congregated in the city's bars and vowed to attack draft offices. On Monday, July 13, 1863, rioting erupted. Blacks were strung up from lampposts, the homes of prominent abolitionists attacked and burned, businesses employing blacks attacked. Altogether, 105 people were killed during the riots; looting and arson were everywhere. The New York police, unused to riots, fought bravely, but could make little headway against the mob. After two days, federal regiments were brought in straight from the battleground of Gettysburg; with their help the rioters were at last subdued.[2]

One of the targets of the mob was Horace Greeley, editor of the antislavery and Republican newspaper, the *Tribune*. On the first day of the riots, a mob formed outside the *Tribune*. Sidney Gay, the managing editor, and other friends of Greeley's tried to persuade him to leave town, but he chose to ignore the rioters and go about his business. That night he went home as usual to the house on 19th Street, owned by his relatives the Sinclairs, where he stayed from Monday through Friday, spending his weekends at Chappaqua with his family. This house was just around the corner from the Gibbonses, on Lamartine Place. Rumors flew that both houses would be attacked that night.[3]

James Gibbons took the precaution of carrying the precious bust of Willie to the house that Samuel and Rachel Brown had rented two doors away and of insisting that Lucy and Julia Gibbons stay dressed all night. He had so far abandoned his Quaker background as to arm himself with a pistol. Rain, however, dampened the ardor of the rioters and nothing happened until mid-afternoon of the second day. Then the peace of the neighborhood was suddenly disturbed by horsemen galloping down the block shouting, "Greeley, Greeley," then "Greeley, Gibbons, Greeley, Gibbons." They were followed by a mob, which filled the street. Two horsemen drew up in front of the Gibbons house and about a dozen men climbed onto the balcony in front of the parlor windows, broke through with pickaxes, and threw chairs and books out the windows.[4] Lucy and Julia, who were both home, had been forewarned and had packed some precious objects as well as clothes. By going over the roof to the Browns they were able to remove these things to safety. But much of priceless value, including the papers, desk, and library of Isaac Hopper were forever lost.[5]

Lucy Gibbons, later Lucy Gibbons Morse, wrote an account of the New York riots in her eighty-eighth year. She told of peeping out of the attic window and watching their books falling like rain. There was fighting in the street, and Lucy was afraid her father had come home and was trying to defend the house.[6]

"Suddenly, a company of soldiers came from Eighth Avenue and marched to Ninth, driving the crowd before them," she wrote. "They marched around the block once, returned, and drove the mob away a second time, and then marched away. As they disappeared one way, the mob returned in full force by another and the looting went on."[7]

Lucy Gibbons described seeing the keyboard of her piano being carried by a man, with sheets of music flying in every direction. A large woman leaned against the garden fence, fanning herself with the lid of a pot she had taken. Suddenly, flames billowed. Having taken everything they wished, the rioters had set fire to the house before leaving the scene. Neighbors, fearing their houses would catch fire, brought buckets of water over the roofs and put out the blaze, but not before it had caused further damage.[8]

Joseph Choate, the friend who had been staying with the Gibbonses, came for the two young women in a carriage, which he parked around the corner. Soldiers did not allow him into the street, so it was necessary for Lucy and Julia Gibbons to climb over the roofs to the last house. The owner was Jewish, and when Mr. Choate asked his permission for the two to climb down through his house he said, "We feel it a privilege to help people who are in so much trouble." When they reached his roof, he was there to greet them and lead the way. His attitude contrasted sharply with that of another neighbor, a Protestant, who refused to lend his carriage the next day to take some of the Gibbonses' clothes to the Choates'. "I refuse to do anything for people who have caused so much trouble in the neighborhood," he said. Lucy Gibbons had grown up in a middle-class Protestant milieu that accepted some antisemitism as a matter of course. Even liberal Quakers and Unitarians were not immune to regarding Jews as a race apart, while the abolitionists never properly addressed the issue. This wartime experience was a lesson in overcoming unthinking prejudice which Lucy remembered all her long life.[9]

Abby and Sarah Gibbons heard news of the New York riot long before they were notified that their house had been sacked. Sarah confessed herself worried sick, but Abby Gibbons thought they might be spared because of the good sense of the family in keeping out of politics. Not until the ship *Keyport* arrived at midnight on July 18 did they hear definitely that their house had been a target of the riot. Julia Gibbons had written to her mother, suggesting that she not come home, but Abby Gibbons was determined to see the damage for herself, and the two packed up and left by the next steamer.[10]

The scene at 19 Lamartine Place was worse than they might have imagined. The mob had thrown all the furniture, including heavy bureaus, out of the windows and set fire to many rooms. The front door was smashed, the marble mantelpieces broken to bits, the water and gas fixtures twisted off, bannisters, window sashes, closet doors carried away, and oilcloth torn from the floors. A heavy mahogany sofa, half burned, and a large ice refrigerator were alone left.[11]

A report of the riot damage made later to the city of New York added details:

The witnesses all agree that a great deal of the furniture was thrown out of the windows, most of it having been previously injured . . . many of the books and papers in the library were used to kindle the fires, placed under the furniture collected for that purpose; others were scattered about and trampled upon . . . the pictures and works of art were mostly defaced or injured in the house. . . . The crockery etc. was demolished in the house. The carpets and oil clothes were greatly injured, and after having been nearly destroyed, were mostly carried away.[12]

With her usual determination, Abby Gibbons set about creating some order in this chaos. Living at her brother John's house, she began the task of attempting to inventory her losses, hoping for some compensation. Meanwhile James oversaw the reclamation of the house. Abby Gibbons was sure that she could never live there again and insisted that a bill of sale be placed upon it. By fall, however, it seemed most practical to move back in, while waiting for a buyer. The local police had collected some of the Gibbonses' things—chiefly chairs without seats, bureaus without drawers, tables without tops—and with these the family camped out until the claim was settled.[13]

Abby Gibbons tried to be philosophical about her "crosses and losses," but so much of her life and her memories of her dead sons were connected to the house on Lamartine Place that she could not throw off her grief. "How few know the utter desolation," she wrote Sarah. She was trying to keep the house, as it had been, alive in her memory, with "every picture in its place, and not a drawer or closet where I could not lay my hand and find what I wanted."[14]

Friends and relatives of the Gibbonses reacted with disbelief and anger to the news of the looting of their home. The fact that Abby Gibbons had been away from home, nursing the sick, including the 69th regiment from New York, at the very moment of the attack, filled her supporters with righteous indignation. Dr. James Walker wrote that the savagery of the mob confirmed his belief in the depravity of humankind. "After all, what is truly divine in man, is not what he is by nature, but what he is by training and culture. Say what we will of the dignity of human nature, a wild man is a wild beast, and a beast of prey." Elizabeth Neall Gay, daughter of Quaker abolitionist Daniel Neall and wife of journalist Sidney Gay, said that with the news, "all my early peace principles were swept away. I, who have meekly borne the brunt of half a dozen mobs . . . [whose father] had suffered in his person the grossest indignities—tar and feathers and rail—at this crisis found myself ready for war." The Honorable John P. Hale wrote of his anger that the Hopper family, who had for generations extended a helping hand to "every form of wretchedness and woe, should be attacked by the very class for whom you have done so much."

The Reverend Octavius Brooks Frothingham preached a sermon praising Abby Gibbons and decrying a mob that would attack her home while she was on the battlefield nursing their sons and brothers.[15]

Although the Gibbonses eventually received some compensation from the city, their losses remained large. A group of their friends, under the leadership of Joseph Choate, undertook to gather up a sum of money on their behalf. One of those Choate wrote to was George Stearns of Boston. By September 1, Choate was able to present a check of $2,750.00 to Abby Gibbons, no small sum in those days. She wrote to thank Choate, saying that the destruction of her home was a light burden compared to what other families were suffering on the battlefield, and that the expression of friendship and the interest in her charities meant as much as the generous help.[16]

Many young men known to the Gibbons family had been killed or wounded at Gettysburg. In addition, word was received soon afterwards that Robert Shaw's 54th Massachusetts Division, for which Abby Gibbons had recruited members, had gone into battle on July 18 at Fort Wagner in Charleston Harbor, South Carolina, sustaining terrible losses. Captain Shaw himself had been killed and lay with his men in a trench at the foot of Fort Wagner. Abby Gibbons felt deeply for his mother, Sarah Shaw, and his sister, Josephine, as well as the other mothers and sisters. It was time to return to her wartime duties, which she regarded as "the call of humanity."

Dr. Heger had been writing her news of the Point, indicating that she was missed. Dr. Clinton Wagner and Dr. John Stearns, who had both been transferred from the Point to the Sanitary Commission, came to call and talk about the war. Clinton Wagner told Abby Gibbons that he had needed her and Sarah badly on the battlefield at Gettysburg, but had not been able to reach them in time.[17]

On a subsequent visit, Wagner brought his sister, Rose. This was Abby Gibbons's first meeting with Rose Wagner. She had forgiven Clinton his southern accent and ways, but she found Rose mannered and theatrical. Rose, however, apparently fell in love with Abby Gibbons and her daughters on the spot. She wrote frequent fervent letters to Abby Gibbons and became an important and troubling factor in the Gibbonses' family affairs.[18]

While in New York, Abby Gibbons had been recruiting nurses to take back with her to the Point to replace the hated "Dixies," and had persuaded two remarkable women to accompany her. They were Jane and Georgeanna Woolsey, members of a prominent and interesting New York family. Their older sister, Abby Woolsey, had been present at Dr. Elizabeth

Blackwell's meeting in New York which formed the Central Association. The sisters had turned their home into an informal headquarters for shipping supplies to the front, and like Abby Gibbons, they had gone to Washington with their supplies and become battlefield nurses. Jane was thirty and Georgeanna twenty-seven when they served as nurses at Gettysburg. Temporarily home in New York after the battle, they were eager for more nursing experience and accepted Abby Gibbons offer of work at Point Lookout. With these two, she returned to the Point on September 13. They were met by enthusiastic soldiers and by Dr. Heger, who had reserved their old quarters, and who gave them supper.[19]

Abby Gibbons lost no time in reacquainting herself with the contraband, particularly with an old friend, Sandy Dorsey, who feared recapture by his master, who lived nearby, and wanted to leave for the north with his wife. Abby Gibbons immediately called on the new general, Gilman Marston, and persuaded him to help her in getting the two fugitives off for Washington on the next boat. She also discovered that one of the "Dixies" had been dismissed, and consequently she had another place to fill. "We are making slow, but I hope sure progress," she wrote to Julia.[20]

Unfortunately, she arrived at a time of turmoil. There was talk of turning the Point over entirely to house Rebel prisoners. Abby Gibbons was indignant. The climate was healthy for her patients; why should they be dislodged to accommodate Rebels. "There is a general outcry. Let us hope it may not be!" she wrote to James.[21]

The news, however, was all too true. In preparation for the change, the Surgeon General, William H. Gardner, had ordered that all nurses ("both of Miss Dix and Mrs. Gibbons selection") be dismissed, except for one to run the diet kitchen and another the linen room. Their places were to be taken by the Sisters of Mercy. Abby Gibbons believed that Surgeon Heger, whom she had so recently regarded as a friend, had requested this order, because as an Austrian he preferred to work with Catholics and had no feeling for the national cause. She and her nurses charged further that Heger had received the order from Acting Surgeon General Charles Crane in return for the favor of covering up the fact that the latter "had been grossly intoxicated on his last visit to the Point."[22]

Abby Gibbons made an immediate trip to Washington to try to use her influence to regain her position at the Point. She soon learned, however, that Gardner's order was not confined to Point Lookout, as she had originally thought. It was army-wide and was designed to place the assignment and direction of women nurses under the medical officers, end the insubordination he felt the Protestant nurses had been creating, and relieve him of troubles with Dorothea Dix. Besides, he argued, what Protestant nurses could compare with the Sisters of Charity for efficiency and faithfulness? Abby Gibbons continued to feel that the Catholic sisters were too submissive, and therefore did not challenge the really miserable medical conditions in many of the hospitals. But she did not have influence enough to override Gardner in this case.[23]

While she was in Washington waiting for a verdict, she visited the camps for the contraband and made a special trip to Arlington, where contraband were living on General Robert E. Lee's former plantation. Here she also visited the National Colored Home for Aged Women and Children, which she had helped to create earlier in the year. Maria Mann, the sister of Horace Mann, was the teacher of some seventeen students, and Abby Gibbons thought the whole affair a grand success. "One day, I passed at the camp where there are 600, living very neatly and many of them paying their own way. They hire out, make baskets, combs etc. I was in their school and their improvement in reading is remarkable. Everything is conducted in a simple and sensible way."[24]

Defeated in her efforts to reverse the decision of the surgeon general, she returned to the Point to face fresh indignities. Dr. Heger dismissed Georgeanna Woolsey and ordered Abby Gibbons to turn her precious stores over to a common storeroom. Gibbons rallied the remaining nurses to make a spirited protest, but it was in vain, and she was forced to say goodbye to her favorite patients and contraband and return in mid-October 1863 to New York.

While Abby Gibbons was going through these painful struggles at the Point, there had been sudden and wonderful news about the Home for Discharged Female Prisoners. A patron had died and left a legacy of $75,000 for its use. This, along with $12,000 the Home realized by selling some railroad bonds, meant that the Home no longer needed to struggle from month to month to meet its budget and might look to moving to a better location. "Many have been our dark days, but faith, patience, and hope will carry us through," Abby Gibbons wrote exultingly.[25]

The only shadow to fall across this rejoicing was the ill health of Catharine Sedgwick, the Home's "First Directress," who resigned in October 1863. Abby Gibbons was sad to see her leave just as the struggles of the Home seemed at last over and good times were ahead. The board wrote her a graceful letter of appreciation, expressing their hope that the separation would only be temporary and that she would remain in spirit their head. Unfortunately, this was not to be. After several years of struggle, Catharine Sedgwick died in 1867.[26]

More great changes were ahead for the Gibbons family. Sarah Gibbons had maintained her engagement to William Emerson all through the war years, waiting for his health to improve so that marriage might be possible. William had spent much of his time travelling, the standard prescription of the day for those with consumption. He got no better, but in the hectic spirit of wartime the couple decided to be wed anyway. This was accomplished very quietly on November 24, 1863. Abby Gibbons wrote to them with well wishes for their new life and thanked them for the dignity and order with which they had conducted their wedding. She was still at heart a Quaker. It was hard to part with her oldest daughter after many months of companionship, but Sarah was not far off, having gone to live at the Emerson home on Staten Island.[27]

Abby Gibbons stayed home through November and December, taking care of the affairs of the German school and preparing materials to be sold at the fair given to benefit the Sanitary Commission, inspired by the old antislavery fairs. She did not forget her problems with Point Lookout, writing to Secretary of War Stanton about the chaplain, Spooner, and to Horace Greeley, asking him to use his influence for the placement of a soldier friend.[28]

In January 1864 she returned to Washington to look into affairs at the Home for Colored Children she had helped to launch and to see old friends. She visited Dr. John Stearns and the Woolsey sisters. The latter promised her a good whiskey punch such as they had enjoyed at Point Lookout.("You know there is something in the air of a hospital which makes whiskey perfectly proper.") She stayed with the Bakers and made further acquaintance with Colonel James Dana of the Quartermaster's Department and his wife, Theresa Dana, the latter on the board of the Home with her. She also called on Charles Sumner and gave him a full account of affairs at Point Lookout, which he promised to look into. At the Capitol she met the sensational young lecturer Anna Dickinson and was impressed by her. After Anna spoke, President Abraham Lincoln was called to the lectern. "He went modestly to the platform and whispered to Vice President Hamlin; then left the hall. Upon which Hamlin who presided said to the audience: 'The President is embarrassed and says he cannot follow so distinguished a speaker.'"[29]

Abby Gibbons spent time on Capitol Hill during this visit, calling upon Senators Grimes and Wilson as well as several members of the House, lobbying for the passage of new legislation covering medical work on the battlefield. She met with General Benjamin Butler, whom she found easy to talk with, and the widow of General Frederick Lander, an ardent abolitionist, who had witnessed in person the refusal of the 54th Massachusetts regiment to accept lower pay than the rest of the U.S. soldiers, and lamented their casualties. She said she wished Abby Gibbons would be put in charge of the general hospital at Hilton Head.[30]

While she was in Washington there was a women's convention at the home for the insane. Abby Gibbons attended and was very interested, but found Dorothea Dix's impromptu speech on nursing objectionable. She wrote Julia that she believed Dix always sought the spotlight and often made a fool of herself thereby. She spent her last days trying to sort out the affairs of the National Home. There were now two factions on the board, those who supported Maria Mann and those who wished to replace her. Abby Gibbons was among the supporters, and her group was strong enough to oust the previous chairwoman. Abby tried to persuade her sister-in-law, Anna Hopper, to take the presidency but Anna turned it down, being busy with the corporation of the newly organized Swarthmore College.[31]

The news from the Emersons was up and down. At first William seemed a lot better and no longer had the dreadful night sweats that went with tuberculosis. Then, in early February, they returned. His doctor advised a change of air, and for a while William considered going to Minnesota. But before he could depart, he took a sudden turn for the worse, and on February 29 he died. He was twenty-nine years of age and had been married to Sarah only three months.[32]

Abby Gibbons had returned to New York early in February in order to look for a new house. The city of New York had finally settled the Gibbonses' claim for damage to Lamartine Place at $8,500; it was now possible to prepare to move. However, the illness and death of her son-in-law and the need to comfort Sarah took precedence over house hunting. With the coming of spring came a call for Sarah and herself to return to the battlefield, thus cutting short the time for grief.[33]

The Army of the Potomac was hammering that May at Lee's forces north of Richmond, and both sides were sustaining heavy losses at Spotsylvania and the Wilderness. Abby Gibbons and Sarah Emerson arrived at Belle Plain on the Potomac on May 21, 1864, and were immediately occupied caring for wounded men who were being transferred from ambulances to a steamer to take them north. Sarah Emerson wrote to her father to describe the scene:

> Their groans, as they were moved from the ambulances, were frightful to hear; and, as they were brought in on their stretchers,

and laid upon the decks made soft with straw, our business was to supply them with ice-water, coffee, milk, punch, farina, bread, crackers, or whiskey, according to their needs; wet their wounds which had not been dressed in days, attend to all their necessities, take last words from dying lips, and promise to write to friends at home the sad tidings.[34]

They slept that night in bunks on the sanitary barges and the next day walked to Fredericksburg through a sea of mud. Here a hospital was assigned to Abby Gibbons and her helpers, with 160 patients lying on a filthy floor. They went to work immediately, improvising beds. "We stole straw to fill ticks, stole boards to make bunks, stole bedsteads, took nails from packing boxes, and yesterday every man was comfortable."[35]

The soldiers called Abby Gibbons "mother" and found the presence of the old lady comforting, Sarah Emerson reported home. Sarah had been near a major battlefield before, but never had she seen so many wounded. Altogether she reported that 23,000 had passed through Fredericksburg and been sent on, 7,166 wounded and 1,000 sick remained in temporary quarters. Agents of the Sanitary Commission were heroic, Sarah felt, washing the men, dressing the wounds, making the patients comfortable. She was, as usual, deeply touched by individual soldiers. A dying boy of sixteen clung to her, saying that she was his only friend, and begging her to take him to her room. When she told him she thought he was too young, he said proudly, "Ask my captain if I did not do good service." Then he died.[36]

As quickly as possible, the men were moved out of Fredericksburg. There were many guerrillas in the area; a raid on the makeshift hospitals was daily expected. After five days Abby Gibbons and Sarah Emerson accompanied many of their patients on a long, jolting ride to Washington, sitting on flatbed railroad cars, with only leafy branches to keep them out of the broiling sun. Long trains of ambulances covered a parallel road, and contrabands trudged along with bundles of possessions on their heads. When they reached Aquia Creek, they loaded their patients onto the *Argo*, which sailed within sight of Washington, then was ordered to return to Alexandria, where they spent an uncomfortable night.[37]

Once they reached Washington and were reunited with some of their patients in a local hospital, Abby Gibbons set up a model diet kitchen with another volunteer Civil War nurse, Clara Thomas. Gibbons was interested in the effect of diet on her patients, observing that some could not tolerate the harsh army fare, and that others were surfeited by the indiscriminate distribution of food and brandy by various commissions that had sprung up in rivalry with the Sanitary Commission. One of these was the Christian Commission, which Abby Gibbons believed pressed so much stimulant on patients that they were sometimes befuddled.[38]

After two weeks, she was ordered to White House, Virginia, along with Sarah and Abby's niece, Maria Hopper. Following a few days of exploration, they settled in a makeshift field hospital at City Point. They were the only women present and were immediately busy cooking and setting the hospital aright as supplies and volunteers arrived by boat. There was fighting nearby, and a black regiment was in the thick of it. Abby Gibbons knew its commander, Colonel Harry Russell, who had been wounded and was himself a patient,and who told her that "never had there been such fighting as by the colored troops."[39]

When they first arrived, the headquarters of General Ulysses S. Grant was a stone's throw from Abby Gibbons's field hospital, and she and Sarah often saw him at a distance. He was aware of them too, and one day, when the temperature stood at one hundred degrees and Sarah was preparing food over a makeshift stove in the broiling sun, he ordered that she be moved under the trees at his headquarters.[40]

Much of their work at City Point was in nursing patients brought to them straight from the battlefield and preparing them to be loaded on ships or trains to be sent back to Washington for longer treatment. Once a train of ambulances five miles long arrived, after being bumped over fearful roads. The suffering of the wounded soldiers was dreadful. "How often I thought of poor Sarah Shaw," Abby Gibbons wrote to *Tribune* editor Sydney Gay. "If she had been with us she would have been ready to exclaim every hour of the day 'Thank God that my dear son was struck down suddenly!'"[41]

After several weeks, the decision was made to evacuate as many patients as possible from City Point, and Sarah Emerson and Abby Gibbons were ordered to board the steamboat *Webster* for a trip to Washington, accompanying 228 patients. It was very hot, and many of the men were sick with diarrhea, but by now the two women were inured to unpleasant sights and smells and did their best to keep the soldiers comfortable on the long, weary trip.

Once returned to City Point in early July, Abby Gibbons began to feel strongly that she was needed at home. There was no rational explanation for the feeling, but it was so strong that she left Sarah Emerson and Maria Hopper in charge and returned to New York for a few days. There she received a telegram that her brother John Hopper, who was in Milton, New

York, where he and his wife and son spent a part of each summer, was very ill and needed her. She immediately set out by train to Poughkeepsie, then took the ferry to Milton. On the way over a man approached her, asking if she was John Hopper's sister. "Are you a doctor?" she asked. "No, an undertaker," he replied. Thus she learned abruptly that her beloved brother, six years younger than herself, had died of a stroke at the age of fifty-seven.[42]

Abby Gibbons wrote of her grief to her close friend and confidante, Elizabeth Gay. "Never let my children know the depth of my sorrow, for I speak the words of peace and resignation to them, as far as I can. How the opposite of what I feel and suffer!"[43]

A week prior to John Hopper's death, Abby Gibbons's friend from Point Lookout, Dr. Clinton Wagner, had written that he had been given charge of an army hospital in Beverly, New Jersey, housing three thousand patients, and wanted her to take charge of the nursing. As soon as John Hopper's funeral was over and his affairs in order, Abby and Lucy Gibbons and Sarah Emerson took the train to Beverly, a village near the east bank of the Delaware River above Camden. Dr. Wagner had found a small ferry house, jutting out over the river, for their use, and here they stayed during their months at Beverly, commuting to and from the hospital by ambulance. Abby complained that it was too luxurious. "Give me camp-life and its privations with the soldier, and under shot and shell. We are outside and have too many comforts."[44]

There was little time to enjoy the luxury however, as the hospital began to fill up with badly wounded and dying patients. "We have 700 patients, eight buried last evening. I closed the eyes of four who arrived in the *Atlantic* from Fortress Monroe not twelve hours before. Barbarous to put dying men off on such a journey," Abby Gibbons fumed. Dr. Wagner had invited her to bring her own nurses, and she had collected as many as she could: the two Woolsey sisters, Clara Thomas, Martha Lever, and Emily Sedgwick. Lucy, whose first nursing experience this was, took charge of the linen room and soon had it arranged elegantly. Anna Hallowell, Lucretia Mott's granddaughter, came to help Abby Gibbons, waiting on her and preparing her meals.

They were all kept busy, night and day, by the arrival of still more patients. Colonel Henry Patten, a Boston abolitionist, was among the wounded. Abby Gibbons saw that he could not live, but he begged her to stay with him, thinking she might somehow pull him through. After the colonel died she wrote to his mother, remembering once more how it felt to lose a son.[45]

With Dr. Wagner's support, and with no "Dixies" to challenge her on the ward, Abby Gibbons enjoyed her nursing tour at Beverly more than her other wartime assignments. Her patients often called her "Mother," and turned to her for the mothering they badly missed, wounded and far from home. As the days passed and the majority of her patients improved, she was glad to see them well enough to be furloughed. A staunch supporter of Lincoln still, she was especially happy to send them home in time to vote in the November 1864 elections.[46]

Abby Gibbons was by now well known for her Civil War nursing. The *Christian Inquirer*, a liberal publication to which the Gibbonses subscribed, ran a short poem that mentioned her:

> Ministering with courage saintly
> Where the heart of man would quail
> There is many an Abby Gibbons
> Many a Florence Nightingale.

The various charitable organizations with which she had worked needed her help. Ellen Collins, still on the board of the Woman's Central Association, begged her to come to the Blackwell Island Hospital to take charge of the kitchen and to supervise the women employed at the hospital who came from the prison to work. When Abby Gibbons did not immediately respond, Collins wrote again to invite her to take over superintendence of the whole hospital. "I hoped that being home and doing this work, plus working with poor women would interest you," she urged.[47]

Maria Mann, head of the Colored Home in Washington that Abby Gibbons had helped to establish, urged her to come and straighten out the deadlocked board of directors. There were two factions on the board, one composed of Emily Howland, Abby Gibbons, Theresa Dana, Sophia Peabody, and others who supported Maria Mann, and one grouped around the volatile Jane Swisshelm, who opposed her. The Swisshelm faction wrote a report to Secretary of War Stanton asking for an investigation. In September Abby left Sarah Emerson in charge at Beverly while she made a flying trip to Washington and managed once more to arrange a compromise settlement for the time being.[48]

Beverly was close enough to New York to enable Abby Gibbons to make occasional visits home to see about the Isaac Hopper Home and the Industrial Schools and to continue looking for a new house, while living temporarily at Lamartine Place. She was determined to move, but was torn between house hunting and her duties at Beverly. Sarah Emerson was managing without her, but one of her nurses, Martha Lever, was very ill with typhoid fever and required nursing care. Martha finally died in November. Sarah Emerson, writing to her father about the sad event, asked rhetorically, "Who can say her life was not given to her country as truly as that of anyone of the band of heroes who have fallen in battle?"[49]

Abby Gibbons's fame as a Civil War nurse resulted in her having a stream of visitors whenever she was home. Society women sought her out, looking for something to do with their time, as well as poor women seeking employment. A representative of the New York Department of Public Charities and Corrections asked her to find a home and job for a reformed prostitute. She kept in touch with several families of contraband whom she had sent north from Point Lookout, and saw to the education of a young black boy, Colbert, an ex-slave of Jefferson Davis's whom she had brought north.[50]

> Judging from the multitude who pass our threshold, it might be supposed we are "in society." All grades, from Mrs. Griffin, to the 40,000 who want situations. The other day, in perfect desperation, after going into the parlor at ten and not leaving until three P.M. I found myself ejaculating, "O Lord, have mercy on me!"[51]

Among the callers at Lamartine Place were some of the doctors and colonels with whom Abby Gibbons had served on the battlefield. Colonel Alfred Hartwell, an old friend of Willie's, came to be nursed. Dr. Wagner left Beverly long enough to make a short visit. Dr. John Stearns kept in close touch.

After a second visit to Washington in November to see about the Colored Home, Abby Gibbons returned to New York to set to work on the dolls for Randall's Island, "the eternal Randall Island dolls," as Julia Gibbons called them. Abby Gibbons was tired and after Christmas fell ill with jaundice, which she may have acquired at the hospital. Just as she began to recover, Lucy was discovered with a case of varioloid, a very mild form of smallpox which was then sweeping New York. She was quite ill and had to have her head shaved. Abby nursed her for three weeks, and would not permit Julia to come home for fear she might contract the disease. Sarah remained at Beverly and kept her informed of the news.[52]

Northern victories were beginning to be regularly reported now, and Abby Gibbons and her friends rejoiced in the news. Sarah Emerson took time off from Beverly to go to Washington to visit friends and attend Lincoln's inaugural in March 1865, where Andrew Johnson was so drunk that he made a stump oration and had to be stopped so that the president could take his vows,

> our dear President who is content to shine with his steady light and leave the brilliant flashes to others. The whole thing was confusion itself—no one to show the foreign ministers where to go and the floor of the Senate so filled by people who did not belong there that the members of the house could not get in. The sun came out just as the president took the oath, an omen that the storm and tempest of the last four years was drawing to a close and the sun of peace about to shine.[53]

As part of the ceremony, Sarah Emerson heard Lincoln's second inaugural speech with its famous lines, "With malice toward none; with charity for all . . . let us strive on to finish the work we are in; to bind up the nation's wounds—to do all which may achieve and cherish a just and lasting peace."

9

"When Johnny Comes Marching Home Again"

The Gibbons family watched the war news eagerly and read with joy about the surrender of Petersburg, then of Richmond, and finally Lee's surrender at Appomattox Courthouse. Like most loyal Unionists, they were stunned on the morning of April 15 to read of the President's assassination by John Wilkes Booth, brother of an actor whom they had seen in the theater in New York. The darkness of the news contrasted with the beauty of the coming of spring. The tragedy caused Abby Gibbons to reflect that in the depths of the bitter war she had at last found healing for herself and was ready to start life anew:

> A sad day this, to so many! but it is bright and beautiful, and every green thing and blooming flower seems to have a peculiar freshness and sweetness, and upon the whole, I feel as I might venture to be grateful for the blessing of life and what it gives to enjoy, and I decided to live on, taking all that comes within my reach;—giving what I can to my limited ability, and endeavoring (according to the words often repeated by "Early Friends," as Uncle John used to say) "to center down in the quiet."[1]

The war had further stretched Abby Gibbons's ties to Friends, early or otherwise. Her beloved father had remained a staunch foe of capital punishment, but she was not sure. Her friend Dr. Clinton Wagner wrote to express the hope that President Andrew Johnson would begin his administration by hanging traitors. Her daughter, Sarah Emerson, travelling in Boston, wrote of the capture of Jefferson Davis and her belief he should be hanged. Abby wavered when it came to the conspirators who had murdered President Lincoln. The day after Booth and Mary Surratt were hanged she wrote to Sarah to comment that the city was very quiet about the conspirators and their fate. "I never would give my voice in favor of any capital punishment, but in this case, would not dare raise my voice against it." She reported that Colbert had been in a butcher store where a woman had said, "They might have given Mrs. Surratt more time." To which the butcher responded, "Why! They didn't give Lincoln *any* time."[2]

The American Anti-Slavery Society met in New York in May 1865. Robert and Harriet Purvis, the black abolitionist couple from Philadelphia whom Abby Gibbons had known as a young woman, stayed with the Gibbonses since no hotel would accommodate them, while the Garrisons stayed this time with Rosa Hopper. Anna Mott Hopper wrote to Abby Gibbons about the Purvises:

> Robert Purvis was at father's last first day and had much to say of his visit to New York and his great admiration for thee and thine. We think him a very entertaining man. I hoped you liked him and his wife. I do not know how they got to your house, for I was very careful not to suggest any thing of the kind when I was asked if I knew of a place where they could stay because I did not know it might suit you to have them.[3]

At this meeting, Garrison declared that the Society should disband, since the war had brought an end to slavery, while another group, under the leadership of Wendell Phillips, proposed to continue until suffrage for the blacks was won. Abby Gibbons and James attended the meeting, but sided with Garrison, and thereafter no longer played a role in the Society, which continued its existence until 1870.[4]

Nevertheless, they kept in touch with their old abolitionist friends. Angelina Grimké Weld and Sarah Grimké often came to stay in New York, and Sarah and Abby Gibbons visited the Welds at Hyde Park, Massachusetts, on their trips to Boston. Here the Welds took care of a third sister from Charleston, South Carolina, who had become destitute during the Civil War, and entertained two Grimké half brothers, Francis and Archibald, sons of their brother and his slave mistress, whom the Welds had heard about and made contact with, after the war was over.[5]

In May 1866, the abolitionists gathered in New York to form an American Equal Rights Association, to work for suffrage for both blacks and women, with the aged Lucretia Mott as chair. By the next year the group was polarized by the introduction of the Fourteenth Amendment and its wording, giving the vote to males only. Some argued that it was "the Negro's hour" and that it was necessary to secure black suffrage in the South immediately to prevent the reestablishment of white supremacy through vigilantes. Others, especially Susan B. Anthony and Elizabeth Cady Stanton, felt betrayed, believing that if suffrage for women were not obtained immediately, it might be many years before it came to be. In January 1868, Anthony and Stanton began to publish a newspaper, *The Revolution*, with the backing of an eccentric Democrat, Francis Train. Something of a Copperhead and racist, Train was regarded by most of the abolitionist pioneers as anathema and his relationship to the Democratic party beyond the pale, since the Republicans were still regarded as the crusaders against slavery. In 1869 Anthony and Stanton founded the National Woman's Suffrage Association, while Lucy Stone, married to Henry Blackwell, formed the American Woman's Suffrage Association.

Abby Gibbons's friendship with the Blackwells, as well as her strong Republican sympathies, caused her to side with the Lucy Stone group. On July 7, 1868, Susan B. Anthony published an open letter in the *Tribune* addressed to the Democratic National Convention, and naming Elizabeth Cady Stanton, Mrs. Horace Greeley, herself, and Abby Hopper Gibbons as a committee of the Woman's Suffrage Association. When she saw this in the *Tribune*, Abby was annoyed because it gave the impression that she was somehow "hitched on to the Democratic party." She felt, however, that a disclaimer would bring more publicity and was inclined to let the matter rest. Her daughter Julia, who was deeply identified with her mother and was often volatile, urged that she write a correction. At first James composed the article, but Abby Gibbons and Julia decided that a "womanly paragraph" was more fitting and sent it off to Horace Greeley, who published it on July 9 as "A Card from Mrs. Gibbons"[6]

By some misunderstanding my name appears on a committee in an appeal to the Democratic Convention now in session in this city. Its use in that connection is made without my knowledge; and whatever my views upon the subject of universal suffrage may be, I wish distinctly to disclaim association with, or approval of, or interest in it, as connected with any body of individuals merely political.[7]

"She finally got worked up to the proper pitch and wrote quite a spicy note to Susan B. for having added her name without authority, etc.," Julia wrote to Sarah. "In the evening Susan B. and Mrs. Stanton came up, apologized, and promised never to do it again. The parties became reconciled and parted the best of friends, but I don't think mother will again appear in that boat."

Abby Gibbons's own account of the incident was somewhat different. She said she had not let out "full sail" against Susan B. because she feared the *Revolution*, but also because she felt that she must be true to all women—"especially such as have stemmed the tide in support of my sisters of every shade and condition."[8]

Whatever position she took publicly, she was widely regarded as a spokesperson for women's rights. Her Quaker friend, Elizabeth Townsend of West Chester, Pennsylvania, wrote to her about the issue:

> This very question of Woman's Rights had been uppermost in my thoughts, and I remembered what Gasparin, that healthful French writer, said: "In every great revolution of opinion, there are always a few fearless ones who start off in advance of the others—these are the Standard-bearers, and instead of ridiculing them, we should honor them for their intrepidity."

> Well, I suppose thee is one of the "Standard-bearers," and be assured, I will not "cast a single stone," although I do not go as far as thee does. Women have "Rights," or at least are entitled to many of which they are deprived; and I have no doubt this question will obtain for them for some privileges which they do not enjoy.[9]

While she did not urge her daughters to join the women's movement, Abby Gibbons did not approve of their making fun of the pioneers, whether the elderly Grimké sisters or Susan B. Anthony. "What you need is patience with Susan B. Anthony and Parker Pillsbury, and others of their kind, who are doing the work you will bless them for, when a few more years are added," she wrote to Sarah and Julia. "Allow them freedom of speech and action, and conventions at watering places if they like . . . be not too proud of your own self to be convicted."[10]

She was concerned also that her daughters were becoming snobs. She herself enjoyed meeting important people and was quite taken with Lady and Lord Amberly, a liberal British couple who visited many of the American reformers in 1867.("I name the Lady first, since she is much more of a woman than her husband is of a man.") But her contact with ex-slaves and prisoners kept her rooted, she believed. "You do not like *'the people'* as I did and do," she wrote Sarah and Julia in 1869. "I like every side of life where there is no clerical hypocrisy, and find among the poorer classes more humanity than among the rich." The next year, when the presence of Horace Greeley as a boarder brought throngs of people of all sorts to her house, she told Sarah it did not bother her. "I am so fond of the *people* and so distrustful of the select and elect, that I take it more composedly than the aristocratic members of the family."[11]

She discussed the *Tribune's* coverage of the Woman Suffrage meetings with Horace Greeley and suggested that it was undignified and unfair. "Of course, they do much they'd better not do, but so does everybody. Reformers are class, and have their privileges, and do what others have not the courage, or are too lazy to do. For myself, knowing them well, I respect and honor the pioneers."[12]

James Gibbons was less inclined to support the women's rights movement. Following the New York riots of 1863, he had become increasingly conservative. He continued to insist on being treated as the head of the household, but he was very much aware that Abby Gibbons was the dominant personality. This seemed to be troubling him in later years. He wrote a long letter to Abby from Germany, commenting on the issue. He said he believed that equality between men and women was a concept already accepted by society, and those who pushed for change were only making matters worse:

> The truth is that any essential difference as to position and rights, between men and woman, is an obsolete thought, a thing of the graveyard, not a thing of the active civilized and cultivated life of the present day. Those "women people" are generally uneducated, unsettled in some way, smart enough to talk without having anything to talk about, very limited in anything like "social science" and about equally gifted in self conceit and self will. In fact they make a sort of "left wing" the special function of which is to fan little sparks of eccentricity and disappointment with a big blaze of fire, which burns up all amiability and gives nothing but "ashes on the lips."[13]

Abby Gibbons's friend and mentor, Dr. James Walker, ex-president of Harvard, was also unsure that the agitation was necessary. He was not in favor of married women voting, but believed that unmarried women should vote, and always should have voted, and that the privilege would surely come to them in time. Abby listened respectfully to both her husband and Dr. Walker, but continued to support the pioneers. Women's rights advocates were urging that women be appointed to local boards to oversee schools and other institutions having to do with women and children, and Abby was a strong advocate of this development. In Boston she met with a group of women who were considering ways and means of having women serve on school committees in Massachusetts. "If I stay in Boston much longer I shall be a woman worshiper. They are grand and glorious and as much above the common level as may be."[14]

In addition to her interest in women's rights, Abby Gibbons continued to be concerned about the condition of blacks in the South. Like many of her fellow abolitionists, she was soon disillusioned with Andrew Johnson's administration. In addition to his drunkenness she was angry at his appeasing attitude toward the South. The fact that Johnson chose to return to its secessionist owner the property in Washington where Maria Mann had sought to conduct a school and home for elderly contraband was proof, she thought, of his sympathies with the Southerners, who were intent, she believed, in returning the condition of the blacks to pre–Civil War status.

The school itself preoccupied her. After many battles with the divided board, Maria had left and started a school for newly freed slaves at Harpers Ferry, but wrote that no one in that town was willing to provide room and board for the "nigger school teacher." The Freedman Committee in Boston did not back her school, so she decided to move on to start a small private school in Washington, to be supported by her former backers. This enterprise, too, came to an end when the black teachers themselves desired to take over management, something Maria Mann said she thought represented "ingratitude and ignorance," revealing the racism that many of the Northern reformers harbored. Abby Gibbons did not comment, but she dropped contact with Maria, who returned to New England and turned her energies in other directions.[15]

Sarah Emerson paid a visit to Washington in the spring of 1866, seeing the Danas and many of the other families with whom she and her mother had made friends during their times at the Capitol. She went to visit Emily Howland, a Quaker abolitionist and women's rights activist, who was living in the Freedmen's Village in Virginia and supervising the schools hastily set up for the children. "She seems to me as genuine a case of philanthropy as we have come across," Sarah wrote to her mother. "Certain it is that she plants herself in most unattractive spots and sticks to her work. Just now she is back at Fort Concord with no neighbors except the colored people."[16]

Abby Gibbons was still in close touch with the Freedmen's Bureau and longed to see for herself the condition of the blacks whose cause she had espoused so vigorously when she was at Point Lookout. In September 1866, she made a nostalgic visit to the Point, taking Lucy with her. She stayed in her old cottage by the shore, now overrun with morning glories, and was greeted as an old friend by many of the officers on duty. She visited the families she had known and the local store, where the blacks traded. She was impressed at first to see them spending money they had earned themselves for their necessities, but soon learned how inadequate that money was.

> This last group work in the field and are paid 37 cents per day; which sum will not pay for meat and meal too. What is needed is that there should be northern settlers to live among them. I wish the energetic, active, humane young men would buy farms here and befriend and protect these poor creatures. To such, they would give their labor without stint, and for reasonable compensation.[17]

She also talked with a black man, Peters, whom she had known at the Point and observed that he had a large fresh scar on his face inflicted by a local "ruffian" who had defrauded him of three dollars. "The law gives no protection whatever to the colored men, and the suffering, by hard treatment and starvation, is horrible," she wrote Sarah.[18]

Was all the sacrifice she had witnessed during the war to be in vain? The only solution that Abby Gibbons could imagine was to work harder to support the freedmen and schools for the newly freed slaves. Ellen Collins was travelling in Virginia to inspect such schools for the Woman's Central Association. With her was Josephine Shaw, who had married Colonel Charles Russell Lowell in 1863 and been widowed a year later. The Association raised money to assist the schools these two recommended. Gibbons solicited donations of food and clothing from friends and packed barrels for the black schools and churches, a practice she continued until 1892.[19]

In addition, Abby Gibbons was concerned about the returning veterans. She received many letters from the soldiers she had nursed. Not a few were looking for work. Many had lost arms or legs and were limited in what they could do. What sort of life, she wondered, had they to look forward to? And what of the widows of those who did not come home at all?

Her practical solution was to organize a "Labor and Aid Society" to supply veterans and their wives with employment. Remembering her experience on the battlefields with the providing of clean linens in abundance, she decided to start with a laundry, add a sewing department, and to couple both with a nursery for children whose mothers were to be employed. She enlisted a number of the prominent women she had worked with in relation to the Isaac Hopper Home and the Industrial Schools, and found a likely site. By February 1866, the laundry was a going enterprise. Abby Woolsey went through it and was pleased with what she saw.

I liked the sweet, clean, sunny look and smell that everything has. I should be very willing to have any washing done in such light, airy quarters. The forewoman was out but I had quite a talk with Woods who recognized my name and said he used to know my sister on the James River when he was storekeeper of the old "Elizabeth." I talk "work and wages" to everybody I meet and I think that for want of any better or other organization, our schools and our church societies ought to have a form of "directory" at least—on which the names of honest hard working women could be entered. . . .There is more help for beggars here than for workers.[20]

Abby Gibbons had hoped to duplicate her laundry all over the city, but the enterprise was slow to become self-sustaining, and donations came in at a trickle. Several members of the board grew anxious about being financially responsible for the institution and insisted that it scale down its operations. Abby battled hard to keep it open, but in 1867, according to Sarah Emerson's version of the story, while Abby was ill and away from the meetings, the board acted without her and closed the laundry.[21]

Her wartime concerns had taken some of her energy away from the Isaac T. Hopper Home. Now that she was back, however, it demanded an increasing amount of her time and energy. The legacy that had been left to the Home was reduced from $75,000 to $50,000 because the will was contested by a son of the anonymous donor. The house on Tenth Street was in bad repair and looked as though it "belonged to the confederacy," according to Abby Gibbons. She decided on a thoroughgoing renovation. To raise additional money she appealed to the New York City Department of Public Charities and Corrections for some form of regular public support. She was somewhat taken aback to be asked if Jews and Catholics were eligible to serve as trustees or managers. The institution had been founded on Quaker principles, she wrote, and was therefore open to all. Catholics had served on the board, and Jews would certainly not be barred. The Home served both Catholics and Jews, but far more of the former than the latter. The faith of the Catholics was never interfered with, as a local Catholic priest would testify. Her appeal was successful, and the Home began to receive a regular allocation from the City. A few years later the State of New York began to allocate money to public charities out of the Supply Bill, and Abby Gibbons organized a group from the Home to go to Albany to lobby for a share of these funds.[22]

She was, according to her daughter, an effective lobbyist, going straight to the point. On a trip home from one such expedition, a member of her group overheard the much-quoted comment from a politician: "When those people want anything, they should send the little Quaker lady; the rest of them could stay at home."

Part of Abby Gibbons's success in Albany and with private donors undoubtedly came from her belief that she was doing people a favor by giving them an opportunity to give. "Thy father thinks I have a good deal of assurance," she wrote Sarah, "While I think it is conferring a privilege to give to worthy charities." In April 1874, she wrote of her lobbying:

> I have been to Albany hobnobbing with Politicians. Sarah Leggett went with me. . . . I was received as an old friend by those I met last year. The Speaker of the House came to me at table in Congress Hall, to let me know he was my friend; and many others did the same. I feel sure of success for Joe Choate gave me such letters as they could not withstand, and said much in praise of those charities in whose interest I was there. I suppose I sent my card to at least thirty; was introduced to all who were important. Hamilton Fish was devotedly kind . . . I talked at least with one hundred of the critters in one day and was glad to get into a chair on the train homeward and turning my book upon all, I slept. That is what you call lobbying and Julie called me a *born* lobbyist. I told the chairman of the finance committee that I was in Albany to tell them how to spend their money.[23]

Abby Gibbons learned later that no appropriation was made that year from the Supply Bill, but that the representative had divided the Excise Fund, giving money to charities. Among these, the Isaac Hopper Home received $5,000 and the Infant Asylum, in which she was also interested, $25,000, the largest gift to any institution. "As much as I could reasonably expect, considering it was through my individual effort," she wrote to her friend Sarah Thayer. "As for the Home, people do not have faith in sinners, but I will stand by them as long as I live."[24]

In 1865 the Isaac Hopper Home had celebrated its twentieth anniversary and revised its constitution and bylaws, making it mandatory for officers of the Women's Prison Association to visit women prisoners in the House of Correction, the prison on Blackwell Island, and Sing Sing. The women had concluded that they needed professional help with this visiting, and a woman doctor, Dr. Mary Greene, had been hired for this purpose, as well as to take care of the residents of the Isaac Hopper Home. The use of a woman physician was part of a statement of the WPA, whose members believed that police matrons should be hired to oversee the arrest and care of women while in jails and to prevent the exploitation of women prisoners.

Interest in the care of women prisoners was spreading among women philanthropists following the end of the Civil War. In Detroit a matron, Emma Hall, was hired in 1868 to supervise a separate shelter for women at the Detroit House of Correction, to serve as a reformatory for prostitutes and wayward girls, and a halfway house for women prisoners once they had achieved parole. The women were treated as members of a family, taught decorum as well as reading and writing, and trained in the domestic arts.[25]

The Shelter in Detroit closed its doors in 1874, but meanwhile in Indiana an evangelical Quaker woman, Rhoda Coffin, with her husband, Charles, began visiting prisons, jails, and workhouses in 1865, to preach. Their visits made them realize how much reform was needed; at the first National Prison Congress, called in Cincinnati in 1870, Rhoda Coffin spoke of the need for prison reform. The governor of Indiana, having heard of the Coffins, asked them to investigate conditions in the men's and women's prisons in Jefferson and Michigan City. In both places they saw conditions that shocked them, and one prisoner described abuses dramatically:

> He told me that a number of the guards had keys to the women's prison and entered when they wished to gratify their lusts. If the women could be bought up they gave them trinkets or goods out of the government stores, if they did not yield, they were reported as incorrigible and stripped and whipped in the presence of as many as wished to look on . . .[26]

The Coffins' report of abuses, delivered to the governor, led to an official investigation by a legislative committee. The governor then drew up a bill calling for a women's reformatory. Rhoda Coffin next undertook a lobbying campaign, enlisting the Indiana Yearly Meeting of the Society of Friends and many others in campaigning for the new reformatory for women prisoners, combined with a shelter for girls. They were successful in seeing that enabling legislation was passed, and Rhoda Coffin became a member of the board supervising construction of the new facility, which was erected and opened for occupancy in October 1873. As first director, the board, on which Rhoda Coffin sat, chose Sarah Smith, a Quaker who had served as a Civil War nurse and later established a refuge for prostitutes, called the Home for the Friendless, in Indianapolis.[27]

Sarah Smith's husband, ten years older than she, came along as steward, but she was clearly the director. One of her first acts was to visit the House of Shelter that Emma Hall was running in Michigan, which can be regarded as the first women's reformatory in the United States. Back in Indianapolis, Sarah Smith and her assistants worked to create a homelike atmosphere, with linen and china on the tables and individual rooms for the inmates. The girls were offered reading and writing and the women, instruction in laundering, sewing, and knitting. Care was taken in placing inmates after parole.[28]

Once the facility was functioning, a new governor appointed an all-male board to oversee operations. This resulted in conflict with the former board; Coffin and her colleagues campaigned for an all-woman board to manage the reformatory and were successful in 1877. Sarah Smith continued as director until her husband's ill health forced her to retire in 1882.[29]

Elsewhere, women were being appointed to boards to oversee women prisoners. One of the first was Elizabeth Buffum Chace, a Rhode Island Quaker, who was appointed to an advisory "Board of Lady Visitors" as a result of her campaign to have women placed on penal boards. She later resigned, charging that the board was without influence, but continued to work for women prisoners. In 1879 she visited New York and toured the Isaac Hopper Home with Abby Gibbons.[30]

All these women approached their charges with a maternal attitude. The prisoners might be actually much older than their advocates, but they were viewed as wayward children, who needed the loving guidance of a mother to bring them into compliance with the demands of Victorian womanhood and away from their former misdemeanors. The language of the new reformatories was that of the family; superintendents spoke of gathering the family together for improving reading or lectures. The new reformatories they were developing were based on a system of maternal justice that was to be part of prison reform for many years to come.[31]

The Women's Prison Association kept in touch with these developments and began to look forward to a time when they too might establish a women's reformatory for New York State. Meanwhile they rejoiced that their pattern for a halfway house for women prisoners was becoming well known. In 1864 Hannah Chickering of Dedham, Massachusetts, had written to Abby Gibbons about establishing an asylum similar to the Isaac Hopper Home in her home town. (Chickering was later to be one of the founders of the Massachusetts Reformatory Prison, in Sherborn.) Following the death of Catharine Sedgwick, the "First Directress," a biographer, Mary Dewey, asked for stories about the Home. And in 1868 Kate Field, a journalist, visited the Home and inspected the Tombs where Flora Foster, a member of the Home board, had been matron for twenty-one years.[32]

Finding placements for Home women continued to be one of Abby Gibbons's chief preoccupations. Many of the residents were still recovering alcoholics, and it was important to place them in the country, the women of the Prison Association thought, far from temptation's way. This was not always possible, and Gibbons was often called upon to locate a local cook or seamstress who had gone off on a spree. Sometimes it was her own servants who disappeared. James Gibbons wrote sarcastically to Sarah to describe the jolly times they were having, with Maria and Lizzy both disappearing "on a high drunk." No doubt, he said, they would be replaced by a new set of hopefuls from the same source."I am an entire and serious convert to the Home as a Spreeing Institution—i.e. it picks up everybody after a spree and fits em out again with a clean character and a new bonnet, and they're just as good after being ground over 20 times as at first and a little better often."[33]

While Abby Gibbons toiled with her charges at the Isaac T. Hopper Home and travelled to Albany on their behalf, James was becoming more well known and respected as a banker and stock broker. His book, *The Public Debt of the United States, its Organization, its Liquidation, and the Financial System*, published in 1867, was well received and he continued to contribute articles to various financial journals. His work demanded travel, including an extended trip to Europe in 1869.[34]

The family had another author. Lucy Gibbons, who had gone to art school, published in December 1869 a children's book, *The Hairy Egg*, containing fairy tales by three friends and her own illustrations. "The stories are poor enough, the illustrations good mainly," Abby Gibbons commented crisply.[35]

Of the three Gibbons daughters, Lucy was the most independent. After her brief venture into matrimony, Sarah seemed content with a life of companionship with her mother, varied by long visits to friends in the Boston and Philadelphia areas. She kept in close touch with the Emerson family, including her late husband's younger brother, Charles, and enjoyed her status as a widow. Julia appears to have been always somewhat immature. She too spent vacations away from the family, but she often complained of homesickness and frequently hurried home early from her adventures. She was given to long periods of depression and mood swings, and Abby Gibbons often worried about her. She sometimes went to the theater with young men, but she was never apparently seriously interested in anyone and accepted the role of single woman happily enough.

Lucy, the youngest, however, showed signs of wanting to break away from home and the strong, sometimes overwhelming influence of her mother. Abby Gibbons did not think of herself as controlling; in fact, she prided herself on giving her daughters leeway and asking their advice. She was such a powerful personality, however, that it took a strong person not to be swept up in her orbit and engulfed in her concerns, whether it was the Isaac T. Hopper Home, or Labor and Aid, or the central place in the life of the Gibbons home still held by the memory of Willie.

Just what happened in the Gibbons family in the late summer and fall of 1868 remains a mystery, for all letters pertaining to it were destroyed, but sometime in that season Lucy Gibbons left home. At first she wrote from Milton, where she was visiting Aunt Rosa, that Rose Wagner was with her there and had shared her bed. Next she said that Rose had left, and she herself was leaving for Poughkeepsie. Then the letters home stopped for over a year. It is possible that she had some sort of nervous breakdown in her efforts to pull free from the grip of the family circle. Hannah Rantoul wrote Abby in November saying she hoped for better news of Lucy, but believed she was afraid to leave her doctor. But whatever the cause of Lucy's leaving, the Gibbonses blamed the break on Rose Wagner.[36]

Rose, the sister of the Dr. Clinton Wagner, with whom Abby Gibbons had served at Point Lookout, had become at first an ardent admirer of Abby's, writing her extravagant letters of praise. She also visited the Gibbons family frequently, in the beginning with her brother, later alone. For a time she and Julia had struck up an intense friendship, and Julia had written of missing her dreadfully whenever they were separated. Then something happened to end this relationship, and Julia asked for her seal ring back. After this, Rose and Lucy became close friends. Abby Gibbons had never liked the woman and worried about her influence on her daughters. "Rose sends Lucy too much of a certain style of reading," Abby Gibbons commented to Sarah.[37]

In the fall of 1869, while James was in Europe, Julia was invited to join the George Baker family for a trip abroad. Writing to James to ask for his permission for Julia to make the trip, Abby Gibbons permitted herself a passionate outburst: "Julia has suffered beyond endurance with her whole head to say nothing of her heart which is deeply touched by all that has come to us by the vilest of men and women, and who in our immediate family has not suffered?" she asked rhetorically. Rose Wagner was evidently the vile woman to whom Abby Gibbons referred. Julia went on the trip and was away until March 1870, though suffering from homesickness.[38]

With her mother, Lucy Gibbons had been attending the church of Octavius Brooks Frothingham, who had separated from the Unitarian church to conduct a wholly independent congregation in New York. George Ripley, the transcendalist and editor of *The Harbinger*, was also a member of this group, introducing and helping to convert its members to the principles of Christian socialism of Charles Fourier. In the spring of 1868, Lucy attended a reception at the home of George Ripley and there met James Herbert Morse, a young teacher with literary interests.

Morse had just talked with Octavius Frothingham about starting a social and literary club, and he asked Lucy if she would be willing to help. A few days later he went with her to a funeral. This was the sedate beginning of a courtship that lasted for several years. As she often had in the past, Lucy spent most of the summer of 1869 at the Newport, Rhode Island, home of John and Jenny Bigelow, a prominent New York family. The Bigelows had spent several years in Paris, where John was the U.S. ambassador, and Lucy liked to speak French with Jenny and teach the children to paint. James Morse came to Newport and called on the Bigelows and Lucy. They spent several days in each other's company. On the last night, waiting for the boat that would take him back to New York, James Morse described hearing Kate Field sing to them from her boat. "We still get glimpses of Eden," he wrote in his journal. "We pass by the gate, but the angel with the flaming sword stands there, and none enter."[39]

Back in New York the friendship progressed, and by December the two were engaged. When James Gibbons returned from his trip to Europe in early January 1870, badly crippled by an attack of rheumatism, Lucy and James Morse came to call.

> Night before last, as I lay in my bed with shoulders enveloped in a wrapper, Mother brought Lucy into the room, my first sight of her for *a year and a half.* All went smoothly, and after a while, I asked of Mr. M. who was in the parlor, and had him invited up. They spent near an hour, and left in good state of mind. Mr. Morse is certainly if I can judge, considerable of a character. We all accept the prospect as one sent from Heaven, and there is every ground for faith that it will so prove.[40]

It was, James said, the undoing of "that wretched coil." Whatever had happened to Lucy, James was going to be her salvation. Abby Gibbons, too, was pleased with James Morse. He was manly, she thought, a leader, and might be taken for Lucy's brother. "If we cannot right all wrongs we can see that she will be gently led into better influences."[41]

James Morse and Lucy Gibbons were married on May 12, 1870, but there was a hitch. Lucy insisted that Rose Wagner attend the wedding, and James Morse backed her up in this. Abby Gibbons was angry, and thereafter relations between the Gibbonses and the Morses were frosty. By June, Abby Gibbons wrote of passing James Morse on the street and only managing civilities.[42]

Shortly thereafter, Lucy wrote to James and Abby Gibbons that she and James Morse were going to Newport, Rhode Island, for a month and then to Hubbardstown, Massachusetts, which was James's home town, and that Rose Wagner was to accompany them. She would like to come by and say goodbye in person, but could not do so while Abby felt so unfriendly toward Rose. Abby Gibbons responded angrily in a letter to Sarah.

> My first impulse was to say you are a couple of children. Stop disciplining the old folks, and practice a little self-discipline and decent control—but after weighing it, decided not to put any-thing on paper, but submit quietly—Julia boiled over and the re-sult was words, not tears, and I was thankful. I must say I was disappointed to find Mr. Morse yet a child.[43]

Abby Gibbons did not relent, and Lucy and James left town without saying goodbye. Abby felt deeply betrayed and regarded Lucy's defection as one of the tragedies of what seemed to her as her own tragic life story.

"I know of no other case on record, or in memory, when the sweetness and beauty of the early years became wormwood and gall, and given us to drink deep through the instrumentality of a shepherd who brutally poisons the lambs of his fold . . . I find myself wondering why a child was not afraid to turn her back without a parting word," Abby wrote to Sarah. Thereafter there was no further communication between the Gibbonses and the Morses for more than a year. Sometime early in 1871, Abby Gibbons heard through Jenny Bigelow that Lucy was pregnant. Her first grandchild, Rose Morse, was born on July 4, with Rose Wagner attending Lucy.[44]

The fact that the baby was named Rose was a bitter blow to Abby Gibbons, but the thought of the baby herself was irresistible. In a few months Abby sent some little shirts for her granddaughter, and Lucy wrote her a prim thank you note. This was the beginning of a reconciliation. By the time the baby was two she was visiting her grandmother and Abby's letters were full of anecdotes about her. "She was holding her doll, when she looked up as roguishly as possible and said: 'Aunty Dule, you're a waxel,' meaning rascal. She was wild with fun and frolic, and so pretty."[45]

Abby Gibbons never called the little girl Rose, preferring Bonnie, and the rest of the family adopted that nickname. In short order, Bonnie became the apple of her grandmother's eye. Abby, who was seventy when Bonnie was born, had not expected grandchildren at all. Now, in rather short order, Lucy presented her with three. A little boy, James Herbert, was born in 1875 and William Gibbons in 1877. Thereafter much of Abby's life was wrapped around these children and visits to the Morse family. Lucy was loving and dutiful to her mother, but she had broken the chains of her childhood, and was never again as fully under her mother's influence as she had once been.

10

An Advocate for Women

After years of skimping, the Gibbonses were now moderately affluent. James Gibbons had continued to rise in the banking world and, in addition, had branched out into financing railroads. In 1870 he was involved in the building of the Delaware Railroad, and in 1871 he became its president. "That project ought to yield him houses & lands, coach & four and every luxury life can afford for surely industry and strength have been given to it without stint," Abby Gibbons commented. Once the railroad's success was assured, she decided that it was time that the family aspire to a "high stoop house." They had finally left Lamartine Place in 1868 and were living in a rented house on West 33rd Street. In 1871 they moved to 111 West 44th Street, where they remained for nine years.[1]

One room of the new house was set aside as a schoolroom, where Julia Gibbons prepared young women to take the examination for entrance into the Radcliffe Annex of Harvard and other colleges. The Gibbons School, which continued for some years, was the first institution in New York to prepare young women for higher education. James Morse also ran a small private school from his home, so the entire family were now taken up with teaching.

This was fitting, for Abby Gibbons continued to see herself primarily as an educator. Although she did not herself return to the classroom, she felt it her duty to educate the public about the needs of the poor, the prisoner, the "fallen woman," and the newly freed slave. In an age that believed fervently in progress, she was sure that when enough men and women understood the facts, they would share of their bounty and correct the many social ills she saw on every hand.

Settled at last and freed of financial anxiety, Abby Gibbons entered into a period of creativity in the field of benevolence, focusing on the

Abby Gibbons in her study. Courtesy of Friends Historical Library, Swarthmore College.

development and support of institutions to meet the needs of those she thought of as less fortunate. She was one of a number of pioneers who developed social institutions prior to the development of professional social work at the end of the century. Although amateurs, these women often sought the help of professionals in developing their services. They particularly turned to the women doctors now being graduated from newly developed medical schools. Abby Gibbons was an active supporter of the Women's Medical College of the New York Infirmary for Women and Children and often secured doctors associated with this institution to work with women prisoners.

Abby Gibbons's divided feelings about the role of women is illustrated by her contact with the women doctors. While proud of her own status as wife and mother and eager to teach domestic skills to the inmates of the Isaac Hopper Home, she was also eager that women prove themselves in the professions. Having met Dr. Mary Putnam, an outstanding pioneer doctor, through the Medical College, she was alarmed when Putnam married Dr. Abraham Jacobi in the summer of 1873. "He is called tyrannical and it is said will assert himself. So all Miss Putnam's years of study and gathered knowledge is in a measure set at naught," she lamented. Fortunately, her predictions did not come true, and Dr. Mary Jacobi continued to practice medicine for many years.[2]

In 1871 Abby Gibbons was among the founding members of the New York Infant Asylum, a home on 61st Street for unwed mothers and orphans. There was such a facility run by the Catholics at 51st and Lexington, but Gibbons and her friends believed there was need of a second asylum primarily devoted to Protestants. Overseen by a woman doctor, Dr. Anna Angel, the Asylum stressed preventive health care and emphasized outdoor recreation and good diet. Abby Gibbons became president of its house committee in 1873 and remained in that post for some years. During her first year in office, she insisted that it accept its first African American infant (although one board member said she hoped they would never sink so low as that) and after several tries she found a wet nurse willing to care for a black baby. She described her visits to the Asylum as one of her "delights," taking great joy in the way she was greeted by the small children whom she called her "runabouts."[3]

Connected with the Asylum was a reception center at Clinton Street and a country home in Mt. Vernon. Here the unwed mothers stayed until ready for delivery. At the Asylum itself, the mothers lived with their infants while arrangements were made for them to be placed in situations or returned to their families. In a number of cases, the Asylum staff and board members influenced the woman to be in touch with the father of her child and persuade him to marry her. Rarely was the mother encouraged to leave the child, although one of the Asylum's benefactors, Olivia Sage, complained that one young woman had deserted an infant and returned the next year, pregnant again.[4]

For Abby Gibbons, the Asylum presented very similar problems to the Isaac T. Hopper Home, and she was once more busy trying to find jobs as domestics for the mothers, in homes where the family was willing to accept an infant. She was also constantly hearing the same horror stories about the abuse of women which she heard at the Home. One family took a teenager as an adopted daughter, and when the wife of the family was away, the husband raped the girl, who returned to the Asylum, pregnant. "These cases are common," Abby Gibbons observed bitterly.[5]

To finance the Asylum, the board members turned to having a fancy ball every January. To Abby Gibbons's Quaker views, the concept of raising money for charity through dancing was distasteful, but her practical side realized it was useful. "The ball is over for the Infant Asylum and nets $11,000 and over. So much for diamonds and empty heads," she wrote Sarah. "Well, it is all right, if there is not mind to work they must dance to the fiddle and keep going from year to year." The next year she reported, somewhat ruefully, that the Asylum Ball had been named the leading ball of the season.[6]

Despite her protestations, Abby Gibbons's views on class were shifting somewhat due to her own affluence and that of many of the men and women with whom she associated. "There will always be the rich and the poor," she wrote "and how liberally the former dispense to the latter!" But she was also attracted to the ideas of Christian socialism as advocated by Charles Fourier and continued to insist that she put her faith in *the people*.[7]

Yet in addition to private charity, she believed that the state must play a role in supporting services to the poor. She visited both city hall and Albany regularly to lobby for the Infant Asylum, as well as for other institutions in which she was involved.

In 1873 Abby Gibbons added a new charity to her list of concerns: the New York Diet Kitchen Association. The idea, born of her Civil War experience, was to provide poor invalids with simple, nourishing meals—beef tea, rice pudding, eggnogs, and the like—on the orders of a physician. The establishment of the first such kitchen in the summer of 1873 was an immediate success. "The Diet Kitchen is an immense comfort to the poor and grows in favor as it becomes known. We rejoice in the fact that no article has been unsupplied," Abby wrote to Julia. Made president of the association, she immediately set out raising money for it. Despite the financial panic of 1873, she found that it was not hard to get contributions by approaching wealthy individuals. Many doctors were interested in the idea and the possibility of duplicating it in other cities. When Gibbons went to Cambridge for her annual visit during Christmas week of 1873, she met an "army of young doctors because of our Diet Kitchen."[8]

Later the board undertook an annual Christmas fair to raise money for the association. Since Abby Gibbons was still making dolls and gathering toys for the Randall's Island orphans, the additional duties of the fair made Christmas a busy season for her, but as usual she rejoiced in having a lot to do. "I hope I shall not drag out a single day, after I cease from daily toil," she wrote her sister. "I shall hang on I know not how long but no mortal living shall stand in the way of my going my own gait day in and day out. Age and circumstance does not deprive me of a knowledge of myself and what I can do."[9]

The Diet Kitchen was a success. Starting with one kitchen in 1873, the charity expanded rapidly until there were four such kitchens functioning in the city of New York. Local hospitals were encouraged to donate a modest sum to the kitchen nearest them, in return for which their physicians were permitted to prescribe diets for indigent patients. As president, Abby Gibbons brought in many prominent women, including William Lloyd Garrison's only daughter, Fanny Garrison Villard, who became president in the twentieth century. She also lobbied successfully in Albany for the kitchens and in 1888 received a sizable bequest for the association.

But these new interests did not replace the Isaac T. Hopper Home in Abby Gibbons's heart. She continued to spend one day a week volunteering her services at the home. She arranged outings for the residents and looked for intelligent women to head the sewing department, or to serve as matron. She continued to find placements for her Home women, and occasionally to encourage women to return for a period when the world outside was too much for them.

The original house on 10th Avenue was woefully overcrowded. In 1874 Abby Gibbons decided the time had come for a new building. She brought her concern to the board of the Home on June 2nd, and was made chair of a committee to look for a new home and act upon her research. She had already spotted a likely house and lot and went to work to raise the additional needed funds. Writing to her friend Sarah Thayer she reported on her success:

[T]o make a long story short of never ceasing toil and trouble through June, I may tell thee that the 1st of July saw us in the new House, Deed executed, and *recorded*. We are rather proud as women, that all was carried forward by remembering the words of General Banks, when speaking of his course toward contrabands. He said his habit was "to *do* and not talk about it."[10]

The new location for the Isaac T. Hopper House, No. 110 Second Avenue, proved commodious, and the organization is still there today.

Conditions on Randall's Island had improved since Abby Gibbons had first begun her Christmas visits there, but not fast enough to satisfy her. "Conditions on the Island condemn the commissioner of gross neglect and inhumanity," she commented after her 1873 visit. "I shall try to do something with the heathen commissioners." Two weeks later she reported that she had written to each commissioner demanding that they change from "dead heads to living men." James told her that he feared she would offend, but instead she received a thoughtful letter of explanation and a request that she meet with an official to devise a plan for reforming some of the abuses she had identified. "And so my wits are active in behalf of a way to give home life to the poor neglected children."[11]

Abby Gibbons's suggestions had a good effect, for two years later she toured Randall's Island, accompanied by the mayor of the city, the commissioners, some reporters, and Louisa May Alcott, to see the many reforms. "We had plenty of everything and the occasion was more satisfactory than usual," Abby Gibbons wrote. Alcott described the trip in a letter to a friend:

> The fog did not daunt me, and I found Mrs. G. on the boat without any trouble. I lost my heart to the dear little lady in five minutes, for she gave the Mayor and the commissioner such a splendid lecture on pauperism and crime that the important gentlemen didn't have a leg to stand upon. I enjoyed it immensely, and the officials appeared no more.
>
> The poor children welcomed her like the sun; and we spent the time in giving out toys and sweeties to the orphans, idiots and babies. It was pathetic yet beautiful to see their happiness as the friend of thirty years came among them, so motherly and sweet; and I am sure a sort of halo surrounded the little black bonnet as she led us from room to room like a xmas good angel in a waterproof.[12]

Still further improvements to the facilities on Randall's Island were to follow at Abby Gibbons's urging. By the end of several decades, the place was transformed, with a large schoolhouse, a greenhouse, three workshops for the boys to learn crafts, a shop for the intellectually impaired to make rope mats, and one-story cottages in place of the three-story buildings Abby Gibbons had always objected to. These changes were widely regarded as the result of her never ceasing to lobby for these poorest of clients.[13]

Abby Gibbons's work with women prisoners had introduced her early to the situation of the fallen woman, or prostitute. Her father, Isaac, had always been especially concerned about the rehabilitation of prostitutes and had been involved, while still living in Philadelphia, with the establishment of the Magdellan Society, providing a home for young women who wished to be rehabilitated. From her father she had learned to believe that these women were almost always the victims of male seducers and of the organized business of vice. Her efforts to rescue young women from prostitution were constant, and her victories a source of pride. Her daughters remembered hearing her tell of meeting a fashionably dressed young woman, who confessed that she was the girl, dressed in boy's clothing, whom Abby Gibbons had discovered in the Tombs and had sent to the country. She had left the past behind and was now married to a banker. Another family story was that of a sixteen-year-old girl who was arrested for performing an illegal abortion on herself. Abby Gibbons had gone to Court, taken the girl under her wing, and placed her in a good home. Male friends who were accosted by youthful prostitutes on the street often sent them to Gibbons for referral.[14]

When she first started working in the prisons, Abby Gibbons discovered to her horror that the practice of prostitution sometimes went on behind prison walls. Many male wardens took advantage of their female prisoners, and sometimes male and female prisoners were allowed to mingle, for a price. There was little separation between first offenders and hardened criminals, and young girls imprisoned for minor theft were housed with seasoned prostitutes, who quickly taught them the trade.[15]

Along with many feminist reformers of the period, Abby Gibbons came to believe that prostitution could be stopped by a campaign to persuade the public of its immorality, and to expose the men involved. As cities began to experiment with laws licensing prostitutes in order to protect their patrons from venereal disease, these women argued that it was wrong to blame the victims. The fact that the women alone were examined, while men, just as likely to be carriers of venereal disease, were not, spoke eloquently to the double standard of the age. Allying themselves with the social purity movement, as it came to be called, they argued that the morality of the nation was being undermined by state law licensing prostitutes. They set themselves the task of serving as watchdogs to call the effort to pass such laws to public attention.

In St. Louis, Missouri, where such a law was tried for four years, from 1870 to 1874, Phoebe Couzzens and Virginia Minor, both suffragists trained in the law, fought a successful battle against regulation, with a host of male and female supporters. Through the National Woman Suffrage Association, Susan B. Anthony and Elizabeth Cady Stanton were early crusaders against state regulation of vice. Lydia Mott, an abolitionist and author, fought regulation in Albany, New York. There were other, scattered pioneer efforts.

In England a similar movement was taking shape under the leadership of a brilliant woman, Josephine Butler, who developed a large network of women interested in women's rights and reform and involved them in her campaign against state regulation of vice. An admirer of William Lloyd Garrison and the antislavery campaigners, she called members of her movement the "new abolitionists." After a successful campaign at home, she began to organize similar groups in Europe and finally to establish an International Federation for the Abolition of State Regulation of Vice.

Abby Gibbons's colleagues in prison reform, Antoinette Blackwell Brown, Elizabeth Blackwell, Emily Blackwell, and Aaron Powell, the former abolitionist turned journalist, heard about Butler's organization and wrote to headquarters in Great Britain asking how they might affiliate. In response they were told that two representatives, Henry J. Wilson and the Reverend J. P. Gledstone, were on their way to New York to confer. Abby Gibbons agreed to call a temporary committee to meet with the gentlemen and discuss the issue.

The meeting occurred in the parlors of the New York Infirmary in the early summer of 1876. Present at the meeting, in addition to Abby Gibbons, were Dr. Emily Blackwell, Elizabeth Gay, Aaron and Anna Powell, Cornelia and William Hussey, and Dr. Anna Lukens, all old friends and most of them former abolitionists. They named their temporary committee The New York Committee for the Suppression of the State Regulation of Vice, agreed to meet in a month at the Isaac Hopper Home, and elected Abby Gibbons president.[16]

The new group was almost immediately involved in an attempt to defeat a bill in Albany to legalize prostitution. Abby Gibbons, by now a seasoned lobbyist, hurried off to see her friends in the state capitol. She and her colleagues were able to defeat the legislation, but it was a long and difficult battle. "The advocates of State Regulation are more numerous and vile than we supposed," she wrote to Aaron Powell.[17]

The committee proved far from temporary and Abby Gibbons continued to act as its president for seventeen years. The move for licensing prostitutes was supported by many medical societies as a means of controlling the spread of disease, and the issue therefore became joined with that of the growing movement toward city, state, and national boards of health. The social purity forces thus found themselves fighting an essential progressive movement, public responsibility for public health, in an effort to oppose the injustice and the double standard of state regulation of prostitution.

In this prolonged battle, members of the social purity movement used the press extensively and circulated pamphlets written by members. "Legal Protection for Young Girls" by Aaron M. Powell, "The State and Girlhood" by Dr. Emily Blackwell," and "Social Purity, the Latest and Greatest Crusade" by Frances E. Willard, president of the Woman's Christian Temperance Union, were among the many titles. Movement members addressed letters especially to the editors of medical journals, and they enlisted the cooperation of such groups as Sorosis, the pioneer New York women's club of which Abby Gibbons's great friend, author Alice Cary, had been the first president.

Abby Gibbons spoke at Sorosis and sent pamphlets to local pastors. In January 1878, when her old friend William Lloyd Garrison was in New York to celebrate the twelfth anniversary of the marriage of his daughter Fannie to journalist/industrialist Henry Villard, she persuaded him to attend an evening affair on the Contagious Diseases Acts at the Isaac T. Hopper Home.[18]

In arguing against state regulation of prostitution, Abby Gibbons and her colleagues in the social purity campaign constantly made the point that women were penalized for the practice of prostitution, while men walked away scot free. In a memorial to the State Assembly in Albany in 1878, the New York Committee asked the legislators to so "amend the laws of the state relating to street walking, excitation to debauchery, and to disorderly houses to make them apply equally to prostitute men as to women."[19]

Abby Gibbons lobbied extensively in Albany against regulation legislation, while Aaron Powell served as watchdog for the New York City Council. The New York City committee also kept its eye on the national scene. When Congress created a national board of health in 1878, members of the social purity movement feared that one aspect of this body's function would be to regulate prostitution.

This put Abby Gibbons and her colleagues in conflict with the American Public Health Association, which believed that a system of regulation, such as that used in Europe, was necessary to stop the spread of venereal disease. Gibbons undertook a spirited correspondence with Dr. Albert Gihon, Medical Director of the U.S. Naval Hospital in Virginia and president of the APHA. At first Dr. Gihon took her to be a man, addressed her as "sir," and asked her to consider the effect of lack of regulation on "your wife." Abby Gibbons straightened out this misunderstanding, but wrote in a heated fashion of "your system of slavery" and its effect on the morality of both slave owners and slave women. Eventually, however, the correspondence became more friendly, Dr. Gihon soliciting Gibbons's ideas of how else to halt the spread of disease. Her response to this letter has not survived, but it is clear that she believed that a campaign for social purity for both men and women was the answer.[20]

Neither side of the social purity campaign converted the other, and in 1882 Congress considered expanding the powers the National Board of Health. Abby Gibbons, aged eighty-one, went to Washington with the backing of the Moral Education Society to lobby against this move and to present the petition of the New York Society. Petitions were also received from other states, and the bill was defeated.[21]

Again, in 1886, when the New York Senate and Assembly were considering a Contagious Diseases Act, Abby Gibbons took the lead in a campaign to defeat the proposal. In a petition to both houses she marshalled all the arguments against the regulation of prostitution and summed up with an eloquent plea for an end to a moral double standard:

The diseases incident to social vice are indeed greatly to be deplored, but they can be permanently lessened only by the promotion of social purity on the part of both men and women. There is no intimation in the bill in question of a purpose on the part of the corporators to do anything to lessen prostitution itself, the source of the devastating disease. No provision is made to discourage, or prevent, the return to a life of debauchery of those whom this corporate board might, with the aid of the police force of New York, placed by the bill at their service, consign to compulsory hospital treatment, at the expense of the taxpaying public. We respectfully submit that it is not part of the proper function of the legislature of the State of New York to authorize medical and police surveillance of the houses of debauchery, in effect, to prepare their inmates for the service of vice and sensuality. Against such ill-judged, immoral legislation, in behalf of the philanthropic Christian manhood and womanhood of the State, we do most earnestly protest.[22]

The energetic campaign of Abby Gibbons and Aaron Powell in New York gave national leadership to the moral purity movement after 1877, and Abby Gibbons's pioneering was recognized at the International Council of Women, meeting in Washington in 1888.[23]

It has been pointed out that the crusaders of the social purity movement, while arguing against the sexual double standard that penalized women and allowed their patrons and abusers to go scot free, actually applied a double standard of their own when it came to treatment. Previously prostitutes and women alcoholics were kept in a prison for a short time, then set free. Abby Gibbons and her colleagues were now arguing that they ought to be sent to a women's reformatory such as the ones established by Rhoda Coffin in Indiana, and by Hannah Chickering in Sherborn, Massachusetts, where they could be educated to a new way of life. These reformatories had been advances over the jails of the period, but the staff treated their inmates as tractable children to be trained and urged indefinite sentences in which this training could take place. Thus, prostitutes arrested and sent to reformatories would actually be deprived of their liberty more harshly than men picked up on any comparable charge. At the time, however, Abby Gibbons and her colleagues never questioned that their efforts were bent entirely to help their fallen sisters.[24]

Abby Gibbons's belief that women should supervise less fortunate women led to her advocacy of the appointment of women to state regulatory boards, a new development in the 1870s. In 1871 her former colleague on the Sanitary Commission, Louisa Lee Schuyler, had organized a State Charities Aid Association to investigate public charitable institutions and had drawn a number of former comrades into the organization. One of these was Josephine Shaw Lowell, who investigated conditions in the jail and almshouse on Staten Island and wrote a blistering report. As a result she was asked to conduct a statewide investigation of the condition of paupers. New York Governor Samuel Tilden was so impressed with her report that he appointed Lowell to the New York State Board of Charities in 1876, the first woman to hold such an office.[25]

Abby Gibbons exulted. "All honor to our Governor, that he has given a woman a place among men! He shall have my vote now and always," she wrote to John Bigelow. In 1882 she backed a bill that required the governor of New York to appoint two or three women to boards of institutions having custody over females and/or children. Supported by several state assemblymen and senators, she sent letters to all relevant committee members, urging that women's domestic talents would create savings in the running of these institutions. Women were already serving on school boards, she pointed out.

Friends in Albany told her that the governor was wavering, fearing that he would not be able to find qualified women, and she decided to address an appeal to him directly:

> A Friend by birth and education, my path in life has been of a character so practical as to leave no doubt as to the feasibility of selecting women of known capacity and sound common sense. In the sect or out of it we claim no superiority on any ground nor do we confine our experience to a limited class. Largely associated with both men and women in charitable work, I have seen the advantage of cooperation and have noted progress in the internal management of the affairs of institutions. This is conceded by our best men who are glad to have women share the responsibilities and active service for which they are especially fitted. And after all, why should it be more difficult to find women than men?[26]

Despite this reasoned appeal, the governor vetoed the bill five days later, saying he still feared that it would be hard to find qualified women willing to accept duties of this sort and that vacancies on the boards would be harmful. Nothing daunted, Abby Gibbons arranged for the bill to be resubmitted the next year and produced testimony from the Massachusetts Board of Health, Lunacy and Charity telling of the improvement in diet at the lunatic asylums following the addition of women to the board. This time the bill passed and was signed by the governor.[27]

In the same vein, in the city of New York, Abby Gibbons and her colleagues persuaded the mayor and council to appoint two women, Grace Hoadley Dodge and Mary Nash Agnew, to the New York City Board of Education in 1886 and lobbied for their reappointment in 1889. "Having a personal knowledge of their way of work, which in many directions, women comprehend as men never can, I do not hesitate to urge, in strong terms, their reappointment," Abby Gibbons wrote the mayor, requesting an interview. When Gibbons was too sick to go to City Hall for the resulting appointment, Mayor Hugh Grant came to her house. She told him she felt sure that women should serve on the school boards, where so many of their sex were represented, and that the opposition came from ignorant and prejudiced minds. "I am glad to lend you the experience of my many years, and believe thoroughly that you will live to take pride in your work," she told him matter-of-factly.[28]

When Mayor Grant reappointed only one of the women, Mary Nash Agnew, Abby Gibbons was disappointed, but congratulated his honor on appointing a married woman.[29]

In 1882 the Women's Prison Association began work on a bill that would make police matrons mandatory. Abby Gibbons first circulated a proposed bill to members of the board of the Isaac T. Hopper Home urging them all to get behind it:

> Why, the very fact that there are no women is sufficient to create a rebellion, and is an insult to the poor wretches who would be wrought upon by the presence and voice of a decent woman. I have seen with my own eyes, and have heard with my own ears, what they are subjected to; and I know of a truth, there are abuses and outrages in all these prisons, that should not be permitted.[30]

Early in 1883 Abby Gibbons began to circulate her bill among lawmakers in Albany. One whom she approached was Theodore Roosevelt. He wrote that he sympathized with the bill, would support it, and work for its passage, but was too busy himself to serve as its sponsor.[31]

Others were less supportive. The police commissioners themselves did not welcome the idea, and there was a problem about the funds to hire the additional women. Abby Gibbons decided that trips to visit the police commissioners were not productive but kept up her lobbying of the New York legislators.

In 1886 Josephine Shaw Lowell joined the struggle. She commissioned Dr. Annie S. Daniel, the attending physician at the Isaac T. Hopper Home, to do a thorough study of the condition of women prisoners in the police stations and prisons of New York. Daniel's explosive report, printed with the proceedings of the Women's Prison Association for 1887, helped to alert the public to the problem. A number of other women now joined the struggle, and in 1888 a bill was passed by the New York State Assembly and the Senate, specifying that women prisoners could be examined only by women.[32]

"Thank you very much for your kind thought of me," Josephine Lowell wrote Abby Gibbons in June 1888. "The passage of that law is a great step gained in the struggle to save degraded women; and I am sure everyone interested ought to be very grateful to you and Dr. Daniel."[33]

The governor, however, vetoed the measure, and it had to be introduced all over again. Not until 1890 was a bill passed, and then to Abby Gibbons's horror she discovered it had not been made mandatory. Another nine months of lobbying was needed before this error was corrected. Despite the length of the struggle Gibbons remained full of good cheer:

> The Police Matrons' Bill is made mandatory, and the committee gives them three months to put it in practice. I have quite a number of applications, with good recommendations; and seem to have friendly relations with the police Board.[34]

Her constant lobbying deepened Abby Gibbons's always keen interest in politics. She had had some personal experience in the political arena in 1870 when Horace Greeley had lived in her house on West 33rd Street, while running for the U.S. Congress, and she had had to fend off political hangers-on from his sick bed. In 1872 Greeley was picked by the liberal Republicans to run for President and also endorsed by the Democrats. The regular Republicans ran Ulysses S. Grant, whom Greeley had supported in 1868, but who was now suspected of scandal. Greeley had tea with the Gibbonses on October 1, and Abby Gibbons had fun teasing him about his Democratic backers and about Grant's fall from grace. Despite the scandals, Grant won and Greeley was defeated. He had done well as a candidate, but had had to leave the campaign trail in September to sit by the bedside of his sick wife. She died a week before the election. Greeley seemed to accept both her death and his defeat, and the day after the election resumed his post as editor of the *Tribune*, but six days later he fell ill again of his recurring fever and died on November 29.[35]

Disgusted with the scandals which marred Grant's second term, Abby Gibbons switched her allegiance in 1876 to Samuel Tilden, whom she had known and lobbied as governor of New York. She was deeply disappointed when he lost the disputed election of March 1877. "Mr. Tilden made a good Governor. He had strength and fitness, and if I am right, with very little knowledge of his character, *he* would have been up and doing, and the world would begin to move. Many are disappointed, and they deserve to be." She had no illusions about Rutherford B. Hayes and was not surprised when he pulled the federal troops out of the South, thus ending the era of Reconstruction.[36]

Her disappointment grew during the four years of Hayes's presidency, as the spoils system seemed to be in control of politics. She was particularly vehement about Senator Roscoe Conkling, who controlled the political machine in New York, and agreed with James when he called Conkling "the personification of the spoils system." When Conkling, who led the "Stalwarts" in the Republican party, supported Grant for the presidential nomination in 1880, she was disgusted and put her hopes in James G. Blaine, the leader of the "Half-Breeds" who brought forward a dark horse, James Garfield. The nomination of Chester Arthur as vice president to appease the Conkling forces made her angry, but she was nevertheless inclined to feel hopeful when Garfield was elected.[37]

Garfield lived up to her hopes by challenging the spoils system in New York State, naming as collector for the port of New York an independent, rather than the Conkling nominee. When Garfield was shot by an assassin on July 2, 1881, she was alarmed and indignant. "Every thought turns to Washington, and while I am in the habit of looking at the bright side, I am unable to feel hopeful. It is too dreadful, and Grant's seeming sympathy I turn from in indignation." She followed the news bulletins on Garfield's health anxiously. When it became clear that he was not going to recover from his wounds, she wrote a letter to Chester Arthur calling on him to resign, if Garfield died, and be elected, rather than taking the office under the cloud of an association in the public mind with Grant and Conkling. "I entreat you with the tenderness of a mother to obey the dictates of the public conscience, and trust to *your own* inward light to guide and guard you," she wrote.[38]

There is no record that Arthur replied to Abby Gibbons's letter. On September 19 Garfield died; the next day Arthur took the oath of office, ending the role of the "Half-Breeds" in U.S. government. Many felt Arthur was independent of the "Stalwart" influence during his presidency, but Abby Gibbons had little interest in him. She was, however, a firm Republican and in 1884 she supported James Blaine and was annoyed at some of her liberal friends who became "Mugwumps" and backed the Democratic nominee, Grover Cleveland.

Despite her interest in politics and in women's rights, Abby Gibbons continued to stay away from the issue of suffrage for women. Writing to a New York State official to urge the importance of appointing women, she made a disclaimer. "Do not understand by this that I am a *Woman Suffragist*. No verily I have never taken action upon that question, though, if men can give the vote to women while I live, I shall cast *mine*. I have not needed to up to this time, as I always *take* what I want."[39]

11

"A Reformatory, Pure and Simple"

Abby Gibbons celebrated her eightieth birthday on December 7, 1881 and received many letters and a sonnet, written by son-in-law James Morse, which began, "Her eighty winters leave an eye serene." In fact, throughout the 1880s, Abby seemed more at peace and more productive than at any other time in her life. While her husband James slowly became morose and eventually lost some of his mental ability, Abby Gibbons became increasingly optimistic and full of energy. As she often said, it was keeping busy that made the difference.

James Gibbons had retired from banking in 1872, although he continued to handle the stock of the Vermont Marble Works. He had long been interested in conservation and devoted himself to a national movement to save the forests, which resulted in the celebration of Arbor Day. He also continued to take careful observations of meteorological conditions five times a day and eventually gave his charts to the Smithsonian Institution. He spent a great deal of time on his papers, trying to reconstruct some of his memoirs lost when the house was sacked in 1863.

As his thoughts turned to the past, he became interested in researching the Gibbons family from which he had sprung. That family had been one of the first Quaker families to settle in Chester County, Pennsylvania. James was delighted when his daughter Sarah gave him a book in which one of his ancestors, Sarah Gibbons, a pioneer Quaker woman persecuted in the Massachusetts Bay Colony, was mentioned:

> Nothing has given me more content of mind with respect to my children than the fact that without any particular instruction ever having been given them on the subject they are nevertheless of sound Quaker opinion. The drawing of the woman getting

whipped at the cart tail may be a true picture of Sarah Gibbons, who was one of eight who arrived at Boston about 10th of August, 1656 and who was whipped from Salem to the other towns near. When brought before Endicott she remonstrated against the jailer's cruelty in keeping her and others without any food for 3 days, and he answered "it mattered him nothing." I have no doubt of our descent from those who came here by that name.[1]

At the urging of friends, James decided to take credit for the song "Three Hundred Thousand Strong," which he had written during the Civil War and had published anonymously, and which was taken to be the work of William Cullen Bryant. His son-in-law, James Morse, helped him clear up the question of authorship by researching an article that appeared in *Century Magazine* for August 1887, giving the story of his writing the song.

None of James's activities kept him wholly occupied, however, and he sank into old age more quickly than Abby, who was nine years older than he. He found life dull and was often anxious, especially when his daughters were travelling. Since the sacking of his house he had become increasingly conservative. He had very little use for the Irish, for the Catholic Church, or for the developing labor unions, and was given to outbursts of indignation. The assassination of James Garfield brought forth a diatribe against Nihilists, the Democratic Party, and the Romish Church. "We need a penal colony . . . only thing to establish moral terror in a large proportion of the immigrant class which now flock to this country."[2]

When Western Union workers went out on strike in the summer of 1883, Abby Gibbons said she saw the uses of such action. "I hope the rich may be made to pay the poor higher wages, though I think a man who is earning his daily bread had better *stick* and take what he can to let his family live." She felt she could not take as much interest as she ought, but wrote to Sarah that "it has given Father a new lease on life."[3]

One might speculate that the long years of being married to a woman as strong and independent as Abby Gibbons had gradually worn away James's self-esteem. Like many men of his era, he undoubtedly grew up expecting women to attend to the nurture of his ego. Abby, in fact, had always treated him with great respect, but her mere ability to be self-motivating and to develop a fame of her own may have been unsettling. His outburst against women's rights, written to Abby while he was travelling in Germany in 1869, showed how far he had moved from the day he supported the feminist/abolitionists of the antislavery movement.

Yet there were many peaceful, companionable days. "We both take our stout daily and have neither want nor care," Abby Gibbons wrote vacationing Sarah, "the house is quiet and neat."[4]

The quiet was threatened in 1880 when the Sixth Avenue elevated was extended to their area. Their house at 111 West 44th was just off the Avenue, and the noise and dirt of the train were dismaying. Finally, in 1880, they moved once more, to a house at 55 West 47th Street nearer Fifth Avenue, and here they ended their days.

More and more, as they grew older, the focus of their life became their three grandchildren. In 1879 James Morse bought a house and land in Cotuit, on Cape Cod. Abby Gibbons was at first appalled at the extravagance of the purchase and thought James Morse should spend more time in New York. In short order, however, she began to look forward to annual visits to Cotuit and to the house, which the Morses named "Bonnie Haven." Sarah, Julia, and James also vacationed at Cotuit. Lucy developed a studio in the barn and, despite her involvement in motherhood, managed to continue to practice her craft each summer. "Was ever a woman so rich at my time of life!" Abby Gibbons exclaimed. "Rich in children and all the blessings children bring!"[5]

To add to her sense of blessing, the New York Yearly Meeting in 1882 heard a proposition to reopen the question of the disownment of Isaac T. Hopper, James Gibbons, and Charles Marriott. Aaron Powell, Abby Gibbons's friend and colleague in the social purity campaign, spoke to the question, saying, "It was important to make the acknowledgment in order that history, when written, might show the better aspects of the transactions of the Society of Friends." Abby Gibbons was delighted and wrote to Powell asking for more information. "An honest admission of error entered upon the records will do much to make the close of life peaceful and happy."[6]

Unfortunately, the proposal came up at the end of Yearly Meeting and Friends decided to hold it over another year and think about it. The matter rested there, and to this day the minute remains on the books.

The center of Abby Gibbons's public life continued to be the Women's Prison Association. After twenty-two years of service, she became the "First Directress" in 1877 and remained so until her death. She wrote the annual reports, raised the money, and brought many of her friends and relations onto the board. Not only were Sarah and Lucy members, but she also involved her niece, Sarah Powell, and added relatives-in-law from the Mott family, including Martha Lord, Lucretia Mott's daughter, Naomi Davis, the wife of Mott's grandson, and Lucy Davis, his daughter.[7]

The Home had added a large laundry department when it moved to 110 Tenth Avenue, and the residents were able to earn money in laundry work while being further trained in laundry skills. Statistics of admissions and referrals were scrupulously kept, with about one-half of the women being sent from the Home to domestic positions. Some, however, returned. At one point the women debated what to do with a certain Annie, who had gone out to service and returned after a binge many times. The women decided to let her stay at the home working in the laundry but receiving no salary.[8]

The regimen at the Home was still puritan, but the board now tried to provide a few luxuries. There were picnics in the summer, for those who were regarded as trustworthy enough, and ice cream for everyone at Christmastime, as requested by one of Abby's grandchildren. There was also an entertainer, sent by Cornelius Vanderbilt, and concerts given by the Young Friends Temperance Society.[9]

In addition to running the Home, the women continued to visit and supervise the various city prisons. The Jefferson Market Prison, where they had once mounted a campaign for reform, was now a model prison they reported, with a matron night and day. The Tombs, where they had visited from the beginning, was beautifully clean, they claimed, and had a room for religious services. The Randall Street Jail in Brooklyn, on the other hand, was a nightmare, with many women crowded together in an inadequate space and a former inmate serving as matron. This woman was accused of selling for profit some garments that the women had made for their own use from materials supplied by the WPA, and Abby Gibbons was asked to be in touch with the president of the police commission to have this culprit replaced.[10]

Dr. Annie Daniel continued to work for the organization, making monthly reports on the condition of the prisons, workhouses, and police stations, and keeping records of the number of women prisoners admitted to prisons during the year. In 1890 she reported an abnormal increase in crime in the city and suggested the need of municipal lodging houses, so that prisons would not be used to house the homeless.[11]

Through the years, the members of the Women's Prison Association had maintained their interest in the movement to establish reformatories for women. They read the reports of Rhoda Coffin and Sarah Smith on the Women's Prison and Reformatory in Indianapolis and of Hannah Chickering at the Massachusetts Reformatory Prison established at

Sherburn, Massachusetts, in 1877. The fact that Dr. Eliza Mosher, a New York Quaker, became the resident physician at this institution and later (from 1880–1883) its superintendent, enhanced Abby Gibbons's interest.

Would it be possible for such an institution to be established in New York? Her friend and colleague, Josephine Shaw Lowell, continued to sit on the state Board of Charities and campaigned from that vantage point for a house of refuge for New York girls and women. Due to her efforts, the Albany legislature passed a bill establishing a "House of Refuge" in 1881, but not until 1887 was the institution built in Hudson, New York. Here for the first time women were housed in cottages, rather than a single prison edifice, and women were hired as staff at all levels. The institution was to be run on the "family plan," with emphasis on developing domestic traits.[12]

By 1889 the House of Refuge was full, and Lowell began pressing for two more such institutions, one in the western part of the state and one in the eastern. As result of her campaign, supported by the WPA, the legislature approved plans in 1890 for a Western House of Refuge in Albion, New York, also to be built on the cottage plan.[13]

Both of these institutions were located far away from centers of population. The legislators were reluctant to establish a reformatory in the east, near New York City. Abby Gibbons and the members of the WPA felt more strongly than ever that a reformatory was needed within commuting distance of the city, where the majority of the women prisoners lived. Using the Hudson House of Refuge as a model, Abby Gibbons persuaded her nephew, Wilson Powell, to draw up a bill for such an institution to serve New York City and its environs, and she presented it to the board of the Women's Prison Association in March 1889. With the approval of her board, she sent the bill to Hamilton Fish to present to the legislature and secured the support of other senators and members of the Assembly, asking for $100,000 for the new institution.[14]

Told by one assemblyman that she ought to enlist the support of some younger women in the cause, she sent her daughter, Lucy Morse, as well as Lucy Davis, off to Albany to lobby for the reformatory. "Pleading in public is a new thing for Lucy and she went with many misgivings," James Morse wrote in his journal. Lucy must have been persuasive, for the Assembly passed the legislation unanimously, and the Senate also approved it. Unfortunately, the governor vetoed it, just as he had done the police matrons' bill. Believing it would not be possible to obtain the new institution until a new governor was elected, the WPA devoted itself to public education on the issue for the next several years.[15]

Meanwhile, Abby Gibbons had domestic problems to attend to. In the summer of 1888, her middle daughter, Julia, now fifty-two, had fallen ill, and Abby had taken her to Mount Washington in New Hampshire to see if the bracing air would do her good. She looked "forlorn," but seemed to recover, and returned to New York for another year of teaching. Abby and Julia spent the next summer at Mount Washington again, and Julia was delighted to learn that four of her pupils had passed the Harvard exams. She once more seemed better, but in the fall she gradually lost ground, and Sarah Emerson took over the school. Early in December the doctor advised a change; since Julia was very weak, it was not possible to go any distance. Instead, Sarah went with her to Lakewood, New Jersey, and there, after several weeks, Julia began to fade. Abby Gibbons hurried to be with her for the last days, and the end came on December 28, 1889.

Julia had been the least independent of Abby Gibbons's daughters and in some way the closest to her heart. Abby thought Julia had the qualities Abby had so much admired in her own mother, Sarah Tatum Hopper, including eyes exactly the same. She had come to depend upon Julia in a thousand ways and felt her loss keenly. She was sick for ten days the following June, attributing her illness to the desolation she felt. "I am waiting for time, which alone can help me. In every relation of life, Julia was pure gold to me, and life can never be the same. It is simply a question of endurance."[16]

Abby Gibbons vacationed in the mountains again that summer but found it hard to pass the time without Julia. She decided to begin work on her memoirs, drawing together an account of her life from the letters she had saved, principally those of the Civil War days. She thought her grandchildren ought to know of the Civil War and the sufferings of both black and white. She asked her friend Sarah Thayer to look at her work and tell her if it was worthwhile, so she might be assured she was not wasting her time. But she was glad when the long summer was over and it was time to get back to what she regarded as real work again.[17]

By the spring of 1891, a new governor was in office and Abby Gibbons turned her energies once more to the creation of a women's reformatory. She began to pepper her friends in the Albany legislature with letters about the institution, and in February 1892 she made a final trip to Albany, accompanied by Martha Mott Lord and Ned Davis.

> We reached the "Kenmore" at 1.20, brushed up a trifle, and went direct to the Capitol, seating ourselves in the Ways and Means Committee Rooms. They came straggling in, gave us a cordial greeting, and I inquired if Chairman Bush was present.

He came forward and took a chair at my side. Of course, I took him by his *extended* hand and said" "Did you receive a letter from me yesterday?" and upon his saying "yes," I said: "You have been against my Bill and I am here to find you converted." Pleasant words were exchanged and instead of *calling me up*, they surrounded us, and in half an hour, the chairman said:

"The bill will have a unanimous vote and will be reported favorably this afternoon," We said and did what we thought was the proper thing, and retired. After I went to my room for the night, a letter was put under my door, which confirmed all he said. We all felt assured of success, as it has no opposition and goes to the Senate; it is said Governor Flower will approve.[18]

Abby Gibbons's optimism was premature. The bill had three separate readings in the Senate, but was hung up in committee. In April she fell ill with erysipelas and lay in bed, worrying about the legislation. Lucy went to see Louisa Lee Schuyler, who set the Charities Aid to work. Joseph Choate, who was often Abby Gibbons's advisor in her dealings with Albany, mobilized support. James Morse, Lucy's husband, wrote a letter to the *Times*, and was also in touch with the *Herald* and the *Tribune*. On the night of April 20, a telegram came for Abby Gibbons telling of the passage of the bill in the Senate and, an hour later, of its passage as amended in the Assembly. The family decided that Abby Gibbons was too ill to be awakened, but told her the next morning. She was elated and announced that she would now get well, so she would be prepared to deal with the implementation of the bill when it was finally signed by the governor.[19]

This happened on the seventeenth of May. "I took the announcement to mother, whose joy was great and deep," James Morse wrote in his journal.[20]

Abby Gibbons's joy was increased when she received a personal letter from the governor, asking for names for the board of managers. She suggested five qualified women and was shocked when only one of those she had named, Alice Sandford, was appointed.

At a meeting of the Women's Prison Association on June 7, the members expressed their indignation that the governor had appointed managers of the reformatory who had no association with their organization. "It is an unheard of thing that the Society which worked for the bill, formulated it, presented it and brought all the influences to bear on its passage should be ignored in this manner," the women complained.[21]

Abby Gibbons swallowed whatever disappointment she felt at not being appointed and wrote to Alice Sandford, who had once been a member of the WPA, congratulating her but complaining that "I do not know what these men will do." A few weeks later, having accepted the situation, she approached a local appointee, David Carvalho, a manager of the city of New York, asking him to call on her and began bombarding him with ideas. They should not consider an old building, but acquire land, where the prisoners could raise fruit, vegetables, and flowers.[22]

> A Reformatory pure and simple is my aim. The word *prison* pray keep in the background. Criminals are made by association and treatment. Let us turn over a new leaf and remember that they are human and, with tact and experience it is possible to "temper the wind to the shorn lamb," and soften the heart of the hardest.

She added that she hoped Carvalho did not think her too free to give counsel, but he would find her glad to receive it as well.[23]

Throughout the summer and fall she corresponded with Sanford and Carvalho, urging them to move on acquiring land for the reformatory. Finally, in December, the board of managers of the new institution took an option on land in Bedford, Westchester County, and agreed to hold a meeting at Abby Gibbons's home to make the final decision about the purchase. "At last! Let us be thankful and rejoice that the good time has come." she wrote. [24]

This sort of youthful enthusiasm on Abby Gibbons's part as she advanced in age was an inspiration to many people. During the long struggle to get the police matrons bill passed and the longer siege for the women's reformatory, she kept in good spirits and encouraged her fellow workers to think positively. As soon as the bills were passed, she was full of plans for their implementation. Few had ever seen a person of ninety so zestful for life.

Abby Gibbons herself regarded aging as a humorous trick time played upon people. She was delighted to have a call, early in 1892, from William Henry Furness, the abolitionist and Unitarian minister she had known all her life. She was in her bedroom at the time but insisted on going down the stairs to meet him.

"Is your hearing good?" the venerable minister asked her.

"Yes," Abby said.

"Then let us sit down and have a chat. I want to talk to someone older than myself. I am four months your junior."[25]

Her sense of humor seemed to come to the fore in her old age. She corresponded frequently with James B. Thayer, a professor who had once been a friend of Willie's. The two disagreed about politics, Thayer supporting Cleveland and the "Mugwumps," while Abby Gibbons urged him to vote for James G. Blaine. In 1888 when he again backed Cleveland and she Benjamin Harrison, she sent him a footstool she had decorated with needlepoint:

> There is time enough always to mend, James
> So a stool of repentance I send, James,
> And make it quite plain,
> Though it may be in vain,
> That there's room for amendment, my friend James.
>
> So put thy two feet on the "rest," James,
> And take a cigar of the best, James,
> And try to find grace
> In the next four years' race
> To vote the right ticket with zest, James.[26]

In 1892, when they were once more on opposite sides, Thayer supporting Cleveland, Abby wrote to James again, urging him to hold on to that stool of repentance—"at the end of the next four years, it will come into play."[27]

One problem of living a long time is that one outlives all one's contemporaries. In 1874 Abby's sister-in-law, Anna Hopper had died, and thereafter her brother, Edward Hopper was morose. Abby wrote to him frequently, inviting him to visit her in New York or at the various vacation spots she haunted. On December 18, 1885, her older sister, Sarah Palmer, with whom she had been close for a lifetime, slipped away. Abby had visited her and said goodbye a month earlier, and then she had cried, but at the news of the death itself she had no tears to shed "for a long life of severe trials and unspeakable pleasures. She had entered her ninetieth year four months before. I shall miss her letters and it seems lonely not to have her to write to in the perfect freedom we practiced towards each other." Two years later it was her quiet sister, Rachel Brown, whom she lost.[28]

Her husband, James, was meanwhile becoming more absentminded, anxious, and irascible. At one point Abby sent him away to spend a vacation, saying that strangers, rather than his family, could do him the most good. The last year was rather difficult, and when he died on October 17, 1892, friends and family spoke of a good and blessed release.[29]

Still, they had been married for almost sixty years, and not to have him by her side was like losing a part of herself. Abby Gibbons had been ill earlier in the fall, and she seemed to her anxious daughter Sally in rather delicate health to sustain this blow. But she was able to arrange for the funeral, to rejoice in the obituaries that appeared in the *New York Times*, the *New York Tribune*, and the *Philadelphia Evening Telegram*, and to respond to the letters of condolence that poured in. By November she seemed like her old self, writing to David Carvalho with advice about securing the property for the reformatory.[30]

She also wrote Alice Sandford, suggesting strategy to get the reformatory moving, and lamenting the inactivity of the men on the board.

> It is very hard for me to reconcile the delay in securing the land and having a *show* of a Reformatory, and I beg thee will tell me how thee feels about it. Womankind is accustomed to go ahead; but to move *man*kind up to the mark is beyond my control of language to set forth.[31]

At Christmastime, as usual, she gathered dolls for Randall's island, and packed a box, as usual, for Hampton Institute. Her colleague at the Infant Asylum, Dr. Anna Angell, had gone to Hampton to train nurses, and Abby Gibbons had done what she could to be of support, remembering the assistance of black nurses during the Civil War. Christmas was a little forlorn without James, but Lucy and James and their three children did everything possible to make it a happy time.

On January 3, she presided at a board meeting of the Isaac T. Hopper Home. She reported on the purchase of the land in Bedford Hills and her hope that the residents would work the ground, raising vegetables, and perhaps even flowers. Of the new institution she said, "It promises well, the managers having liberal ideas in regard to the matter. It is hoped much good will come of it."[32]

After the meeting there was time for a word with Alice Sandford. "Be sure, Alice that thee makes it a Reformatory and not a prison," she said.

On the way home from this meeting she caught a cold, which spread to her chest. She was to have chaired a meeting of the Diet Kitchen Association on January 11, but wrote to her old friend Florence Baker, asking her to take the chair in her place. "There will be little to do aside from reading the Report and accompanying papers by Mrs. White, and I am very sure of thee, and of all, going on full as well as if I were with you."[33]

Trying to get over the cold, which was turning into pneumonia, she stayed in her bedroom on January 11, but kept at her desk, finishing her correspondence and leaving all her affairs in order. On the fourteenth she felt ill enough to stay in bed and on the sixteenth she died, peacefully, asking toward the end if "Father," or James, was in the room.

Lucy and Sally accompanied their mother to her final resting place in Greenwood Cemetery, next to James and Willie and Julia and the two little boys the Gibbonses had earlier lost. Nearby was the grave of her father, Isaac T. Hopper. Her daughters had arranged for Abby's tombstone to bear the words she spoke at her father's memorial service, "She had finished her work and it was meet she should have rest."

There were lengthy obituaries in the *New York Tribune, The Boston Evening Transcript*, the *Philanthropist*, and the *Friends Intelligencer*. Her friend Sarah Thayer wrote a long piece in the *Charities Review* for May 1893. But more touching to her daughters were the letters that came pouring in from old friends, many of them former friends of Willie's who were now themselves approaching sixty. One of these was Robert Rantoul, recently elected mayor of Salem:

> But regrets are vain. Nobody taught better than your mother in her daily life and bearing the lesson of high courage. I should feel ashamed, in her presence, if anything had the sound of repining. We are to be up and doing, ready for what comes, rejoicing in the good, but cast down by nothing. This, it seems to me, is her legacy—this the lesson of a life too brave and noble for language.[34]

The Women's Prison Association's February meeting was devoted to mourning and honoring their lost leader. "Never expressive of religious sentiments, her life was full of religion in its best and highest sense. Never was a woman more reluctant than she to have her name appear in connection with her good works," one member said. Another added, "She had that most essential gift, knowing when to let go."[35]

The WPA also sought to honor her by urging that the new reformatory be named after her:

> No woman in this country has a stronger claim to respect and gratitude, and probably no one has carried on to such an advanced age works of reform and philanthropy. It seems fitting that the Woman's

Reformatory around which centered so much of her thought and effort during the last months of her life should be called, as has been suggested, by her name.[36]

The Reformatory was not opened until 1901, and it was then called "Bedford Hills." But it was modelled on the cottage plan, just as Abby Gibbons had hoped, and the cottage for inmates under twenty-one was called "Gibbons" in her honor. Abby would have been pleased by the appointment of Katherine Bement Davis, a social worker and penologist, as first superintendent of the new institution. Under Davis's thirteen-year administration, Bedford Hills became a model reformatory, "the most active penal experiment station in America,"according to one observer.[37]

Many years later, during World War II, the U.S. Navy commissioned a Liberty Ship, the *Abigail Hopper Gibbons*, in honor of her Civil War nursing and her founding of Bedford Reformatory.

As Abby Gibbons had once told her son Willie, every human being has her gifts. Hers was to find women in despair and restore them to dignity so that they could "enjoy of life's little flowers." In trying to exercise this gift she had come up against injustices, which she sought to remedy. She was an innovator, and the reforms she began lived on long after her day. At a time before the profession of social work had been born, she was one of a small group of women who stepped forward to meet perceived needs and to enlist the energies and the money of many people to meet those needs.

During a period of growing awareness of women's rights, she served as a role model to many women. The network of women reformers she built in New York around the issues of women in prison became a powerful force for women needing help in many areas of life. These Victorian women reformers made many mistakes in their approach to their less fortunate sisters. But they served as foremothers of later reformers who have maintained their feminist zeal and understood the problems better.

As one of the newspapers said of her at the time of her death, "When the story of her life is written, as it assuredly will be, it will be known that she had more than a man's courage, combined with more than a woman's tenderness. She was such an exceptional character that nature gives but few of them to any single generation."[38]

Notes

——

Introduction

1.   Sarah Hopper Emerson, *Life of Abby Hopper Gibbons Told Chiefly Through Her Correspondence* (New York: Putnam, 1897) [Hereafter, Emerson] II, p.180.

2.   See Barbara Berg, *The Remembered Gate: Origins of American Feminism: The Woman and the City, 1800–1860* (New York: Oxford University Press, 1978); Jill Conway, "Women Reformers and American Culture, 1870–1930," in *Our American Sisters: Women in American Life and Thought*, ed. Jean E. Friedman and William G. Shade (Boston: Allyn & Bacon, 1976); Nancy Hewitt, *Women's Activism and Social Change, Rochester, New York 1822–1872* (Ithaca: Cornell University Press, 1984).

3.   Lori Ginzberg, *Women and the Work of Benevolence: Morality, Politics, and Class in the Nineteenth Century United States* (New Haven: Yale University Press, 1990), p. 5.

4.   The most important source of information on the life of Abby Hopper Gibbons are the *Abby Hopper Gibbons Papers 1801–1893*, RG5/174, at the Friends Historical Library, Swarthmore College [Hereafter, Gibbons Papers]. In 1897 her daughter, Sarah Hopper Emerson, published a selection of her letters in *The Life of Abby Hopper Gibbons; Told Chiefly Through Her Correspondence* in two volumes. (New York: Putnam, 1897). While very useful, these volumes suffer from the fact that Emerson edited her mother's letters heavily and left out all sensitive material.

5.   Abby Gibbons to Sarah Emerson, July 8, 1865, Gibbons Papers.

6.   Emerson I, p. 256. Elizabeth Cady Stanton, Susan B. Anthony, Matilda Gage, *History of Woman Suffrage* (New York: Fowler, 1881), I, p. 688;

174 *Notes*

Abby Gibbons to Sally Emerson, July 7, 1868; Julia Gibbons to Sally July 9, 1868, Gibbons Papers.

7.   Abby Gibbons to Sarah Emerson, July 29, 1869, Emerson II, p. 157.

8.   Nicole Hahn Rafter, *Partial Justice: Women in State Prisons, 1800–1935,* (Boston: Northeastern University Press, 1985), p. xxii.

9.   Estelle B. Freedman, *Their Sisters Keepers: Women's Prison Reform in America, 1830–1930* (Ann Arbor: University of Michigan Press, 1981), pp. 162–168; Negley Teeters, *They Were in Prison* (Philadelphia: John Winston Company, 1937), p. 249; Minutes, Women Friends' Association for Visiting the Penitentiary, Baltimore Monthly Meeting, Baltimore Yearly Meeting, Quaker Collection, Haverford College, Haverford [Hereafter QC]; *Memoir of Elizabeth T. King, with Extracts from Her Letters and Journal* (Baltimore: Armstrong & Berry, 1859); Elma Holloway, "A History of the Howard Institution of Philadelphia," typescript, QC; C. (Catherine) Hare, *Life and Letters of Elizabeth Comstock* (London: Headley Brothers, 1895); Margaret Hope Bacon, *Valiant Friend; the Life of Lucretia Mott* (New York: Walker & Co. 1980), p. 127.

10.   Emily Manners, *Elizabeth Hooton: First Quaker Woman Preacher, 1600–1672* (London: Headley Brothers, 1914), pp. 14–15.

11.   See Jack D. Marietta; *The Reformation of American Quakerism, 1748–1783* (Philadelphia: University of Pennsylvania Press, 1984); Negley Teeters, *The Cradle of the Penitentiary: the Walnut Street Jail at Philadelphia 1773–1835* (Philadelphia: Pennsylvania Prison Society, 1955).

12.   Jack Marietta, "Egoism and Altruism in Quaker Abolition," *Quaker History* 82, 1 (Spring 1993): pp. 12–13.

13.   At Westtown Boarding School, founded in 1799, Greek and Latin were introduced for the boys in 1830; girls were not allowed to study Latin until 1855. Helen Hole, *Westtown Through the Years* (Westtown, Pa., 1942), pp. 165, 172.

14.   See Marilyn Dell Brady, "The Friendly Band: Quaker Women's Benevolence and the Poor in Late Eighteenth Century Philadelphia (Master's Thesis, Texas Christian University, 1978); John Cox, *Quakerism in the City of New York* (New York: 1930), pp. 176–177.

15.   June Rose, *Elizabeth Fry: A Biography* (London: Macmillan, 1980), pp. 81–122, 134–136.

16.   Rose, *Elizabeth Fry,* pp. 182–185; Bacon, *Valiant Friend,* pp. 94–95.

17.   *A Memorial of the Monthly Meeting of Friends of Philadelphia for the Western District: concerning Mary Wistar, deceased* (Philadelphia: J. Rakestraw, 1846).

18. Roberts Vaux to Mary Waln Wistar, n.d. Historical Society of Pennsylvania.

19. Teeters, *They Were in Prison,* pp. 249–266; Holloway, "History of Howard Institution," typescript, QC; Obituary notice, *Friends Review* 10 (1857): p. 569.

20. *Memoir of Elizabeth T. King, with Extracts From Her Letters and Journal* (Baltimore: Armstrong & Berry, 1859).

21. W. David Lewis, "Eliza Wood Farnham," in Edward and Janet James et al. *Notable American Women, 1607–1950,* 3 Vol. (Cambridge, Mass.: Belknap Press, 1971) [Hereafter *NAW*], I, pp. 598–600. Rhoda Coffin Johnson, ed., *Rhoda M. Coffin: her reminiscences, addresses, papers and ancestry* (New York: The Grafton Press, 1910), pp. 157–159, 263.

22. "Eliza Mosher," *Medical Woman's Journal* (May 1925).

23. See Elizabeth Chace Wyman, *Elizabeth Buffum Chace and Her Environment,* 2 Vols. (Boston: W. B. Clarke, 1914).

24. Mary Dewees,"Martha Falconer," in *NAW* I, pp. 594–596.

Chapter I. *Her Father's Daughter*

1. Emerson II, pp. 23–27.

2. See Lydia Maria Child, *Isaac Hopper: A True Life* (London, 1853) [hereafter, Child]; Margaret Hope Bacon, *Lamb's Warrior, the Life of Isaac Hopper* (New York: Thomas Y. Crowell, 1970); and Daniel E. Meaders, *Kidnappers in Philadelphia: Isaac Hopper's Tales of Oppression, 1780–1843* (New York: Garland Publishing, Inc. 1994).

3. *New York Tribune,* January 19, 1893.

4. Child, Preface, p. v. Margaret Morris Haviland, speech at the Friends Historical Association, May 1993, Newton Square Meeting, based on her Ph.D. dissertation, "In the World but not of the World: the Humanitarian Activities of Philadelphia Quakers 1790–1820," University of Pennsylvania, 1994.

5. Child, p. 31; Emerson I, p. 172.

6. Child, p. 27.

7. Ibid., pp. 15, 47.

8. Ibid., p. 383.

9. Ibid., p. 417.

10.   Minutes, Woodbury [New Jersey] Monthly Meeting of the Religious Society of Friends, August 11, September 15, September 18, October 13, 1795; Monthly Meeting of Friends of Philadelphia for the Southern District, December 23, 1795; microfilm, FHL.

11.   Minutes, June 28, 1796, Pennsylvania Abolition Society, housed at the Historical Society of Pennsylvania. [Hereafter, PAS]; minutes, Philadelphia Monthly Meeting for the Southern District, Jan. 23, 1799.

12.   Child, pp. 126–129; 139–145.

13.   Minutes, Acting Committee, Papers relating to slaves purchased and manumitted by M. C. Cope, Thomas Harrison, and Isaac Hopper 1787–1838. Papers concerning court actions brought by Thomas Harrison and Isaac T. Hopper against the slave schooners *Eliza* and *Sally*, 1803–1804; Case of Thomas Harrison and Issac T. Hopper v. the brig *Tyrphrena*, 1805. Reel 22 and 23, PAS.

14.   *The Diary of Elizabeth Drinker*, ed. Elaine Forman Crane (Boston: Northeastern University Press, 1991), III, p. 1644.

15.   Minutes, Guardian of the Poor, September 16, 1799 to September 18, 1803, Philadelphia City Archives.

16.   Minutes, Pennsylvania Prison Society, November 31, 1800; December 29, 1800; August 2, 1802; December 5, 1803, Historical Society of Pennsylvania.

17.   See Negley Teeters, *The Cradle of the Penitentiary* (Philadelphia: Temple University Press, 1955).

18.   Ibid.

19.   Child, pp. 237–241.

20.   Hopper Genealogical Chart, FHL, Emerson I, p. 12.

21.   Emerson I, p. 9.

22.   Child, p. 210; Haviland dissertation and speech.

23.   Minutes of Philadelphia Monthly Meeting for the Southern District, July 24, 1816. "Our friend Sarah Hopper having been at times engaged in public communication in our meeting for worship for a considerable time past, her situation obtained the consideration of the meeting, and it being believed that a gift of ministry has been disposed to her, the meeting unites in recommending her to the care and sympathy of the Quarterly meeting of ministry and elders"; Margaret Hope Bacon, *Mothers of Feminism: The Story of Quaker Women in America* (San Francisco: Harper & Row, 1986), pp. 139–144.

24.   Emerson I, p. 13.

25.   Walter Merrill, ed., *The Letters of William Lloyd Garrison* (Cambridge: Belknap Press, 1971–1981), V. VI, p. 567; Emerson I pp. 3–4.

26.   Emerson I, p. 5.

27.   Emerson I, p. 7.

28.   Emerson I, pp. 12–13; also, Isaac T. Hopper to Sarah Hopper at Weston, July 20, 1811. Sarah Hopper Palmer Papers (1705–1883), RG5/115. FHL The two accounts differ considerably.

29.   Ibid.

30.   Emerson I, pp. 19–20.

31.   Edwin Wolf 2nd, *Philadelphia: Portrait of an American City* (Philadelphia Library Company, 1990), pp. 123–141.

32.   Women's Minutes, Philadelphia Monthly Meeting for the Southern District, February 21, 1810; May 12, 1812; December 12, 1812; December 27, 1820, Microfilm, FHL. Sarah Hopper, "to dear my parents," October 7, 1811, Sarah Hopper Palmer papers, FHL.

33.   Abby Hopper to Sarah, September 21, 1810. Gibbons Papers;

34.   Abby Hopper to Sarah, July 1, 1811, Gibbons Papers.

35.   In regard to Elizabeth Hopper, see John Hopper to Abby Gibbons October 27, 1865, Gibbons Papers. Minutes, Pennsylvania Prison Society, 1804.

36.   Minutes, Philadelphia Monthly Meeting for the Southern District, August 28, 1811 and September 28, 1811, Microfilm, FHL; Minutes, General Meeting, 1800–1824, Reel 1, PAS.

37.   Minutes, Philadelphia Monthly Meeting for the Southern District, September 1811, and October 1811, Microfilm, FHL.

38.   Minutes, Philadelphia Monthly Meeting for the Southern District, November 1817, December 1820, December 1821, Microfilm, FHL; Bacon, *Valiant Friend*, pp. 34–35; Emerson I, p. 22.

39.   Ibid., p. 52.

40.   Emerson I, p. 8.

41.   Ibid., p. 23.

42.   Minutes, Philadelphia Monthly Meeting for the Southern District, January 12, 1816; February 23, 1820, Microfilm, FHL.

43.   Robert Wells, "Quaker Marriage Patterns in a Colonial Perspective," *William and Mary Quarterly* 2, 9 (1972): pp. 415–442.

44.   Emerson I, p. 9.

45.   Ibid.

46.   Child, pp. 294–295.

47.   Abby Gibbons to James Gibbons, September 23, 1869, Gibbons Papers.

48.   Emerson I, p. 41.

49.   Emerson I, p. 7.

50.   Lee Chamber-Schiller, *Liberty a Better Husband; Single Women in America, 1780–1840* (New Haven: Yale, 1978). Emerson I, p. 58.

Chapter II.   *The Abolitionist/Feminists*

1.   See Larry Ingle, *Quakers in Conflict: the Hicksite Reformation* (Knoxville; The University of Tennessee Press, 1986).

2.   See Bliss Forbush, *Elias Hicks, Quaker Liberal* (New York: Columbia University Press, 1956).

3.   See Ingle, *Quakers in Conflict.*

4.   Elias Hicks to Isaac T. Hopper, June 1, 1824, Elias Hicks manuscripts, FHL.

5.   Teeters, *They Were in Prison*, pp. 248–249.

6.   Ingle, *Quakers in Conflict*, pp. 196–201.

7.   Minutes, Philadelphia Monthly Meeting for the Southern District, February 28, 1827; May 23, 1827; July 25, 1827; August 29, 1827. FHL.

8.   Sarah Hopper Palmer to Abby Hopper, December 18, 1831, Gibbons Papers.

9.   Child, p. 296.

10.   Ibid.

11.   Abby Hopper to Isaac T. Hopper, November 7, 1829; Abby Hopper to Rachel Hopper, February 2, 1830, Emerson I, pp. 21–23, 25–26; Isaac Hopper to Abby Hopper April 30, 1830, Gibbons Papers.

12.   Chambers-Schiller, *Liberty: A Better Husband*, pp. 117–118.

13.   See John A. Kouwenhoven, *Columbia Historical Portrait of New York* (New York: Doubleday, 1953).

14. Gibbons Genealogical Papers, FHL.

15. Abby Hopper to Jonathan and Sarah Palmer and Sisters Susan and Elizabeth, September 8, 1830, Emerson I, p. 30.

16. Abby Hopper to William and Deborah Wharton, October 19, 1831, Gibbons Papers.

17. Mary B. Thomas to Abby Hopper, July 1, 1830, Emerson I, p. 27.

18. Abby Hopper to Sarah Palmer, Sept. 17, 1830, Gibbons Papers.

19. Isaac Hopper, *Defense of Isaac T. Hopper Against the Aspersions of Marcus T. C. Gould* (New York, 1831).

20. Dillwyn Parrish and Edward Hopper to Abby Hopper, Sept. 7, 1831, Gibbons Papers.

21. James Gibbons to Isaac Hopper, November 9, 1831, Emerson I, p. 53.

22. Isaac Hopper to James S. Gibbons, December 9, 1831; Sarah Palmer to Abby Hopper, Second day morning, 1831, Emerson I, pp. 54–59.

23. Abby Hopper to the Palmers et al., February 14, 1832, Emerson I. p. 59.

24. Emerson I, pp. 71–72.

25. Ibid. The wedding dress has been preserved and is at FHL.

26. Abby Gibbons to Samuel and Rachel Brown, November 6, 1833, Emerson I, p. 76.

27. James Gibbons to Abby Gibbons, November 11, 1833; July 10, 1836; Emerson I pp. 81–83, 86.

28. Isaac Hopper to "my dear daughter Abigail Hopper Gibbons," July 19, 1833, Gibbons Papers.

29. Carolyn Williams, "The Female Antislavery Movement: Fighting Against Racial Prejudice and Promoting Women's Rights in Antebellum America," in *The Abolitionist Sisterhood: Women's Political Culture in Antebellum America*, ed. Jean Fagan Yellin and John C. Van Horne (Ithaca: Cornell University Press, 1994).

30. New York City Anti-Slavery Society, Address of the New York City Anti-Slavery Society to the People of the City of New York. West & Trow, 1833, Library Company of Philadelphia; Minutes, Philadelphia Female Anti-Slavery Society, January 1838, PAS.

31. Abby Gibbons to "The Family at home," November 26, 1833, Emerson I, p. 76, Gibbons genealogical papers, FHL.

32.   Sarah Palmer to Rachel Brown, n. d. (circa January 23, 1834); Abby Gibbons to Rachel Brown, March 3, 1833 (misdated, should be 1834); Emerson I, pp. 78–79.

33.   Abby Gibbons to Rachel and Samuel Brown, April 1833 (should be 1834), Emerson I, p. 81.

34.   Linda K. Kerber, "Abolitionists and Amalgamators: The New York City Race Riots of 1834." *New York History* V. XLVIII, 1 (January 1967), Child, p. 315.

35.   Abby Gibbons to "My dear Brother," Nov. 28, 1834, Gibbons Papers, FHL; James Gibbons to Abby Gibbons, July 10, 1836; Abby Gibbons to Sarah Palmer, December 18, 1837, Emerson I, pp. 83–89.

36.   Child, pp. 319–320.

37.   Dorothy Sterling, ed., *Turning the World Upside Down: The Anti-Slavery Convention of American Women held in New York City May 9–12, 1837* (New York: Coalition of Publishers for Employment Inc., 1987); Dorothy Sterling, *Ahead of Her Time: Abby Kelley and the Politics of Antislavery* (New York: W. W. Norton, 1991), pp. 44–47.

38.   List of Founding Members, December 1833, Philadelphia Female Anti-Slavery Society, PAS. Sterling, *Ahead of Her Time* p. 46.

39.   *Turning the World Upside Down*, p. 12.

40.   Ibid., p. 13.

41.   Ibid., p. 7.

42.   *History of Pennsylvania Hall which was Destroyed by a Mob, May 17, 1838*, ed. Samuel Webb. Philadelphia, 1838. Joseph Sturge, *A Visit to the United States* (London: 1841), 45–47.

43.   *History of Pennsylvania Hall.*

44.   *Proceedings, Third Anti-Slavery Convention of American Women* (Philadelphia, 1839), p. 9; Sarah Palmer to Abby Gibbons, March 31, 1839, Gibbons Papers.

45.   Sarah Palmer to Abby Gibbons, n. d., Emerson I, p. 97; Lucretia Mott to Abby Kelley, March 18, 1839, Abby Kelley Foster Letters, American Antiquarian Society.

46.   Aileen Kraditor, *Means and Ends in American Abolitionism: Garrison and His Critics in Strategy and Tactics, 1834–1850* (New York: Vintage Books, 1967), p. 49.

47.   Amy Swerdlow, "Abolition's Conservative Sisters: The Ladies New York City Anti-Slavery Societies, 1834–1840," in *The Abolitionist Sisterhood*, pp. 31–44.

Chapter III. The Woman Question

1. Kraditor, *Means and Ends in American Abolitionism*, p. 69.

2. Edward Hopper to Abby Gibbons, May 19, 1840, Gibbons Papers.

3. William Lloyd Garrison to Helen Garrison, May 15, 1840, *Letters*.

4. Lydia Maria Child to E. R. Loring, February 28, 1842, *Selected Letters of Lydia Maria Child*, ed. Milton Meltzer and Frances Holland (Amherst, Mass. Massachusetts Press, 1982), p. 163; James Gibbons to my dear Abby, August 7, 1840, Gibbons Papers.

5. Abby Gibbons to Anne and Deborah Weston, March 23, 1841, Emerson I, p. 99.

6. See Lawrence Friedman, *Gregarious Saints: Self and Community in American Abolitionism, 1830–1870* (Cambridge: Belknap, 1982); Benjamin Quarles, *Black Abolitionists* (New York: Oxford University Press, 1969).

7. James Gibbons to Sarah Palmer, November 28, 1840, Emerson I, p. 97.

8. Emerson I, p. 246.

9. See Meaders, *Kidnappers in Philadelphia.*

10. Childs, *Life of Isaac Hopper*, p. 341.

11. Ibid.

12. "Tales of Oppression, XVI," *National Anti-Slavery Standard*, March 25, 1841.

13. Bacon, *Valiant Friend*, pp. 106–107.

14. Minutes, New York Association for the Relief of those held in Slavery and the Improvement of Free People of Color, Jan. 26, 1840, New York Yearly Meeting Records, (RG 4/51) FHL.

15. Isaac T. Hopper to Sarah H. Palmer, June 29, 1839, Isaac T. Hopper Papers, FHL.

16. "Sermon," preached by George F. White, 1838, Cherry Street Meeting Room," FHL.

17. Anna Davis Hallowell, *James and Lucretia Mott: Life and Letters* (Boston: Houghton Mifflin, 1896), pp. 206–207.

18. Edward Hopper to Abby Gibbons, May 19, 1840, Emerson I, pp. 95–96.

19.   "Rare Specimen of a Quaker Preacher," *National Anti-Slavery Standard*, March 25, 1841.

20.   Ibid.

21.   Margaret Hope Bacon, *Lamb's Warrior: The Life of Isaac T. Hopper* (New York: Thomas Y. Crowell, 1970), pp. 131–135.

22.   Sarah Palmer to Abby Gibbons, n. d. October, 1841. Emerson I, pp. 108–109.

23.   Abby Gibbons to Isaac Hopper, June 14, 1841; to Sarah Palmer August 16, 1841, Gibbons Papers.

24.   Abby Gibbons to the Monthly Meeting of New-York, June 1, 1842, Gibbons Papers.

25.   Abby Gibbons to Sarah Palmer, June, 1 1842, Gibbons Papers.

26.   Child, *Isaac Hopper*, p. 397.

27.   Lucretia Coffin Mott to Richard and Hannah Webb, February 25, 1842, Anti-Slavery Papers, Boston Public Library. (BPL)

28.   Thomas Drake, *Quakers and Slavery* (New Haven: Yale University Press, 1950), p. 158.

29.   Abby Gibbons to my Dear Daughter, March 24, 1865, Gibbons Papers.

30.   Isaac T. Hopper to Susan Hopper, November 26, 1844, Isaac T. Hopper Papers.

31.   Abigail Hopper Gibbons to Ellis Gray Loring, May 24, 1842, Anti-Slavery Papers.

32.   Lydia Maria Child to Maria Chapman, May 11, 1842; Child to Loring, Oct. 29, 1842, *Selected Letters*.

33.   Child, *Selected Letters*.

34.   Lydia Maria Child to Abby Hopper Gibbons, November 6, 1842, Gibbons Papers; Child to Ellis Loring, April 4, 1843, *Selected Letters*.

35.   Isaac Hopper to Susan Hopper, November 26, 1844, Gibbons Papers.

Chapter IV. Our Imprisoned Sisters

1.   Child, *Isaac T. Hopper*, pp. 427–428.

2.   Minutes, New York Prison Association, January 1845, New York Prison Association Records, Manuscripts and Archives Division, The New York Public Library (NYPL). Astor, Lenox, and Tilden Foundations.

3. Child, *Isaac Hopper*, p. 411.

4. Minutes, NYPA, January 1845 (NYPL).

5. Negley Teeters, *They Were in Prison*, pp. 249–257.

6. Freedman, p. 16.

7. Rafter, *Partial Justice*, p. xxv.

8. Teeters, *They Were in Prison*, p. 188.

9. Harriet Martineau, *Retrospect of Western Travel* (London: Saunders and Otley, 1838) I, pp. 124–125.

10. Marmaduck B. Sampson, *Rationale of Crime* (originally published 1845, reprinted 1973, Montclair, New Jersey,) "Introduction by W. David Lewis," pp. ix–xxiii.

11. Georgiana Bruce Kirby, *Years of Experience; an Autobiographical Narrative* (New York: Putnam, 1887, reproduced on microfilm Connecticut Research Publications, "History of Women" Reel 46, no. 3420), pp. 193,197, 199.

12. Dorothea Dix, *Remarks on Prisons and Prison Discipline in the United States* (originally printed 1845, Second edition Montclair, New Jersey: Patterson Smith, 1967), p. 107; Freedman, *Their Sisters Keepers*, p. 30.

13. W. David Lewis, "Eliza Wood Burnham Farnham," in *NAW* I, p. 600.

14. Caroline M. Kirkland, *The Helping Hand* (New York: Scribners, 1853), p. 40.

15. Ibid., pp. 32–33, 56.

16. Ibid., pp. 62–63; Emerson I, pp. 149–150.

17. James Gibbons to Caroline Weston, June 17, 1849, Emerson I, p. 150.

18. Kirkland, pp. 114–115.

19. Emerson I, p. 259.

20. Langley Carleton Keyes, "Caroline Matilda Stansbury Kirkland," in *NAW*, II, pp. 337–339.

21. Richard Welsh Jr., "Catharine Sedgwick," in *NAW* III, pp. 256–258.

22. Mary S. Benson, "Sarah Platt Haines Doremus," *NAW* I, pp. 500–501.

23. Elizabeth H. Thomson, "Elizabeth Blackwell" and "Emily Blackwell," *NAW* I, pp. 161–167; Emerson II, pp. 254, 328, 347; *Philadelphia Inquirer*, August 11, 1871.

24. Kirkland, *The Helping Hand,* p. 51.

25. Kirkland, p. 128; Women's Prison Association Annual Report, 1863–1864, pp. 7–8. (NYPL)

26. See for instance Jane Addams's books such as *Democracy and Social Ethics* (1902).

27. Rafter, *Partial Justice,* p. xxii.

28. Abby Gibbons to Sarah Gibbons, April 3, 1874, Gibbons Papers.

29. WPA Annual Report, 1863–1864, p. 7.

30. Twentieth Annual Report, WPA, 1865.

31. Abby Gibbons to Dear Daughter Sarah, May 3, 1856, Emerson I, p. 229.

32. Abby Gibbons to Willie, May 6, 1854, Emerson I, p. 187.

33. Abby Gibbons to Sarah Palmer, "12th mo. 1854," Gibbons Papers.

34. Abby Gibbons to Catharine Sedgwick, September 17, 1857, Emerson I, pp. 265–266.

35. Stanton, Anthony, and Gage, *The History of Woman Suffrage* I, p. 688.

36. Emerson I, pp. 134–136; Julia Gibbons to Willie Gibbons, May 7, 1850, Gibbons Papers.

37. Abby Gibbons to Willie, March 13, 1854, Emerson I, pp. 180–181.

38. Abby Gibbons to "Sally," May 3, 1856; Ferdinand Luis to Mrs. Gibbons, May 9, 1859; Emerson I, pp. 229, 275; Ginzberg, *Women and the Work of Benevolence,* p. 120.

39. Ginzberg, *Women and the Work of Benevolence,* p. 120.

40. First Annual Report Presented to the New York Anti-Slavery Society, May 12, 1854, by the Executive Committee, New York Anti-Slavery Office, 1854, Library Company of Philadelphia.

41. Walter Merrill, *The Letters of William Lloyd Garrison,* V. IV, p. 12; Stanton, Anthony, and Gage, *History of Woman Suffrage* III, pp. 557–558.

42. Abigail Hopper Gibbons to Reverend Samuel May Jr., May 26, 1858, Antislavery Papers. (BPL).

43. Ginzberg, *Women and Benevolence,* p. 120.

Chapter V. *"Losses and Crosses"*

1. Abby Gibbons to Susan Hopper, November 2, 1845, Emerson I, p. 131–132.

2. Abby Gibbons to Sally, September 22, 1879, Emerson II, p. 204.

3. Abby Gibbons to Sarah Palmer, May 26, 1847, Emerson I, p. 140.

4. Abby Gibbons to Willie, August 12, 1847; May 11, 1848; September 11, 1849; August 14, 1851, Emerson I, p. 142, 145, 151, 154.

5. Abby Gibbons to Willie, August 12, 1842, Emerson I, p. 141–142.

6. New York City Directories; Abby Gibbons to Sarah Palmer, May 22, 1851, Gibbons papers; William Lloyd Garrison to Helen Garrison, September 5, 1853, *Letters*.

7. See Kouwenhoven, *Columbia Historical Portrait of New York.*

8. Abby Gibbons to Sarah Palmer, May 22, 1851, Gibbons Papers.

9. James Gibbons to My dear Children, November 18, 1851; Abby Gibbons to my dear children, November 21, 1851; December 19, 1851; December 29, 1851; January 12, 1852, Gibbons Papers.

10. Child, p. 480.

11. Abby Gibbons to Sally and Julia, January 13, 1852; John D. Russ to Mrs. Gibbons, July 9, 1852, Emerson I, pp. 159, 164.

12. Abby Gibbons to Sarah Palmer, December 1852, Emerson I, 191, 193.

13. Miss Sedgwick to Mrs. Gibbons, September 29, 1853, Emerson I, p. 174.

14. Abby Gibbons to Julia, 1853, Emerson I, p. 172.

15. William Lloyd Garrison to the *Liberator*, Oct. 15, 1858; William Lloyd Garrison to Helen Garrison, Feb. 16, 1854, *Letters*.

16. Abby Gibbons to Willie, March 13, 1854, Emerson I, pp. 179–181.

17. Abby Gibbons to Willie, March 25, 1854, Emerson I, p. 185.

18. James Gibbons to Willie, May 17, 1855, Emerson I, pp. 195–196.

19. Abby Gibbons to "ever dear Will," December 11, 1855, Emerson I, p. 204.

20. Theodore Tebbets, *A Memoir of William Gibbons* (New York, 1856), pp. 85–86.

21.   Ibid., p. 88.

22.   Abby Gibbons to unknown, 1856, Gibbons Papers.

23.   James Gibbons to My dear Edward, March 18, 1856, Gibbons Papers.

24.   Abby Gibbons to my dear brother and sister, April 7, 1856, Gibbons Papers.

25.   Abby Gibbons to Dear Daughter Sarah, May 3, 1856, Gibbons Papers.

26.   *The Century* 3-24-1860, article on abolition of slavery and meteorological readings by J. S. Gibbons; April 28, 1860, J. S. Gibbons, publisher.

27.   Abby Gibbons to Julia and Lucy, August 24, 1854, Emerson I, pp. 271–272.

28.   Abby Gibbons to Edward Hopper, October 20, 1857, Gibbons Papers.

Chapter VI. *"The Calls of Humanity"*

1.   Quarles, *Black Abolitionists*, p. 201; Sterling, *Ahead of Her Time*, p. 281.

2.   Allan Nevins, *Ordeal of the Union: A House Dividing, 1852–1857* (New York: Charles Scribner's Sons, 1947), p. 431.

3.   Frank Preston Stearns, *The Life and Public Service of George Luther Stearns* (Philadelphia: Lippincott, 1907), p. 124.

4.   See Stearns biography.

5.   Rosa DeWolf Hopper to Abby, July 17, 1856, Gibbons Papers.

6.   Bacon, *Valiant Friend*, p. 185; Dorothy Sterling, *Ahead of Her Time*, p. 335.

7.   George L. Stearns to Mrs. Gibbons, May 18, 1857, Emerson I, pp. 261–263; Abby Gibbons to Aaron and Anna Powell, August 4, 1882, Emerson II, pp. 225–226.

8.   Ibid.

9.   Abby Gibbons to Miss Sedgwick, September 17, 1857, Emerson I, p. 265.

10.   Abby Gibbons to My dear Julia, May 17, 1857, Gibbons Papers.

11.   Lucy to Sally, then Abby to Sally, August 14, 1859, Gibbons Papers.

12.   Abby Gibbons to "My kind and ever dear Mary," April 5, 1858, Gibbons Papers.

13.   Bacon, *Valiant Friend*, p. 185.

14.   Bacon *Valiant Friend*, p. 181; Henrietta Jacquette, ed. *South After Gettysburg: The Story of a Civil War Nurse*; (New York: Thomas Y. Crowell, 1937); Hare, *Life and Letters of Elizabeth Comstock*; Johnson, *Rhoda M. Coffin*, p. 258.

15.   Sarah H. Palmer to Abby Gibbons, May 5, 1861, Emerson I, p. 292.

16.   Ginzberg, *Women of Benevolence*, pp. 140–141.

17.   Lucy McKim to Ellen Wright, October 1, 1862, Box 14, folder 370; McKim to Wright, May 27, 1864, Box 29, folder 802; Garrison Family Papers, Sophia Smith Collection, Smith College, Northampton, Massachusetts; Robert D. Cross, "Louisa Lee Schuyler," *NAW* III, p. 246; Robert H. Bremner, "Josephine Shaw Lowell," *NAW* II, p. 439.

18.   Ginzberg, *Women of Benevolence* p. 141; Robert Bremner, "Ellen Collins," *NAW* I, pp. 360–362.

19.   Abby Gibbons's "War Journal," Emerson I, pp. 296–299. Portions of this journal seem to have been put together by Abby Gibbons toward the end of her life from Gibbons family letters exchanged during the war, perhaps to expand the war diary Abby Gibbons wrote that she was keeping but which has subsequently disappeared. Large portions of the journal can be traced to specific letters among the Gibbons Papers.

20.   Ibid.

21.   "War Journal," Emerson I, p. 300.

22.   Abby Gibbons to My Dear Children, November 24, 1861, Gibbons Papers.

23.   "War Journal," Emerson I, p. 301.

24.   Linus Pierpont Brockett and Mary C. Vaughn, *Woman's Work in the Civil War* (Philadelphia: Zeigler, 1867), p. 470.

25.   See Elizabeth Brown Pryor, *Clara Barton: Professional Angel* (Philadelphia: University of Pennsylvania, 1987).

26.   See Helen Marshall, *Dorothea Dix: Forgotten Samaritan* (Chapel Hill: University of North Carolina, 1937).

27.   Abby Gibbons to My Dear Daughter Lucy, May 14, 1862, Gibbons Papers.

28.   Abby Gibbons to Family at Home, April 21, 1862, Gibbons Papers.

29.   John Hopper to Sarah Palmer, April 18, 1862, Gibbons Papers.

30.   Abby Gibbons to Julia Gibbons, April 9, 1862, Gibbons Papers.

31.   See Marshall, *Dorothea Dix: Forgotten Samaritan.*

32.   Abby Gibbons to my dear children, April 4, 1862, Gibbons Papers.

33.   Sarah to Home, April 6, 1862; Abby Gibbons to Julia, April 9, 1862; Abby Gibbons to John Hopper, April 27, 1862, Emerson I, pp. 318, 320, 326.

34.   Abby Gibbons to dear children, July 18, 1862, Gibbons Papers.

35.   Abby Gibbons to My dearest Lucy, April 27, 1862; Abby to my dearest brother, May 1, 1862, Gibbons Papers.

36.   James M. McPherson, *Battle Cry of Freedom; the Civil War Era* (Oxford University Press, 1988), p. 457; "War Journal," Emerson I, p. 332.

37.   "War Journal," Emerson I, p. 332.

38.   Abby Gibbons to Sally, June 13, 1865, Gibbons Papers.

39.   "War Journal," Emerson I, p. 332.

40.   *National Anti-Slavery Standard*, June 7, 1862; "War Journal," Emerson I, p. 335; McPherson,*Battle Cry of Freedom*, p. 457.

41.   "War Journal," Emerson I, pp. 333–336.

42.   "War Journal," Emerson I, p. 338.

Chapter VII.   *"Take the News to Mother"*

1.   Abby Gibbons to James Gibbons, July 13, 1862, Gibbons Papers; "War Journal," Emerson I, p. 339.

2.   "War Journal," Emerson I, p. 341.

3.   "War Journal," Emerson I, p. 342.

4.   Aunt Rosa to My darling Sally, July 21, 1862, Gibbons Papers.

5.   "War Journal," Emerson I, p. 340.

6.   "War Journal," Emerson I, p. 345.

7.   Sarah Gibbons to Dear Family, July 22, 1862, Gibbons Papers.

8.   "War Journal," Emerson I, p. 346.

9.   Ibid., p. 357.

10.   Sarah to Dear Family, July 22, 1862; also "War Journal," Emerson I, p. 352.

11.   Ibid.

12.   "War Journal," Emerson I, p. 353.

13.   "War Journal," Emerson I, p. 354.

14.   Ibid.

15.   Abby Gibbons to My dear J., August 6, 1862, Gibbons Papers.

16.   "War Journal," Emerson I, pp. 367–368, 372.

17.   Ibid., p. 365.

18.   Abby Gibbons to James Gibbons, August 5, 1862; James Gibbons to Abby Gibbons, August 13 and 15, 1862, Gibbons Papers.

19.   Abby Gibbons to Lucy Gibbons, August 9, 1862; "War Journal," Emerson I, p. 372.

20.   "War Journal," Emerson I, pp. 389–390.

21.   Sarah Gibbons to dear father, September 16, 1862; Sarah to Dear Julia, September 19, 1862, Gibbons Papers.

22.   Abby Gibbons to my dear daughter Julia, September 16, 1862, Gibbons Papers; Emerson I, p. 377.

23.   Abby Gibbons to Dear J, August 5, 1862; to My dear husband and children, August 10, 1862; To People, August 13, 1862; to dear Lucy, August 18, 1862; to James, August 31, 1862, Gibbons Papers.

24.   James Gibbons to Dear People, August 7, 1862; to Dear A., August 19, August 21, August 24, August 28, August 30, 1862, Gibbons Papers.

25.   Abby Gibbons to Dear Julia, September 3, 1862; Sally to Dear Father, September 7, September 16, 1862; Sarah to Dear Lucy, September 10, 1862; Lucy to Dear Mother, October 2, 1862, Gibbons Papers.

26.   "War Journal," Emerson I, p. 378.

27.   Lucy to my darling mother, August 24, 1862, Gibbons Papers; McPherson, *Battle Cry of Freedom*, p. 492; see Lillian Schissel, ed., *Conscience in America: a Documentary History of Conscientious Objection in America, 1757–1967* (New York; Dutton, 1968).

28.   Sally to Lucy, October 5, 1862, Gibbons letters.

29.   Abby to Julia, September 3, 1862, Gibbons Papers.

30.   Dr. James Walker to Abby Gibbons, January 22, 1863, Emerson I, p. 385.

31.   Clinton Wagner to Abby Gibbons, January 16, 1863, Gibbons Papers.

32.   Abby Gibbons to Dear Ones All, February 1, 1863, Gibbons Papers.

33.   Abby Gibbons to Dear Ones All, February 1, 1863; Abby to My dear J., February 6, 1863, Gibbons Papers.

34.   Abby Gibbons to Julia, February 12, 1863, Gibbons Papers.

35.   "War Journal," Emerson I, p 391.

36.   Abby Gibbons to Dear Ones All, February 21, 1863, Gibbons Papers.

37.   "War Journal," Emerson I, p. 393.

38.   "War Journal," Emerson II, pp. 9, 12, 20.

39.   "War Journal," Emerson II, p. 3.

40.   Ibid.

41.   Ibid.

42.   "War Journal," Emerson II, p. 39.

43.   "War Journal," Emerson II, p. 6.

44.   "War Journal," Emerson II, pp. 6, 15–18.

45.   "War Journal," Emerson II, pp. 23–27.

46.   Clinton Wagner to Abby Gibbons, May 10, 1863, Gibbons Papers.

47.   Colonel Rogers to General Lockwood, May 27, 1863, Gibbons Papers; "War Journal," Emerson II, p. 25.

48.   "War Journal," Emerson II, p. 2.

49.   "War Journal," Emerson II, p. 3; Gibbons to Dear J., May 21, 1863, Gibbons Papers.

50.   "War Journal," Emerson II, p. 33.

51.   James Gibbons to Dear A. and S., June 30, 1863, Gibbons Papers.

52.   Dr. Clinton Wagner to Abby Gibbons, July 29, 1863, Gibbons Papers.

Chapter VIII. The Draft Riots

1.   See Iver Bernstein, *The New York Draft Riots: Their Significance in American Society and Politics in the Age of the Civil War* (New York: Oxford University Press, 1990).

2.   McPherson, *Battle Cry of Freedom*, pp. 609–611.

3.   Lucy Gibbons Morse, "Personal Recollections of the Draft Riot of 1863," Gibbons Papers.

4.   Ibid.

5.   Ibid.

6.   Ibid.

7.   Ibid.

8.   Ibid.

9.   Ibid.

10.   Sally to Dear Father, July 16, 1863; Abby to dear ones all, July 17, 1863, Gibbons Papers; Emerson II, p. 53.

11.   Lucy Gibbons to Her Aunt Anna, July 17, 1863, Emerson II, pp. 50–51.

12.   Bernstein, *New York City Draft Riots*, p. 26.

13.   Ibid.

14.   Abby Gibbons to Lucy, August 19, 1863, Emerson II, p. 60.

15.   James Walker to Abby, September 14, 1863, Gibbons Papers; Emerson II, pp. 55, 58; *National Anti-Slavery Standard*, August 1, 1863, p. 4.

16.   Abby Gibbons to Joseph Choate, September 10, 1863; Emerson II, p. 64.

17.   Abby Gibbons to my dear daughter, September 7, 1863, Gibbons Papers.

18.   Ibid.

19.   Anne L. Austin, *Woolsey Sisters of New York: A family's involvement in war and a new profession* (Philadelphia: Philosophical Society, 1971), pp. 94–95; Abby Gibbons to Dear Ones, September 13, 1863, Gibbons Papers.

20.   Abby Gibbons to Dear Julia, September 17, 1863, Gibbons Papers.

21.   Abby Gibbons to James Gibbons, September 13, 1863, Emerson II, p. 72.

22.   Memorandum, October 6, 1863, "Protestant nurses protest their dismissal and replacement with 'Sisters of Mercy,'" Gibbons Papers.

23.   William Quentin Maxwell, *Lincoln's Fifth Wheel: the Political History of the United States Sanitary Commission* (New York: Longman's, 1956), pp. 66–69.

24.   Abby Gibbons to Lucy, September 26, 1863, Emerson II, p. 74.

25.   Abby Gibbons to Julia Gibbons, October 2, 1863, Gibbons Papers; Abby Gibbons to Sally, October 23, 1863, Emerson II, p. 79.

26.   Abby Gibbons to Miss Catharine M. Sedgwick, October 13, 1863, Gibbons Papers.

27.   Abby Gibbons to My Dear Children, November 12, 1863, Gibbons Papers.

28.   Abby Gibbons to Secretary of War Edwin Stanton, n.d., Gibbons Papers; Emerson II, p. 79.

29.   Georgie Woolsey to Abby, January 9, 1864, Gibbons Papers; Abby Gibbons to Lucy, January 18, 1864, Emerson II, p. 81.

30.   Mrs. Lander to Dear Madam, January 27, 1864, Gibbons Papers.

31.   Anna Mott Hopper to Dear Abby, January 18, 1864; Abby to Julia, January 24, 1864, Gibbons Papers.

32.   Emerson II, p. 78; John Hopper to Abby Gibbons, March 29, 1864, Gibbons Papers.

33.   Abby Gibbons to Sarah Emerson, February 1, 1864, Gibbons Papers.

34.   Sarah to My Father, May 18, 1864, Emerson II, pp. 88–89.

35.   Sarah Emerson to James Gibbons, May 26, 1864, Emerson II, p. 92.

36.   Ibid.

37.   Ibid.

38.   Abby Gibbons to Dear Ones at Home, June 12, 1864, Gibbons Papers; Abby Gibbons to Lucy, July 1864, Emerson II, p. 101.

39.   Abby Gibbons to My Dear Julia, June 18, 1864, Gibbons Papers.

40.   Abby Gibbons to Dear Ones at Home, June 15, 1854, Gibbons Papers.

41. Abby Gibbons to Sydney Howard Gay, May 31, 1864, Emerson II, p. 98.

42. Abby Gibbons to Elizabeth Gay, August 4, 1864, Emerson II, pp. 103–104.

43. Ibid.; Emerson II, pp. 105–106.

44. Abby Gibbons to Julia, August 17, 1864, Emerson II, pp. 110–111.

45. Abby Gibbons to Julia, September 14, 1864, Emerson II, pp. 113–114; J. B. Patten to Abby Gibbons, September 14, 1864, Gibbons Papers.

46. Sally to Her Father, October 16, 1864, Emerson II, p. 118.

47. Ellen Collins to Abby Gibbons, September 8, 1864, and September 17, 1864, Gibbons Papers.

48. Maria Mann to Abby Gibbons, September 27, 1864; Mary Donaldson to Abby Gibbons, September 28, 1864, Gibbons Papers.

49. Sarah Emerson to James Gibbons, November 12, 1864, Emerson II, p. 119.

50. Isaac Bell to Abby Gibbons, January 25, 1864, Gibbons Papers.

51. Abby Gibbons to Sally Emerson, December 16, 1864, Emerson II, p. 122.

52. Abby Gibbons to Sarah Emerson, January 1865, Emerson II, pp. 124–126.

53. Sally Emerson to Abby Gibbons, March 8, 1865, Gibbons Papers.

Chapter IX. "*When Johnny Comes Marching Home Again*"

1. Abby Gibbons to Sarah, April 19, 1865, Gibbons Papers.

2. Dr. Clinton Wagner to Abby Gibbons, April 20, 1865; Sally Emerson to Abby Gibbons, May 16, 1865; Abby Gibbons to Sally Emerson, July 7, 1865, Gibbons Papers.

3. Anna Hopper to Abby Gibbons, May 30, 1865, Gibbons Papers.

4. Abby Gibbons to my dear daughter, April 27, 1865, Gibbons papers.

5. Sally to my Dear Mother, May 25, 1865, Gibbons Papers. Gerda Lerner, *The Grimké Sisters from South Carolina; Pioneers for Woman's Rights and Abolition* (New York: Schocken Books, 1967), p. 359.

6. New York *Tribune*, July 7 and 9, 1868; Emerson, II, p. 151.

7. Ibid.

8. Julia to Sally, July 9, 1868, Gibbons Papers; Emerson II, p. 151.

9. Elizabeth Townsend to Abby Gibbons, June 3, 1869, Emerson II, pp. 153–154.

10. Abby Gibbons to Sally, July 29, 1869, Emerson II, p. 157.

11. Abby Gibbons to Julia, November 15, 1867; Abby Gibbons to Sally, July 29, 1869, Emerson II, pp. 149, 157, 159–160.

12. Abby Gibbons to Sally, August 1, 1869, Emerson II, p. 158.

13. James Gibbons to Abby Gibbons from Hamburg, October 31, 1869, Gibbons Papers.

14. Abby Gibbons to Dear Ones, November 16, 1867, Gibbons Papers.

15. Elizabeth Peabody to Abby Gibbons, August 17, 1865; Elizabeth Peabody to Theresa Dana, September 18, 1865; Maria Mann to Abby Gibbons, January 30, 1866, July 25, 1868, Gibbons Papers.

16. Judith Breault, *The World of Emily Howland: The Odyssey of a Humanitarian* (Millbrae, Cal.: Les Femmes, 1976); Sarah Emerson to Dear Mother, May 28, 1866, Gibbons Papers.

17. Abby Gibbons to Sally from Point Lookout, September 18, 1866, Emerson II, p. 145.

18. Ibid.

19. Abby to Sarah W. Adam, November 1, 1888; Mrs. Frederick Billings to Sarah Emerson, circa January 1893, Emerson II, pp. 268, 346.

20. Abby Howland Woolsey to Abby Gibbons, February 17, 1867, Gibbons Papers.

21. Emerson I, p. 250.

22. Abby Gibbons to Sarah, May 18, 1865; Abby to and from the Commissioner of Public Charities and Corrections, June 27, 1867, June 26, 1868, Gibbons Papers, Emerson II, pp. 179–180.

23. Abby Gibbons to Sarah Emerson, March 4, 1874, Gibbons Papers.

24. Abby Gibbons to Dear Sarah, April 3, 1874, Gibbons Papers.

25. Rafter, *Partial Justice*, pp. 24–28.

26. Johnson, *Rhoda Coffin*, p. 151.

27. *Coffin*, pp. 258–260.

28. Rafter, pp. 25–32.

29. *Coffin*, pp. 157–159, 263.

30. Wyman, *Elizabeth Buffum Chace*, II, p. 104.

31. See Estelle Freedman, *Maternal Justice: Miriam Van Waters and the Female Reform Tradition* (Chicago: University of Chicago Press, 1996).

32. Hannah Chickering to Abby Gibbons, April 4, 1864; Abby Gibbons to Dearest Julia, March 18, 1870, Gibbons Papers; Abigail Hopper Gibbons to Flora, February 14, 1868, Anti-Slavery Papers.

33. James to Sally, November 3, 1870, Gibbons Papers.

34. E. J. Cutter to James Gibbons, August 4, 1867, Gibbons Papers.

35. Abby Gibbons to Julia, December 17, 1869, Gibbons Papers.

36. Lucy to My Dear Mother, August 17, August 23, September 2, September 7, 1868; Hannah Rantoul to Abby Gibbons, November 8, 1868, Gibbons Papers.

37. Rose Wagner to Abby Gibbons, July 20, 1864; Rose Wagner to Abby Gibbons, July 27, 1864; Julia Gibbons to Mother, September 3, 1864; Abby Gibbons to my dearest daughter, November 28, 1864, Gibbons Papers.

38. Abby Gibbons to Dear J., October 24, 1869, Gibbons Papers.

39. Journal of James Herbert Morse, Vol. I, pp. 106–109, September 14, 1869, New-York Historical Society. (Hereafter Morse Journal.)

40. James Gibbons to Julia Gibbons, January 12, 1870, Gibbons Papers.

41. Abby Gibbons to Julia, February 31, 1870, Gibbons Papers.

42. Abby Gibbons to Sally, June 14, 1870, Gibbons Papers.

43. Abby Gibbons to My dear daughter Sally, June 17, 1870, Gibbons Papers.

44. Abby Gibbons to Sarah Emerson, June 23, 1870, Gibbons Papers.

45. Abby Gibbons to Sally, October 17, 1873, Emerson II, p. 169.

Chapter X. *An Advocate for Women*

1. Abby Gibbons to Julia, January 14, 1870; George Baker to Abby Gibbons, March 3, 1871, Gibbons Papers. New York City Directory.

2.   Abby Gibbons to Sally, September 5, 1873, Gibbons Papers.

3.   Abby Gibbons to my Dear Daughter, July 18, 1873, Gibbons Papers; Abby Gibbons to Sally, March 27, 1874; Abby Gibbons to Sally, August 13, 1879, Emerson II, pp. 181, 202–203.

4.   Minutes of House Committee, New York Infant Asylum, February 14, 1878, Rare Books (NYPL).

5.   Abby Hopper Gibbons's Diary-journal, relating to the operation and management of the New York Infant Asylum in New York City, p. 1, n.d., Abigail Gibbons Papers (NYPL).

6.   Abby Gibbons to Sally, January 16, 1874, Gibbons Papers.

7.   Abby Gibbons to Elizabeth Gay, September 6, 1892, Emerson II, p. 313; Abby Gibbons to Sally, July 29, 1869, Emerson II, p. 157.

8.   Abby Gibbons to Julia, August 1, 1873; Abby to my dear daughter, December 30, 1873, Gibbons Papers.

9.   Abby Gibbons to my dear sister, May 22, 1877, Gibbons Papers.

10.   Abby Gibbons to Sarah Thayer, July 4, 1874, Emerson II, p. 184.

11.   Abby Gibbons to Sarah Thayer, January 16, 1874, Gibbons Papers.

12.   Aaron M. Powell, *Reminiscences* (New York: Carlon Press, 1899), pp. 240–241.

13.   Mrs. Margaret Davis to Sarah Emerson, January 13, 1894, Emerson II, p. 331.

14.   Emerson I, pp. 258–259.

15.   David J. Pivar, *The Purity Crusade; Sexual Morality and Social Control, 1868–1900* (Westport, Conn.: Greenwood Press, 1973), p. 86.

16.   Pivar *The Purity Crusade*, p. 68.

17.   *The Philanthropist* VIII, 2, New York, February 1893, p. 1.

18.   Invitation to William Lloyd Garrison, signed by Abigail Hopper Gibbons, President, January 1, 1878, Anti-Slavery Papers; William Lloyd Garrison to Helen, January 4, 1878, in *Letters*, Vol. VI.

19.   New York Committee for the Prevention of Licensed Prostitution. No State Regulated Vice. New York [n.p.] 1878, Library Company of Philadelphia.

20.   A. L. Gihon to A. H. Gibbons, Feb. 18, 1880, April 29, 1880, Abby Hopper Gibbons correspondence (WPA).

21. Pivar, *Purity*, pp. 87, 97; *The Philanthropist* VIII, March 3, 1893, p. 7.

22. *Alpha*, May 1, 1886, p. 13.

23. *Report of International Council of Women, Washington, D. C. March 25 to April 1, 1888* (Washington, D. C.: Fugus H. Darby, printer, 1888), pp. 252–257.

24. Rafter, *Partial Justice*, pp. 47–48.

25. Robert Bremner, "Josephine Shaw Lowell," *NAW*, II., pp. 437–439.

26. Abby Gibbons to His Excellency, May 12, 1882, WPA, Correspondence by Directors, 1845–1983.

27. The Honorable William Letchworth to Abby Gibbons, January 22, February 20, 1883, Director's Correspondence, WPA.

28. Abby Gibbons to the Honorable Hugh J. Grant, November 8, November 19, 1889, Emerson II, pp. 277–278.

29. Abby Gibbons to the Honorable Hugh J. Grant, November 22, 1879, Emerson II, p. 279.

30. Abby Gibbons to Anna Powell, March 16, 1883, Emerson II, p. 228.

31. Theodore Roosevelt to Abby Gibbons, February 28, 1883, Gibbons Papers.

32. William Rhinelander Stewart, *The Philanthropic Work of Josephine Shaw Lowell* (New York: Macmillan, 1911), pp. 320–324.

33. Josephine Shaw Lowell to My dear Mrs. Gibbons, June 5, 1888, Emerson II, p. 262.

34. Abby Gibbons to Anna Powell, March 25, 1891, Emerson II, p. 293.

35. Abby Gibbons to Sarah Thayer, November 3, 1870, Emerson II, p. 159; Abby Gibbons to Sally, October 1, 1872, Emerson II, p. 166.

36. Abby Gibbons to John Bigelow, April 18, 1877, Emerson II, pp. 192–193.

37. Abby Gibbons to John Bigelow, September 22, 1876; James to My Dear Sally, September 9, 1881, Gibbons Papers.

38. Abby Gibbons to the Honorable Chester Arthur, August 22, 1881, Gibbons Papers.

39. Abby Gibbons to D. N. Carvalho, August 5, 1892, Emerson II, p. 309.

Chapter XI. "A Reformatory, Pure and Simple"

1. James Gibbons to Sarah Emerson, July 1, 1883, Gibbons Papers.

2. James to My dear Daughter Sally, February 7, 1881, Gibbons Papers.

3. Abby Gibbons to My dear daughter Sally, July 28, 1883, Gibbons Papers.

4. Abby Gibbons to my Dear daughter Sally, August 13, 1879, Gibbons Papers.

5. Abby Gibbons to Lucy Morse, Emerson II, p. 205.

6. Abby Gibbons to Aaron Powell, Emerson II, p. 223.

7. WPA Minutes, Oct. 5, 1889, Dec. 2, 1890.

8. WPA Minutes, March 5, 1892.

9. WPA, Annual Reports, 1878, 1885, Minutes, March 4, 1890.

10. WPA Minutes, February 4, 1889, November 5, 1889, May 6, 1890.

11. WPA Minutes, November 4, 1890.

12. Stewart, *The Philanthropic Work of Josephine Shaw Lowell* pp. 306–307; Freedman, *Their Sisters Keepers*, pp. 56–57.

13. Ibid.

14. Abby Gibbons to Anna Powell, March 12, 1889, Emerson II, p. 270.

15. Morse Journal, Volume VIII, March 1889, p. 112.

16. Abby Gibbons to Anna Powell, June 9, 1890, Emerson II, p. 283.

17. Abby Gibbons to Sarah Thayer, July 12, 1890, Emerson II, p. 284.

18. Abby Gibbons to Edward Hopper, February 26, 1892, Gibbons Papers.

19. Morse Journal, Vol. IX, pp. 82–83, April 22, May 17, 1892.

20. Ibid.

21. WPA Minutes, June 7, 1892.

22. Abby Gibbons to Alice Sandford, June 8, 1892; Abby Gibbons to David Carvalho, August 2, 1892, Emerson II, pp. 301, 307.

23. Ibid.

24. Abby Gibbons to Alice Sandford, December 20, 1892, Emerson II, p. 323.

25. Tribute by James Herbert Morse, Emerson II, p. 345.

26. Abby Gibbons to James B Thayer, 1886, Emerson II, p. 247.

27. James B. Thayer to Mrs. Gibbons, November 13, 1892, Emerson II, p. 319.

28. Abby Gibbons to Anna Powell, December 30, 1885; Abby Gibbons to Susan Hopper, November 25, 1887, Emerson II, pp. 244–245, 259.

29. Emerson II, p. 317.

30. Abby Gibbons to David Carvalho, November 16, 1892, Emerson II, p. 320.

31. Abby Gibbons to Alice Sandford, December 1, 1892, Emerson II, p. 321.

32. WPA Minutes, January 3, 1893.

33. Abby Gibbons to Florence Baker, January 9, 1893, Emerson II, p. 324.

34. Robert Rantoul to Sally Emerson, January 20, 1893, Gibbons Papers.

35. WPA Minutes, February 7, 1893.

36. N.D. Miscellaneous, Gibbons Papers.

37. W. David Lewis, "Katherine Bement Davis," *NAW* I., pp. 439–440.

38. New York *Tribune*, January 19, 1893.

Bibliography

Primary Sources

Manuscript Collections

Abigail Hopper Gibbons Papers. Friends Historical Library, Swarthmore College (FHA).

Antislavery Papers. Boston Public Library.

Abby Kelley Foster Papers. American Antiquarian Society.

Minutes, Guardian of the Poor. Philadelphia City Archives.

Lloyd Family Papers. Quaker Collection, Haverford College, Haverford, Pa. (QC)

Isaac T. Hopper Letters. Quaker Collection, Haverford College, Haverford, Pa.

Abigail Gibbons Papers. Manuscripts and Archives Division, The New York Public Library, Astor, Lenox, and Tilden Foundations. (NYPL)

Journal of James Herbert Morse. New-York Historical Society.

Minutes, New York Monthly Meeting. FHA.

Minutes, Monthly Meeting for the Southern District. FHA.

Minutes, New York Association for the Relief of those held in Slavery and the Improvement of Free People of Color. FHA.

Records, New York Prison Association. Manuscripts and Archives Division, The New York Public Library, Astor, Lenox, and Tilden Foundations.

Minutes, Women's Meeting, Philadelphia Monthly Meeting for the Southern District. FHA.

Minutes, Pennsylvania Abolition Society. Historical Society of Pennsylvania (HSP).

Minutes, Pennsylvania Prison Society. HSP.

Minutes, Annual Reports, and Correspondence, Women's Prison Association Records. Manuscripts and Archives Division, The New York Public Library, Astor, Lenox, and Tilden Foundations. (WPA)

Miscellaneous manuscripts. Radcliffe College.

201

National Archives and Record Service, Washington, D. C.
Sarah Hopper Palmer Papers. FHL.

Secondary Sources

Books

Austin, Anne L. *The Woolsey Sisters of New York; a family's involvement in the Civil war and a new profession (1860–1900)*. Philadelphia: American Philosophical Society, 1971.
Bacon, Margaret Hope. *Lamb's Warrior*. New York: Thomas Y. Crowell, 1970.
———. *Valiant Friend: The Life of Lucretia Mott*. New York: Walker and Company, 1980.
———. *Mothers of Feminism: The Story of Quaker Women in America*. San Francisco: Harper & Row, 1987.
Berg, Barbara. *The Remembered Gate: Origins of American Feminism*. New York: Oxford University Press, 1978.
Bernstein, Iver. *The New York Draft Riots: Their Significance in American Society and Politics in the Age of the Civil War*. New York: Oxford University Press, 1990.
Blake, McKelvey. *American Prisons*. Montclair, N.J.: Patterson Smith, 1968.
Breault, Judith Colucci. *The World of Emily Howland: Odyssey of the Humanitarian*. Millbrae, Cal.: Les Femmes, 1976.
Brockett, Linus Pierpont, and Mrs. Mary Vaughn. *Woman's Work in the Civil War: a Record of Heroism, Patriotism, and Patience*. Philadelphia: Zeigler , McCurdy and Company, 1867.
Cazden, Elizabeth. *Antionette Brown Blackwell: A Biography*. Old Westbury, N.Y.: The Feminist Press, 1983.
Chambers-Schiller, Lee. *Liberty A Better Husband: Single Women in America: the Generations of 1780–1840*. New Haven: Yale University Press, 1984.
Child, Lydia Maria. *Isaac T. Hopper, A True Life*. Boston: John P. Jewett, 1853.
Cox, John. *Quakerism in the City of New York*. New York: 1930.
Crane, Elaine Forman, ed. *The Diary of Elizabeth Drinker*. Boston: Northeastern University Press, 1991.
Dix, Dorothea Lynde. *Remarks on Prison and Prison Discipline in the United States*. Reprinted from the 2nd ed., 1845. Montclair, N.J.: Patterson Smith, 1967.
Drake, Thomas. *Quakers and Slavery in America*. New Haven: Yale University Press, 1950.
DuBois, Ellen, ed. *Elizabeth Cady Stanton, Susan B. Anthony: Correspondence, Writings, Speeches*. New York: Schocken Books, 1981.

Emerson, Sarah Hopper, ed. *Life of Abby Hopper Gibbons Told Chiefly Through her Correspondence.* New York: G. P. Putnam, 1896.

Farnham, Eliza W. Notes and illustrations to M. B. Sampson, *Rational of Crime and its Appropriate Treatment. Being a Treatise on Criminal Jurisprudence Considered in Relation to Cerebral Organization.* From the 2nd ed. New York: D. Appleton and Company, 1846. Reprinted, Montclair, N.J.: Patterson Smith, 1973.

Flexner, Eleanor. *Century of Struggle: The Woman's Rights Movement in the United States.* Cambridge, Mass.: Belknap Press, 1959.

Forbush, Bliss. *Elias Hicks, Quaker Liberal.* New York: Columbia University Press, 1956.

Foster, Edward Halsey. *Catharine Maria Sedgwick.* New York: Twayne Publishers, 1974.

Freedman, Estelle B. *Their Sisters Keepers; Women's Prison Reform in America.* Ann Arbor: University of Michigan Press, 1981.

———. *Maternal Justice: Miriam Van Waters and the Female Reform Tradition.* Chicago: University of Chicago Press, 1996.

Friedman, Lawrence. *Gregarious Saints: Self and Community in American Abolitionism, 1830–1870.* Cambridge: Cambridge University Press, 1982.

Fry, Elizabeth. *Elizabeth Fry: Life and Labors of the Eminent Philanthropist, Preacher and Prison Reformer*, compiled from her journal and other sources by Edward Ryder. Pawling, N.Y.: E. Walker's Sons, 1883.

Gilfoyle, Timothy. *City of Eros: New York City: Prostitution and the Commercialization of Sex, 1790–1920.* New York: Norton, 1992.

Ginzberg, Lori. *Women and the Work of Benevolence: Morality, Politics, and Class in the Nineteenth-Century United States.* New Haven: Yale University Press, 1990.

Greene, Dana. *Suffrage and Religious Principle: Speeches and Writings of Olympia Brown.* Metuchen, N.J.: Scarecrow Press, 1984.

Johnson, Rhoda Moorman. *Rhoda Coffin: her reminiscences, addresses, papers, and ancestry.* New York: The Grafton Press, 1910.

Hallowell, Anna Davis. *Lucretia and James Mott, Life and Letters.* Boston: Houghton, 1884.

Hare, C. (Catherine) *Life and Letters of Elizabeth Comstock.* London: Headley Brothers, 1895.

Harris, Jean. *"They Always Call Us Ladies": Stories from Prison.* New York: Scribners, 1988.

Hawkes, Mary Q. *Excellent Effect: The Edna Mahan Story.* Laurel, Md.: American Correctional Association, 1994.

Heilbrun, Carolyn G. *Writing a Woman's Life.* New York: Norton, 1988.

Hersh, Blanche. *Slavery of Sex: Feminist-Abolitionists in America.* Urbana, Ill.: University of Illinois Press, 1978.

Hewitt, Nancy Ann. *Women's Activities and Social Change: Rochester, New York, 1822–1872.* Ithaca: Cornell University Press, 1984.

Hole, Helen. *Westtown Through the Years.* Westtown, Pa.: Westtown School, 1942.

Holloway, Elma. "A History of the Howard Institution of Philadelphia," typescript, Quaker Collection, Haverford College Library.

Hopper, Isaac. *Defense of Isaac T. Hopper Against the Aspersions of Marcus T. Gould.* New York: Privately Published, 1831.

Ingle, Larry. *Quakers in Conflict: The Hicksite Reformation.* Knoxville: University of Tennessee Press, 1986.

Jacquette, Henrietta, ed. *South After Gettysburg: The Story of A Civil War Nurse.* New York: Thomas Y. Crowell, 1937.

James, Edward and Janet, eds. *Notable American Women:1607–1950.* Cambridge: Belknap Press, 1971.

King, Elizabeth. *Memoir of Elizabeth T. King, with Extracts from her Letters and Journal.* Baltimore: Armstrong & Berry, 1859.

Kirby, Georgiana Bruce. *Years of Experience: An Autobiographical Narrative.* New York: Putnam, 1887. Microfilm, New Haven, Conn.: Research Publications 1977. History of Women, Reel 146, No. 3420.

Kirkland, Caroline M. *The Helping Hand.* New York: Scribners, 1853.

Kouwenhoven, John. *A Columbia Historical Portrait of New York.* New York: Doubleday, 1953.

Kraditor, Aileen S. *Means and Ends in American Abolitionism.* New York: Vintage Press, 1967.

Lekkerkerker, Eugenia Cornelia. *Reformatories for Women in the United States.* The Hague: J. B. Wolters, 1931.

Lerner, Gerda. *The Grimké Sisters from South Carolina: Pioneers of Woman's Rights and Abolition.* New York: Schocken Books, 1967.

Lewis, Orlando Faulkland. *The Development of American Prisons and Prison Customs, 1776–1845 with Special Reference to Early Institutions in the State of New York.* Albany: Prison Association of New York, 1922.

McPherson, James M. *Battle Cry of Freedom: the Civil War Era.* New York: Oxford University Press, 1988.

Manners, Emily. *Elizabeth Hooton: first Quaker woman preacher(1600–1672).* London: Headley Brothers, 1914.

Marietta, Jack. *Reformation of American Quakerism.* Philadelphia: University of Pennsylvania Press, 1984.

Marshall, Helen. *Dorothea Dix: Forgotten Samaritan.* Chapel Hill: University of North Carolina, 1937.

Martineau, Harriet. *Retrospect of Western Travel.* London: Saunders and Otley, 1838.

Maxwell, William Quentin. *Lincoln's Fifth Wheel: The Political History of the United States Sanitary Commission.* New York: Longman's, 1956.

Meaders, Daniel E. *Kidnappers in Philadelphia: Isacc Hopper's Tales of Oppression 1780–1843.* New York: Garland Publishing, Inc. 1994.

Melder, Keith. *Beginnings of Sisterhood: The American Woman's Rights Movement, 1800–1850.* New York: Schocken Books, 1977.

Meltzer, Milton, and Patricia G. Holland, eds. *Lydia Maria Child: Selected Letters, 1817–1880.* Amherst: University of Massachusetts Press, 1982.

Merrill, Walter, and Louis Ruchames, eds. *The Letters of William Lloyd Garrison.* Cambridge: Belknap Press, 1971–1979. 6 Volumes.

Nevins, Allan. *Ordeal of the Union: A House Dividing, 1852–1857.* New York: Charles Scribners Sons, 1947.

Pivar, David. *Purity Crusade: Sexual Morality and Social Control 1868–1900.* Westport, Conn.: The Greenwood Press, 1973.

Powell, Aaron. *Reminiscences.* New York: Caulon Press, 1899.

Pryor, Elizabeth Brown. *Clara Barton: Professional Angel.* Philadelphia: University of Pennsylvania Press, 1987.

Quarles, Benjamin. *Black Abolitionists.* New York and London: Oxford University Press, 1969.

Rafter, Nicole Hahn. *Partial Justice: Women in State Prisons, 1800–1935.* Boston: Northeastern University Press, 1985.

Rose, June. *Elizabeth Fry.* New York: Macmillan, 1980.

Sampson, Marmaduke B. *Rationale of Crime.* New York: 1845.

Schissel, Lillian ed. *Conscience in America; a Documentary History of Conscientious Objection in America 1757–1967.* New York: Dutton, 1968.

Sklar, Kathryn Kish. *Catherine Beecher.* New Haven: Yale University Press, 1973.

Smith-Rosenberg, Carol. *Disorderly Conduct: Visions of Gender in Victorian America.* New York: Knopf, 1985

Stanton, Elizabeth, Susan B. Anthony, Matilda Gage. *History of Women Suffrage.* New York: Fowler,1881–1922.

Stearns, Frank Preston. *The Life and Public Service of George Luther Stearns.* Philadelphia: Lippincott, 1907.

Sterling, Dorothy, ed. *Turning the World Upside Down: The Anti-Slavery Convention of American Women, Held in New York City, May 9–12, 1837.* New York: Coalition of Publishers for Employment, 1987.

———. *Ahead of Her Time; Abby Kelley and the Politics of Antislavery.* New York: W. W. Norton, 1991.

———. *We Are Your Sisters: Black Women in the Nineteenth Century.* New York: Norton, 1984.

Stewart, William Rhinelander. *The Philanthropic Work of Josephine Shaw Lowell.* New York: The Macmillan Company, 1911.

Tebbets, Theodore. *A Memoir of William Gibbons.* New York: "Printed for his Friends," 1856.

Teeters, Negley. *The Cradle of the Penitentiary*. Philadelphia: Temple University Press, 1955.

———. *They Were in Prison*. Philadelphia: John Winston, 1937.

Tharp, Louise Hall. *The Peabody Sisters of Salem*. Boston: Little, Brown, 1950.

Webb, Samuel, ed. *History of Pennsylvania Hall which was Destroyed by a Mob on the 17th of May, 1838*. Philadelphia: 1838.

Wolf, Edwin. *Philadelphia: Portrait of an American City*. Philadelphia: Library Company, 1990.

Wyman, Lillie B.C., and Arthur C. *Elizabeth Buffum Chace, 1806–1899: Her Life and Environment*. Boston: W. B. Clarke Co., 1914.

Yellin, Jean Fagan, and John C. Van Horne, eds. *The Abolitionist Sisterhood: Women's Political Culture in Antebellum America*. Ithaca: Cornell University Press, 1994.

Index

207

KITTY LINDSAY
LEARNING RESOURCES CENTER
RICHLAND COMMUNITY COLLEGE
ONE COLLEGE PARK
DECATUR, IL